Letts

Revise GCSE
History

ling

004941754 1

Contents

Chapter 7 New World 1945–2000

Chapter 8 Britain 1919–1978

Chapter 9 Russia and the Soviet Union 1914–1941

Chapter 10 Germany 1918–1945

Chapter 11 The USA 1919–1980

This book and

This book is suitable for students studying the following courses:

- AQA B (Modern World History)
- Edexcel A (The Making of the Modern World)
- OCR B (Modern World)
- WJEC Route A (History) – Selected topics only
- WJEC Route B (History) – Selected topics only
- CCEA (History) – Selected topics only

	AQA B	Edexcel A	OCR B	WJEC A	WJEC B	CCEA
Specification number	4047	2HA01	J417	4270A	4270B	4010
Terminal papers	2 x 105 min. papers, each 37.5%	3 x 75 min. papers, each 25%	1 x 120 min. paper 45% / 1 x 90 min. paper 30%	3 x 60 min. papers each 25%	3 x 60 min. papers each 25%	1 x 120 min. paper 50% / 1 x 75 min. paper 25%
Controlled Assessment	25% (Unit 3)	25%	25%	25%	25%	25%
			Specification Reference Numbers			
Chapter 1 How British society changed 1890–1918						
1.1 Poverty and the Liberal Government	Unit 3	Unit 3	Unit A972	Units 1/2		
1.2 Votes for women	Unit 3	Unit 3	Unit A972	Units 1/2		
1.3 The Home Front during the First World War			Unit A972	Units 1/2	Unit 2	
Chapter 2 The First World War 1914–1918						
2.1 The causes of the First World War	Unit 1	Unit 1	Unit A971			
2.2 How the failure of the Schlieffen Plan led to stalemate	Unit 3	Unit 3	Unit A971	Units 1/2		
2.3 The other fronts	Unit 3	Unit 3	Unit A971			
2.4 How victory was achieved	Unit 3	Unit 3	Unit A971			
Chapter 3 The failure of international peace 1919–1939						
3.1 The peace settlements 1919–1923	Unit 1	Unit 1	Unit A971			
3.2 The League of Nations 1919–1936	Unit 1	Unit 1	Unit A971			
3.3 Why international peace had collapsed by 1939	Unit 1	Unit 1	Unit A971			Unit 1
Chapter 4 The Second World War 1939–1945						
4.1 The early years in Europe and Africa	Unit 3	Unit 3*	Unit A972	Unit 3*		Unit 1*
4.2 The entry of the superpowers: victory in Europe and Asia	Unit 3	Unit 3*		Units 1/2	Unit 1	
4.3 The war at home	Unit 3	Unit 3	Unit A972			
Chapter 5 The Cold War begins 1945–1960						
5.1 Who was to blame for the Cold War?	Unit 1	Unit 1	Unit A971	Unit 3		Unit 2
5.2 How did the Cold War develop 1945–1960?	Unit 1	Unit 1	Unit A971	Unit 3		Unit 2

your GCSE course

The following table shows how the topics in this book map to the units of the different exam specifications. (*Only parts of the topic are relevant to the course. Please refer to the exam board specification for full details.*)

Topic						
Chapter 6 Tension and détente 1960–1980						
6.1 Who won the Cuban Missile Crisis?	Unit 2		Unit 3	Unit A971	Unit 1	Unit 1
6.2 Why did the USA fail in Vietnam?	Unit 2		Unit 3	Unit A971		Unit 2
6.3 Détente	Unit 2		Unit 3	Unit A971		Unit 1
Chapter 7 New World 1945–2000						
7.1 Opposition to Soviet control in Eastern Europe	Unit 2		Unit 3*	Unit A971	Unit 1	Unit 1
7.2 Gorbachev and the collapse of the Soviet Union	Unit 2		Unit 3	Unit A971	Unit 1	Unit 1
7.3 Northern Ireland 1968–2000	Unit 1			Unit A971		Unit 2
7.4 Arab–Israeli conflict 1948–1995			Unit 3	Unit A971		Unit 2
7.5 The Iraq war, 2003				Unit A971		
7.6 Terrorist or freedom fighter?						Unit 2*
Chapter 8 Britain 1919–1978						
8.1 Depression and unrest in the 1920s and 1930s		Unit 1	Units 1/2	Unit A972	Unit 3	Unit 3
8.2 The reconstruction of Britain in the 1940s and 1950s		Unit 1	Units 1/2		Unit 3	Unit 3
8.3 The transformation of society between 1950 and 1980		Unit 2*		Unit A972	Unit 3	Unit 3
Chapter 9 Russia and the Soviet Union 1914–1941						
9.1 Russia before the First World War	Unit 1		Units 1/2	Unit A971	Unit 2	Unit 2
9.2 The impact of the First World War on Russia	Unit 1		Units 1/2	Unit A971	Unit 2	Unit 2
9.3 March to November 1917	Unit 1		Units 1/2	Unit A971	Unit 2	Unit 2
9.4 The Bolshevik victory: October / November 1917	Unit 1		Units 1/2	Unit A971	Unit 2	Unit 2
9.5 Bolshevik rule and its impact 1918–1928	Unit 1		Units 1/2	Unit A971	Unit 2	Unit 2
9.6 The nature of Stalin's dictatorship	Unit 1			Unit A971	Unit 2	Unit 2
Chapter 10 Germany 1918–1945						
10.1 The weakness of the Weimar Republic	Unit 1	Unit 1	Units 1/2/3	Unit A971	Unit 2	Unit 2
10.2 Hitler's rise to power	Unit 1	Unit 1	Units 1/2/3	Unit A971	Unit 2	Unit 2
10.3 Nazi control of Germany 1933–1945	Unit 1	Unit 1	Units 1/2/3	Unit A971	Unit 2	Unit 2
10.4 Life in Nazi Germany 1933–1945	Unit 1	Unit 1	Units 1/2/3	Unit A971	Unit 2	Unit 2
Chapter 11 The USA 1919–1980						
11.1 Boom and slump in the USA 1919–1941	Unit 1		Unit 3	Unit A971	Unit 2	Unit 2
11.2 The 'Great Society' 1945–1980			Unit 3	Unit A971	Unit 3	Unit 2
Downloadable pdfs						
• China, c.1930–1976	Unit 1		Units 1/2	Unit A971		
• End of Empire, c.1919–1969				Unit A971		

www.lettsandlonsdale.com

*Only parts of the topic are relevant to the course. Please refer to the exam board specification for full details.

1 How British society changed 1890–1918

The following topics are covered in this chapter:

- **Poverty and the Liberal Government**
- **Votes for women**
- **The Home Front during the First World War**

1.1 Poverty and the Liberal Government

LEARNING SUMMARY

After studying this section you should be able to understand:

- how attitudes to poverty were changing
- how the Liberal Government introduced reforms
- how effective the Liberal reforms were

The problem of poverty

AQA B	✗
EDEXCEL A	✗
OCR B	✓
WJEC A	✓
WJEC B	✗
CCEA	✗

Attitudes towards poverty in the 19th Century

Governments adopted laissez-faire policies in the 19th Century, doing little to help the poor. There were various reasons for this:

- Their intention was to keep taxes down.
- Governments thought that the poor should take care of themselves. Poverty was not the concern of the state.
- They thought poverty was caused by sin, e.g. idleness and drink, so it was people's own fault.

> **KEY POINT**
>
> A **laissez-faire** policy means that a government should not interfere in the lives of ordinary people, in order to provide the maximum of personal freedom. Therefore, helping the poor, sick or elderly was not the government's concern.

Workhouses had been provided in most big towns and they were intended to discourage the poor from asking for help. The workhouses were often like prisons, keeping people in worse conditions than they would experience outside the workhouse. Families were split up, discipline was harsh and food was scarce and poor.

The people in the workhouses were usually the very young or very old and so they were unable to do anything to bring themselves out of poverty.

Figure 1.1 Workhouse women

Many **charities** were set up to try to provide help for the poor. For example:

- By 1900 over 100 **Dr Barnardo's Homes** had been set up to help destitute children.
- Homes for the **homeless** were provided by many charities, e.g. the London Congregational Union provided shelters in London's docklands. Hundreds of men queued each evening, trying to get in.

However, voluntary organisations were quite incapable of providing enough relief, so government attitudes needed to change in order to help the poor.

Why did attitudes towards poverty change?

There were several reasons why attitudes towards poverty changed:

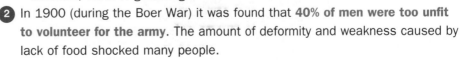

1. The work of two social reformers was particularly influential in the 1900s.
   - **Charles Booth** was appalled by the slums of the East End of London in the 1880s. He began to gather information that would challenge people's indifference and persuade them to do something. Detailed questions were asked in every house in the area and his first report was published in 1889. Booth found the causes of poverty to be old age, sickness, unemployment and low wages rather than idleness or drink. He went on to publish 17 volumes of evidence between 1898 and 1903.
   - **Seebohm Rowntree**, the son of the York chocolate manufacturer, decided to do a similar survey in York. His book, *Poverty, a Study of Town Life* showed that about one third of people lived in poverty, mostly because wages were too low or the wage-earner of the family was ill, old or dead. Social research like this showed that the huge scale of poverty in Britain was too great for charities to cope with. The government would have to act to support, not to punish, because generally poverty was not caused by idleness, drink or gambling.
2. In 1900 (during the Boer War) it was found that **40% of men were too unfit to volunteer for the army**. The amount of deformity and weakness caused by lack of food shocked many people.

The significance of these two reformers was not only that they helped change attitudes, but also that they provided the evidence and created a new concept of the causes of poverty.

③ Political parties were now more aware of the power of the working class vote created by the extension of democracy. A particular group of Liberal MPs, an important part of Liberal governments after 1905, supported **New Liberalism**. They believed that attitudes of laissez-faire and self-help had to give way to government action to tackle poverty. In 1900, the Labour Representation Committee had been formed, which became the **Labour Party** in 1906, with 52 MPs. Liberals now had to compete for the working class vote so they had to deal with working class poverty.

④ New Liberalism had two important leaders – **David Lloyd George** (Chancellor of the Exchequer 1908–1915) and **Winston Churchill**. Their passion and commitment helped to get reforms through Parliament.

The Liberal reforms

AQA B	✗
EDEXCEL A	✗
OCR B	✓
WJEC A	✓
WJEC B	✗
CCEA	✗

The Children's Charter

Figure 1.2 Children outside their home in a slum area of a British town.

A series of Acts made up the Children's Charter:

- The **1906 School Meals Act** allowed local education authorities to provide free meals for poor children and to help pay for meals of other pupils.
- The **1907 School Medical Service** was set up to provide regular school medical inspections. Free medical services could be provided for children by the local education authority.
- The **1908 Children's Act** banned children from public houses and from buying cigarettes. Child offenders would be tried in special juvenile courts and imprisoned in special centres (Borstals) so that they would not have to enter adult prisons.

> **KEY POINT**
>
> The 1906 School Meals Act and the 1907 School Medical Service were **permissive**. They did not force local authorities to do very much.

The Old Age Pensions Act

The introduction of the **old age pension in 1908** meant that many old people would no longer be condemned to the workhouse just because they could no longer work. The pension was given to people over 70 with an annual income of under £21 a year, while a reduced pension was given to those on an income above £21. The full pension was just 25p per week.

The unemployed

Unemployment was a particular problem so various measures were introduced:
- **1909, Employment Exchanges.** These were set up to help people find jobs.
- **1909, Minimum Wages.** Wages were fixed for people working in 'sweated industries', e.g. dressmakers where there weren't any trade unions.
- **1911, Health Insurance.** For workers who earned less than £160 a year, their employers and the government paid a weekly amount into a fund. The fund would then pay for free medical treatment and sickness benefit of 50p per week for up to six months.
- **1911, Unemployment Insurance.** This was a compulsory scheme for industries such as building and shipbuilding where workers were often laid off in bad weather (this covered about 4 million workers). Workers and their employers paid a weekly amount to gain a benefit of 35p per week for up to 15 weeks a year.

Figure 1.3 Unemployment threatened public order as well as poverty

How important were the Liberal reforms?

Important	Not very important
• They established the principle that society, through the government, had a responsibility to help the poor. In this way the reforms were the foundations of the welfare state. • They established an agreement on the causes of poverty – low wages, sickness, unemployment and old age – and did something about them. • The reforms helped a lot of people, effectively helping in the worst cases of poverty.	• The reforms left out too many people, e.g. you had to be very poor indeed to qualify for the old age pension; health insurance did not include women or farm workers; unemployment insurance was only for certain trades; free school meals could be provided but many education authorities chose not to do so. • The Poor Law was not reformed, therefore, many poor people still had to go into a workhouse.

However, there was strong opposition to these reforms from landowners and taxpayers and if the Liberals had tried to make more radical changes, their proposals would have been defeated in Parliament.

The political results of the reforms

Lloyd George decided that the rich needed to pay towards the cost of the reforms.

The People's Budget 1910: Lloyd George intended to increase income tax, impose a supertax on the very rich and tax the sale of land. His proposals gained a huge majority in the House of Commons, but were defeated in the House of Lords (which was made up of great landowners with hereditary titles, who would have had to pay for the tax increases, especially on land).

> **KEY POINT**
>
> The members of the House of Lords had not been elected, but had inherited titles and seats. Many were very conservative in outlook and did not believe that the government should help the poor.

By rejecting the Budget, the House of Lords provoked a confrontation with the Commons. Why should the Lords be allowed to reject a bill supported by the elected House of Commons? After a general election in 1910, which the Liberals narrowly won, the Lords accepted the budget.

The reform of the House of Lords: The Liberals were now determined to force reform on the House of Lords, so they called a second general election in 1910 over the issue, which again they narrowly won. In 1911, the **Parliament Act** was passed, although the Government had to threaten the Lords with the creation of 500 extra peers to force it through. The Parliament Act was very significant:
• It removed the power of the Lords to discuss money bills (including budgets).
• It removed the right of the Lords to reject bills for longer than two years.
• It reduced the time between general elections from a maximum of seven to five years.

Payment for MPs was also agreed in a separate Act. MPs would be paid £400 per year, which meant that ordinary working men could afford to serve.

Figure 1.4 Lloyd George as a giant, as seen in Punch, 1909

PROGRESS CHECK

1. What is the correct term for government policy that tries not to interfere with the life of the ordinary person?
2. Which researcher found that poverty was not normally caused by idleness, drink or gambling?
3. Why wouldn't every poor child receive a free school dinner after the Liberal Reforms?
4. Why were some industries targeted for Unemployment Insurance, whilst others were left out?
5. What stopped the House of Lords from defeating the Budget each year?

5. The Parliament Act, 1911, prohibited the discussion of money bills.
4. The Unemployment Insurance only targeted industries that suffered from seasonal layoffs, e.g. building and shipbuilding.
3. Because Education Authorities were not forced to provide them (permissive).
2. Charles Booth.
1. Laissez-faire.

1.2 Votes for women

LEARNING SUMMARY	**After studying this section you should be able to understand:** • the position of women at the beginning of the 20th Century • the differences between the campaigns of the Suffragists and the Suffragettes • the arguments used for and against giving women the vote • the value of women's work during the First World War • why some women were given the vote in 1918

The position and aims of women at the beginning of the 20th Century

AQA B	✓
EDEXCEL A	✓
OCR B	✓
WJEC A	✓
WJEC B	✓
CCEA	✗

Women's position in 1900

In 1900 women still did not have the vote, but their position had improved over the previous years:

1870s	Women began to qualify as **doctors**.
1878	London University allowed women **equality in taking degrees**.
1882	The Married Women's Property Act allowed women to **own their own property**, after they married.
1886	The Guardianship of Children Act allowed women to claim **guardianship of their children** if their marriage broke up.
1888	Women were allowed to **vote** in some **local elections**.
1894	Women could **vote** in all local elections and stand as **candidates**.

> **KEY POINT**
>
> In 1900 women could neither vote in national elections nor become MPs.

The campaign for **women's suffrage** began in the 1850s and by the 1870s it had spread countrywide, mostly among the working class. Even so, by 1900 only a minority of people thought that women should have the vote.

The Suffragists

The **National Union of Women's Suffrage Societies** (**NUWSS**) was formed in 1897 by **Mrs Millicent Garrett Fawcett**, from hundreds of different suffrage groups throughout the country. Its members were known as **Suffragists**:
• Suffragists aimed at **equality with male voters**, only 60% of whom had the vote in 1900.
• They **campaigned peacefully**, relying on reasoned argument in public meetings, leaflets and petitions. They met politicians and argued their case.
• In elections, they **supported candidates** who favoured votes for women, putting up male candidates against Liberals who were opposed to votes for women.
• They trained women to speak at public meetings.
• They held huge **demonstrations**, e.g. in 1907 the 'Mud March' of over 3,000

women in London. Seeing women marching in public was shocking to many people at the time.

The Suffragists were careful not to antagonise men – they wanted to convert public opinion, arguing that reform would be for the good of everyone. They were very well organised and numbers grew fast under paid organisers, who co-ordinated campaigns across the country. In 1910 they collected a petition of 280,000 signatures.

The Suffragettes

Mrs Emmeline Pankhurst had been a member of the Manchester Suffrage Society, but in 1903 she formed the **Women's Social and Political Union** (**WSPU**), which she led with her daughters, Christabel and Sylvia. Mrs Pankhurst had become impatient with the slow progress being made by the Suffragists and the Liberal Party. The leader of the Liberal Party, Henry Asquith, refused to give support to women's suffrage so attempts in the House of Commons by 1912 had come to nothing:

- Suffragettes wanted women to have the vote on the same basis as men.
- They wanted wise social reforms and thought that women could apply pressure to carry these through.
- They believed in 'deeds not words', so when it became obvious that the Liberal Government would not introduce reform, they turned to violent methods. For example, they used megaphones to heckle Liberal candidates in by-elections, and in 1905 Christabel was arrested for hitting and spitting at a policeman.
- They would not allow men to join the WSPU.

Figure 1.5 An early Suffragette demonstration in London

The NUWSS and the WSPU worked together at first, but as the WSPU became more violent, Mrs Fawcett realised that they were losing support in Parliament and with the public. However, the NUWSS worked hard to win back support and had over 100,000 members by 1914. The NUWSS continued to campaign quietly, gaining members and supporting the Conciliation Bill (see page 14).

The Suffragist and Suffragette campaigns

AQA B	✓
EDEXCEL A	✓
OCR B	✓
WJEC A	✓
WJEC B	✓
CCEA	✗

1908	When he became Prime Minister, Henry Asquith challenged the suffrage societies to prove that they had widespread support. So both organisations held large **marches** in London, which were attended by hundreds of thousands of women. While the NUWSS march was peaceful, the **WSPU demonstration led to stones being thrown** through the Prime Minister's windows in Downing Street. The women responsible were sent to prison, but they became heroines to their fellow suffragettes. From then onwards confrontation grew – women stepped up the violence while the Government found excuses to do nothing. A group of Suffragettes broke into the House of Commons. They were caught and each sentenced to three months in prison.
1909	In prison, Suffragettes went on **hunger strikes**. At first the authorities released them (they couldn't afford to let them die), but they later started to **force feed** them. This involved forcing a tube down their throat, which was unpleasant and they retaliated by trying to barricade their cells.
1910	The Government introduced the **Conciliation Bill**, which the Suffragists and Suffragettes had helped to draw up. For the moment there was a truce, but the Government delayed the Bill and patience ran out. The Suffragettes organised a **mass hunger strike** in prisons throughout the country.
1911	After a **window-smashing campaign**, causing thousands of pounds worth of damage, hundreds of Suffragettes were sent to prison where they went on hunger strikes.
1912	**Public buildings were bombed**, chemicals were poured into post boxes destroying thousands of letters and telephone wires were cut.
1913	**Lloyd George's house was damaged by a bomb**: Mrs Pankhurst was sentenced to three years in prison. **Emily Davidson** threw herself in front of the King's horse at the Derby. She died four days later. **The Cat and Mouse Act** was passed, allowing the Government to release hunger strikers from prison, but then re-arrest them when they had recovered. But the violence and hunger strikes continued.
1914	The First World War began and both the NUWSS and WSPU ended their campaigns.

Arguments for and against giving women the vote

AQA B	✓
EDEXCEL A	✓
OCR B	✓
WJEC A	✓
WJEC B	✓
CCEA	✗

Even in 1914 opinion was still divided over whether women should have the vote.

For:
- Women now had the education and often the experience to make good voters – some women were now doctors or teachers. They were also allowed to vote in local elections, so why not in national ones?
- Women were gaining the vote in other Commonwealth countries, e.g. Australia and New Zealand, while one in four states in the USA had already given women the vote.
- Women's interest in social reform would benefit the poor.

Against:

- Women were considered to be too emotional, their brains were not suitable for making political decisions and they would neglect their duties at home. The Suffragette campaign proved their irresponsibility.
- Only 60% of men had the vote (to be eligible they had to be householders living in the constituency for one year). Therefore, it would be irrational to give all women the vote.
- Just giving the vote to propertied women would benefit the Conservative Party. But the Conservatives feared that the majority of women would vote Liberal or even Labour.

Did the Suffragettes help or hinder votes for women?

AQA B	✓
EDEXCEL A	✓
OCR B	✓
WJEC A	✓
WJEC B	✓
CCEA	✗

Historians differ over the question of whether the Suffragette movement helped or hindered their cause. There has recently been discussion of the Suffragettes as terrorists, while the popular press still regard them as heroines.

Helped	Hindered
<ul><li>The NUWSS had been campaigning for years, but had never managed to gain the vote.</li><li>The Suffragette methods put the campaign on the political agenda.</li><li>The Suffragette campaigns made sure that once the war was over the issue would return; women would now be given the vote at some point.</li></ul>	<ul><li>The Suffragettes' activities gave Asquith the excuse he needed not to give women the vote: the government could not be seen to give in to violence.</li><li>They convinced many people that women were irresponsible.</li><li>The principle of female suffrage had been agreed in 1913, but the extremism of the Suffragettes disgusted many Liberal MPs.</li></ul>

Gaining votes for women

AQA B	✓
EDEXCEL A	✓
OCR B	✓
WJEC A	✓
WJEC B	✓
CCEA	✗

Women's war work

By ending their campaigns as soon as the First World War was declared, both groups reassured the Government of their loyalty – helping Britain was their first duty. Both Mrs Fawcett and Mrs Pankhurst campaigned for women to help the war effort.

Women helped in all areas of life, but some industries in particular:

- The munitions factories had thousands of women employed doing dangerous jobs.
- Many women became nurses. Women served close to the Front Line and huge numbers were recruited.
- The Women's Land Army had 16,000 women enrolled by 1918.

Initially men's trade unions had resisted the employment of women. By 1915 over 100,000 women had registered as available for work, but only 5,000 had been employed. Then in 1916, male conscription was introduced and the country could not do without female labour. Women proved that they were quick to learn new skills and adept at work, often doing the job better than the men they replaced.

Figure 1.6 Women working on the Home Front.

Women gained the vote, 1918

Through their war work, women had proved that they were not weak, fragile or stupid. Even Asquith was now convinced that women had played a crucial part in winning the war. Lloyd George had replaced Asquith as Prime Minister in 1916 and he was far more sympathetic to women getting the vote.

Men who had been away fighting had lost their right to vote because they had not been living in Britain. The law, therefore, had to be changed, extending the male franchise and giving the opportunity for women to be included.

The **1918 Representation of the People Act**…
- gave the vote to women aged 30 and over and men aged 21 and over
- allowed women to stand for election as MPs.

If women had been allowed to vote at 21 they would have outnumbered men and many people thought that women in their 20s were still 'too silly' to vote.

PROGRESS CHECK

1. What could married women not do before 1882?
2. What was the name of the leader of the Suffragists?
3. How many members did the NUWSS have by 1914?
4. Why did the Conciliation Bill fail?
5. At what age could women vote after 1918?

1. Own their own property.
2. Mrs Millicent Garrett Fawcett.
3. Over 100,000
4. Because Henry Asquith delayed the Bill.
5. 30 and over.

1.3 The Home Front during the First World War

LEARNING SUMMARY

After studying this section you should be able to understand:

- how the Government recruited volunteers and why people joined
- how the country was organised to fight a war
- how the war affected civilian life
- the British public's attitude to the peace treaties

Recruitment

AQA B	✓
EDEXCEL A	✓
OCR B	✓
WJEC A	✓
WJEC B	✗
CCEA	✗

In Britain in 1914 there was **huge enthusiasm** for the war:

- People in Britain believed that it was right to fight for 'poor little Belgium' against the aggression of the German army.
- Britain had not been involved in a major war for several generations and people thought that war would be glorious, as at Waterloo. Ordinary people did not think they would be personally involved, but volunteers would fight heroically in distant lands. They did not expect that millions would be killed and that Britain would be bombed.
- Most people were very proud of their country and wanted to defend it.

KEY POINT

No one realised the seriousness of the situation because they were used to easy victories in colonial wars. Everyone thought it would be over by Christmas.

Britain's army was small, and there was no conscription, so volunteers were needed urgently. There was such enthusiasm that men rushed to join – 300,000 joined in August 1914.

The Government organised recruitment by various methods:

- They encouraged people from the same area, factory or business to join up together in **'Pals' battalions** of the Territorial Army, e.g. 'Glasgow Corporation Tramways' battalion, or the 'Accrington Pals'.
- They used **propaganda** to persuade men to sign up and to get women to encourage them. Propaganda methods included posters, speeches, newspaper advertisements, parades and public meetings.

The most famous example of propaganda was the poster of Lord Kitchener (the Secretary of State for War) pointing his finger with the slogan, 'Your country needs you'. Some posters were aimed at women and suggested that their men were cowards if they did not join up, even that their children would be ashamed of them in the future. Some women, often Suffragettes, gave men who weren't in uniform white feathers, implying that they were cowards. Propaganda whipped up hatred against the Germans and prolonged the myth that life in the trenches was heroic and glamorous.

Figure 1.7 'Your Country Needs You' poster

These voluntary conscription campaigns were so successful that women had to step in to take over the jobs of over 2.5 million men, who had joined up by 1916. However, this huge recruitment was not enough:

- So many men were being killed that more recruits were needed, but the number of volunteers dropped after news of the 1915 battles.
- There was alarm about the effect of volunteering in certain social and age groups e.g. that a generation of Public school boys aged 18 to 25 would be lost.

In 1916 the Government introduced **conscription**:

- This allowed for the recruitment of all men aged 18 to 41 into the armed services in an organised and fair way.
- Men in essential work (reserved occupations, e.g. farming, railways) were exempt.
- Conscientious objectors had to justify why they would not fight.

Organising the country for war

AQA B	✓
EDEXCEL A	✓
OCR B	✓
WJEC A	✓
WJEC B	✗
CCEA	✗

The Defence of the Realm Act (DORA) 1914

In order to win the war, the Government thought it must take **special powers** to concentrate the country's efforts. The Defence of the Realm Act allowed the government to curtail some individual freedoms:

- The press were **censored** in order to control the news and to keep people in support of the Government.
- The Government could take whatever **property** it needed for the war effort, e.g. factories, land and resources. In 1917, the Government ordered an extra 2.5 million acres of land to be ploughed for growing food.
- People were **restricted** from certain activities, e.g. talking about military matters in public, buying binoculars, trespassing in sensitive areas (e.g. railways and bridges) and ringing church bells.

In 1918 the Act was extended to introduce **food rationing**.

The impact of war on civilian life

AQA B	✓
EDEXCEL A	✓
OCR B	✓
WJEC A	✓
WJEC B	✗
CCEA	✗

Civilian casualties

The First World War was the first time that people at home had suffered from indiscriminate bombardment (though not to the extent they would during the Second World War):

- In 1914, east coast towns such as Scarborough, West Hartlepool and Lowestoft were shelled. In Scarborough alone 137 people were killed and hundreds more wounded.
- From 1915 German Zeppelins bombed towns in south-east Britain, causing hundreds of casualties.

Shortage of food

Early food shortages were caused by hoarders, but later shortages were mainly caused by the blockade by German submarines, which stopped food reaching Britain. These blockages rose to become a real threat in 1917 during the period of unrestricted submarine warfare. Food prices rose steeply, with long queues at food shops. Many could not afford to buy food and suffered from malnutrition.

> Some historians argue that the poor had a better diet after rationing was introduced than they had been used to in peacetime.

This situation was improved by the following:

- A convoy system was introduced, which began to break the blockade.
- Rationing was introduced in 1918. A weekly ration per person was one pound of meat and half a pound of sugar. Bacon, butter and cheese were also rationed. This improved the situation so that even the poor were able to have a healthy diet.

Britain's attitude to the peace treaties

AQA B	✓
EDEXCEL A	✓
OCR B	✓
WJEC A	✓
WJEC B	✗
CCEA	✗

By the end of the war about 703,000 soldiers and civilians had been killed and 1,663,000 wounded, and most people in Britain were determined on revenge. During the 'Khaki Election' in 1918, politicians competed in their demands for the punishment of Germany.

Lloyd George, as Prime Minister, had promised that Germany should pay the whole cost of the war. However, he later realised that Britain could not afford to destroy the economy of her main trading partner. This left him under constant pressure to be more harsh, while the peace treaties failed to satisfy Britain's thirst for revenge.

PROGRESS CHECK

1. Who was the Secretary of State for War in 1914?
2. Give an example in which DORA was used to misinform the public.
3. What did DORA prevent people from buying?
4. Which town suffered from severe bombardment in 1914?
5. When rationing was introduced in 1918, how much sugar could an individual buy each week?

5. Half a pound.
4. Scarborough.
3. Binoculars.
2. It censored anything likely to lower morale, e.g. conditions in the trenches.
1. Lord Kitchener.

Sample GCSE questions

Study the following sources.

Source A   **Source B**

Source C: Extract by George Coppard, a soldier during the First World War.

Rumours of war broke out and I began to be interested in the Territorials tramping the streets in their big strong boots. Although I seldom saw a newspaper, I knew about the assassination of Archduke Franz Ferdinand at Sarajevo. News placards screamed out at every street corner and military bands blared out their martial music in the main streets of Croydon. This was too much for me to resist, as if drawn by a magnet I knew I had to enlist right away.

Source D: From Lloyd George's War Memoirs

The populace caught the war fever. In every capital they clamoured for war…
On Monday afternoon I walked with Mr. Asquith to the House of Commons to hear Grey's famous speech. The crowd was so dense that no car could drive through it…
It was distinctly a pro-war demonstration. I remember observing at the time: 'These people are very anxious to send our poor soldiers to face death; how many of them will ever go into battle themselves?'

Source E: From a speech by Lord Montague to the House of Lords, July 1917

It was absolute humbug to talk of London being an undefended city. The Germans had a perfect right to raid London. London was defended by guns and aeroplanes and it was the chief centre for the production of munitions… The right line for the government to take was: 'This is a war of nations, and not alone of armies, and you must endeavour to bear the casualties you suffer in the same way as the French and Belgian civil populations are bearing the casualties incidental to this kind of warfare.'

Sample GCSE questions

Source F: A female eyewitness of Zeppelin raids, being interviewed in 1980.

The airship was on fire and it was floating down. I could only think of the people inside it being roasted to death. I was disgusted to see kind, good-hearted British people dancing in the street as the men in that airship were dying. When I said it was a terrible thing, my friends said, 'But they are Germans, they're the enemy, they've been bombing us!' This was what the war did, it turned gentle people into monsters.

(a) Study Source A. Why was this poster published in Britain in 1915? Use the source and your knowledge to explain your answer.

The poster was printed to recruit soldiers. We can tell this because it says at the bottom: `Join the Army at once and help stop an air raid'. It was printed in 1915, before conscription began in 1916, and during the first Zeppelin raids on the south-east of Britain. The picture shows St. Paul's in London, so it is suggesting that if a man joined the Army he would be helping to stop the bombing of London. Perhaps they intended to imply that it would be cowardly to `be killed at home by a bomb'   **(6)**

> This is a good answer because it uses and directly quotes from the source. The answer also uses some knowledge of 1915 to put the source into its context.

(b) Study Sources A and B. Is one poster more useful than the other to a historian studying the importance of bombing in Britain during the First World War? Use the sources and your knowledge to explain your answer.

Source A is more useful, because it is first-hand evidence that proves that people were worried about Zeppelin attacks in 1915. It was printed that year, and it suggests that Zeppelin attacks were significant enough to worry a potential recruit: `It is far better... killed at home by a bomb'.

Source B is less convincing because it only shows what the Germans wanted to do, rather than the effect of what they actually did. They wanted to threaten British shipping and ports, but there isn't much evidence to suggest that they did this. Perhaps this was a piece of German propaganda – they wanted the people at home to think this was what they were actually doing, while in fact they were killing women and children. This source may be quite reliable, because one can compare it with Source E, in which Lord Montague thinks that the Zeppelins were after economic targets. But that doesn't make it as useful as Source A.   **(8)**

> This compares the usefulness of both sources using information from both and evaluating both with the focus on the importance of bombing. It corroborates Source B with Source E, which is a useful way of establishing reliability, and clearly evaluates it in comparison.

Sample GCSE questions

(c) Study Sources C and D. How far do these sources disagree about support for the war? Use the sources to explain your answer.

Both the sources agree that the war was supported. In Source C, although Coppard rarely saw a newspaper, he was attracted first by `Territorials tramping the streets in big strong boots´, and later by placards and military bands. There is no evidence that he was interested in the international causes.

Source D is in agreement that the war was supported: `It was distinctly a pro-war demonstration.´ However, Lloyd George doubts that people will sign up to join the Army: `how many of them will ever go into battle themselves?´ So what Coppard takes as being inevitable, Lloyd George doubts. It is also implied in Source D that the politics of the war are important, because the crowd has gathered around Parliament. Coppard clearly thought this less important: `I seldom saw a newspaper´. So these sources agree that there was support, while suggesting different reasons for that support. **(6)**

There is no need to use any of your knowledge directly. First answer how the sources agree, then explain how they disagree. Use details from the sources to illustrate your arguments. Try to conclude with a direct statement of 'How far...'

(d) Study Sources E and F. Is one source more reliable than the other about attitudes in Britain towards Zeppelin raids? Use the sources and your knowledge to explain your answer.

I am sure that Lord Montague would not intentionally lie to the House of Lords, but there is nothing here to say that this attitude is typical. He says: `The Germans had a perfect right to raid London.´ This is in contrast to Source A, in which the propaganda poster clearly suggests both terror and revenge as motives for enlistment. I know that there is plenty of evidence to suggest that people generally thought that `the Hun´ was a `beast´ and was not right to target civilians: `Remember Scarborough´ was used on another poster. So, if Source E is reliable about what Lord Montague thought, it is not reliable for British attitudes in general.

Source F does not seem very reliable either. The eye witness records that her friends thought differently from her, and she was only interviewed in 1980, by which time her view of Germans would have softened. Even if she was telling the truth, there is no real evidence that this view was typical.

Neither of these sources can be very reliable for attitudes in Britain in the general sense, but they do corroborate each other in that they show that there were individual views and that not everyone was convinced by the propaganda image of the crazed German beast. **(9)**

This answer compares each source with the candidate's own knowledge and with other sources. An account written at the time is not necessarily typical, while an account written many years later is not necessarily unreliable. Look for points of reliability, as well as unreliability.

2 The First World War 1914–1918

The following topics are covered in this chapter:

- **The causes of the First World War**
- **How the failure of the Schlieffen Plan led to stalemate**
- **The other fronts**
- **How victory was achieved**

2.1 The causes of the First World War

LEARNING SUMMARY

After studying this section you should be able to understand:

- how the alliance system made war more likely
- how colonial rivalry created tension between the Great Powers
- why problems in the Balkans could not easily be solved
- how far the Kaiser should be blamed for the conflict
- the importance of the arms race, 1900–1914

The importance of the alliance system

AQA B	✓
EDEXCEL A	✓
OCR B	✓
WJEC A	✗
WJEC B	✗
CCEA	✗

The formation of opposing alliances

Until 1870 Germany had been a group of small states with no central control, but in a series of wars Count von Bismarck had unified Germany under the autocratic control of the Kaiser (Emperor). A war with France in 1870 had created a permanent state of **rivalry between Germany and France** since Germany had taken Alsace-Lorraine from France, so Bismarck was keen to build alliances that would keep France isolated. At first he successfully allied Germany to Austria–Hungary, Russia and Turkey, depriving France of any useful friends (Britain was not interested in continental alliances). But when Bismarck was dismissed in 1890, Kaiser Wilhelm II allowed the alliance with Russia to lapse – this was a very serious oversight.

By 1914, Germany was the most powerful industrial nation in Europe at the head of the **Central Powers: an alliance of Austria–Hungary, Turkey and Italy**. France naturally felt isolated by German diplomacy, more so because she was falling behind in the growth of industry and population. During the 1890s she developed closer and closer ties with Russia, helping to finance the growth of industry there.

At first this almost forced Britain into the German alliance, because Britain was worried by Russian ambitions in India, but when Russia was soundly defeated by Japan in 1904–1905, Britain realised that an association with France would be better than complete isolation in Europe. In 1904, Britain and France sorted out their colonial disagreements and began a no-strings-attached friendship, called an 'Entente'. In 1907 this loose group was joined by Russia in the '**Triple Entente**'.

informal alliance.

> **The Triple Entente:** This agreement didn't bind them to fight in each other's wars, but it did bind them not to fight each other.

Did the alliances preserve peace?

Certainly neither of the alliances was intended to cause war: both had been formed for reassurance, rather than for aggression, and yet their effects were bad:

- Both groups began to assume that the other was a **potential threat** and made contingency plans, which would involve fighting whole alliances rather than individual countries.
- Arms were built up competitively in '**arms races**' to give each group an advantage. This increased nationalist tension, making war seem inevitable.

The importance of colonial rivalries

Some historians believe that the First World War was about colonies: which Great Power would rival Britain in size of empire – France or Germany? Certainly, had Germany been able to take the French Empire in Africa to add to her own, small empire, she would have become a much greater colonial threat to Britain.

France and Germany were in competition to take control of Morocco. The Kaiser, suffering a setback at the **Conference of Algeciras** in 1906, thought that Britain and France were working together to exclude Germany. When, in 1911, the French tried to take over Morocco, the Kaiser sent a gunboat (the Panther) to **Agadir**. Britain didn't want the German navy to take a base in the Mediterranean and called another conference at which Britain and France stood together. France took Morocco, while Germany was compensated in central Africa. While all appeared friendly, the Kaiser never again appeared in Britain, while France and Britain agreed to use their navies to **defend each other's interests**: the French would defend the Mediterranean, while the Royal Navy would defend France's Atlantic and North Sea coasts. The Entente became more like an alliance.

Trouble in the Balkans

The Austro–Hungarian and Russian Empires were both trying to take advantage of the small states left since the Turkish Empire had lost control of the area between Austria, Greece and Bulgaria. The first crisis occurred in 1908, when Austria took over Bosnia and Herzegovina. Russian protests were only silenced when Germany supported Austria. Perhaps this victory made Austria over-confident?

During a series of small wars in 1912–1913, Serbia emerged as the strongest country in the Balkans with a strong army and close ties with Russia. **Austria was hoping for a chance to crush Serbia** by 1914, but this was fraught with danger, because the Serbs were both Slav and Orthodox and so had close ties to the Russians. The murder of Archduke Franz Ferdinand and his wife Sophie at Sarajevo was blamed on Serbia. With German backing, Austria issued a ten-point ultimatum, which Serbia could not possibly accept and retain her independence. Austria declared war on Serbia on 28th July 1914.

Figure 2.1 The collapsing Turkish Empire

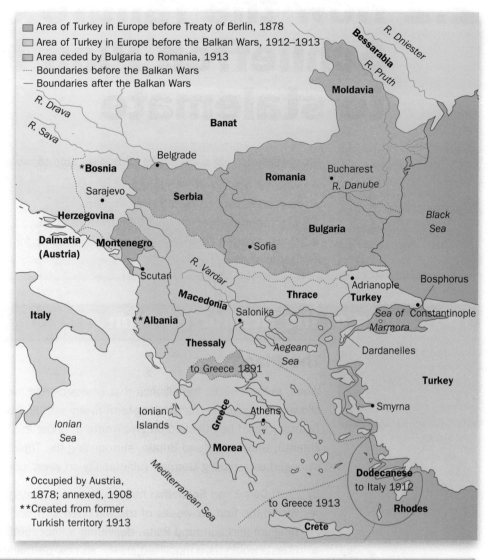

- Area of Turkey in Europe before Treaty of Berlin, 1878
- Area of Turkey in Europe before the Balkan Wars, 1912–1913
- Area ceded by Bulgaria to Romania, 1913
- ···· Boundaries before the Balkan Wars
- — Boundaries after the Balkan Wars

*Occupied by Austria, 1878; annexed, 1908
**Created from former Turkish territory 1913

The German connection

AQA B	✓
EDEXCEL A	✓
OCR B	✓
WJEC A	✗
WJEC B	✗
CCEA	✗

Though Germany was blamed unfairly for starting the war once she had lost it in 1919, historians do now blame Germany for several reasons:

- Germany had constructed the alliance of the **Central Powers**, which did oblige its members to go to war together.
- Germany got herself involved in a **naval arms race** with Britain and a **military arms race** with Russia, both of which made war seem inevitable.
- Germany was **challenging Britain and France for colonial power**.
- Germany felt threatened by Russia when Russia mobilised to help Serbia, but rather than attacking Russia, **she invaded France through Belgium**, making the war much greater than it would have been. Historians think that Germany wanted to forestall being overtaken by Britain and Russia and decided on a pre-emptive strike.

> It is more important to know how each country was brought into the war, than to know who was to blame.

However, Germany was not entirely to blame:

- Austria wanted war with Serbia.
- Russia mobilised troops on the German front as well as against Austria.
- Britain and France did not make a clear statement whether they would, or would not support Russia or each other. Germany was, therefore, taking rational precautions to avoid being caught in the middle.

2.2 How the failure of the Schlieffen Plan led to stalemate

LEARNING SUMMARY

After studying this section you should be able to understand:

- why the Schlieffen Plan failed
- how stalemate caused trench warfare
- why the stalemate on the Western Front lasted so long
- to what extent General Haig should be blamed for the losses in the Battle of the Somme

The failure of the Schlieffen Plan

AQA B	✓
EDEXCEL A	✓
OCR B	✓
WJEC A	✓
WJEC B	✗
CCEA	✗

The Plan

When, in the 1890s, the alliance that Bismarck had arranged with Russia was allowed to lapse, Germany's long-term rivalry with France became more dangerous: Germany could be attacked on **two fronts** at once. In 1907 Russia joined the Triple Entente, with France and Britain, surrounding the Triple Alliance to which Germany belonged and making German vulnerability an even more urgent consideration.

By 1905 **Count von Schlieffen** had developed a strategic plan to avoid this threat:
- Within the first six weeks of the war, Germany would attack France through Belgium and surround Paris, delivering a knockout blow.
- Russia would have mobilised slowly, so now Germany could concentrate on her.

Why the Plan did not work in 1914

The Plan did not work for several reasons:
- On 3rd August **von Moltke attacked** with over 1 million men through Belgium, but the Belgian army resisted, slowed down his advance and, therefore, the element of surprise was lost.
- To German surprise, **Britain honoured the Treaty of London 1839**, which obliged Britain (and Germany) to protect Belgian independence. The British Expeditionary Force was sent to Belgium, where it slowed the German advance at Mons.
- On 19th August **Russia attacked Germany much sooner than expected**. Germany was forced to weaken her attack on France by moving 100,000 men to East Prussia.
- While the German army continued its advance, it was **too weak to envelop Paris** to deliver the knockout blow. Instead it was met by both the British and the French armies at the **Battle of the Marne** and forced to retreat to the Aisne River.

> **KEY POINT**
>
> The failure of the Schlieffen Plan was decisive in the whole course of the war. It forced Germany onto the defensive until 1918.

Figure 2.2 The failure of the Schlieffen Plan

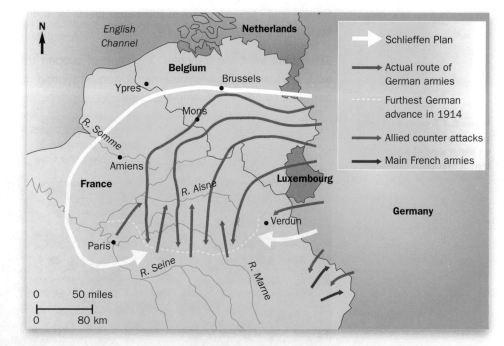

Stalemate

AQA B	✓
EDEXCEL A	✓
OCR B	✓
WJEC A	✓
WJEC B	✗
CCEA	✗

The race to the sea and stalemate

After the German retreat, both sides raced to outflank the other, quickly extending the battle front towards the English Channel. The main confrontation was at the **First Battle of Ypres**, in November, in which thousands died, but neither army could break through the other.

As the advances stopped, both sides brought up artillery and machine guns, driving their opponents to seek safety in **trenches**. Soon these extended from the English Channel to Switzerland.

Figure 2.3 The Western Front stretched from Belgium to Switzerland

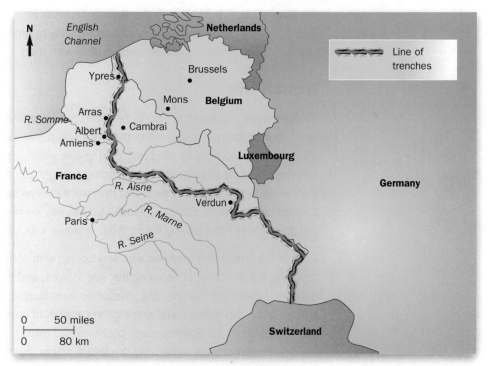

There was a 'stalemate' because neither side could now advance. The Western Front would remain in almost the same place for the next three years, until stalemate was broken in 1918.

Behind the front line trenches, a system of support trenches and supply dumps were gradually built. Reinforcements were stationed nearby, connected to the front line by communication trenches.

Figure 2.4 A cross-sectional view of a trench and an aerial view of a trench system.

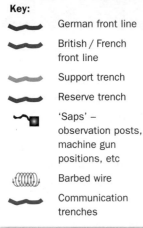

Front-line trenches 2 metres deep sandbags at top for protection

Parapet
Wooden periscope
Lee Enfield rifle
Sandbags
Fire step
Wooden or iron support
Dug-out
Duck boards
Mud and water

Key:

- German front line
- British / French front line
- Support trench
- Reserve trench
- 'Saps' – observation posts, machine gun positions, etc
- Barbed wire
- Communication trenches

No-Man's Land

'**No-Man's Land**' lay between the British / French front line, and the German front line. This was protected by lines of barbed wire to slow down enemy attacks, pitted by shell holes and often impassable with mud.

Trench life

Soldiers were supposed to rotate between the front line, reserve and company 'rest', but often they remained in the front line for weeks, or even months. Trench life was made horrible by mud and cold in the winters, but in the summers the soldiers could be blisteringly hot. Flooding brought the additional hazard of trench foot, while in the summer, flies and rats were everywhere, as was the smell from corpses and sewage. Soldiers usually had to rely on poor, tinned food or hard biscuit. Danger from enemy fire or from disease was constant.

Most of the time in the trenches was very boring, with constant hard work repairing and supplying the trenches, or repairing the wire in front, and never time to rest properly. However, when there was fighting, casualties were terrible because the only way was to attack across 'No-Man's Land' running the gauntlet of enemy artillery and machine-gun fire. The Battle of the Somme alone cost over 1.2 million casualties; 57,000 were killed, wounded or captured among the British troops on the first day alone.

Gas warfare

Among many new weapons developed to break the stalemate, gas was the worst. The Germans first used **chlorine gas in 1915**. At first the wind was used to blow the gas over their opponents' trenches, but later **mustard gas** was developed, which was delivered in shells. By now a gas mask on its own was insufficient, since mustard gas burned exposed skin, as well as blinding and even killing if breathed in.

> **KEY POINT**
>
> Gas was used in huge amounts by both sides, as the war progressed, but it didn't create a breakthrough.

Why did the stalemate last so long?

It was much easier to defend than to attack:

* **Machine guns** and artillery were tremendously powerful, but they were difficult to move forward over the churned-up land of 'No-Man's Land'. This meant that attackers were easily mown down as they couldn't fire back so effectively, and couldn't communicate with their own artillery.
* Attackers were slowed down by **barbed wire**, **mud**, **shell-holes** and debris in 'No-Man's Land', while horses could not survive a charge across it.
* The further attackers advanced, the more they outdistanced their **supplies and reinforcements** whereas defenders could quickly bring up reinforcements and had supplies to hand.
* This was the first time that war had been fought like this: never before had firepower been so devastating. Generals and other officers had to develop tactics to overcome these difficulties and **success took a long time**, during which men continued to be sent to their deaths.
* The biggest tactical mistake was often that enemy trenches were 'softened up' by **heavy bombardment** before an attack, alerting the enemy to have reinforcements ready and rarely killing many well dug-in defenders.

> You will need to know why stalemate developed and why it lasted so long.

The Battle of the Somme

AQA B	✓
EDEXCEL A	✓
OCR B	✓
WJEC A	✓
WJEC B	✗
CCEA	✗

General Haig's Plans

Haig replaced General French as **commander of British forces** in December 1915. He had made his reputation as a cavalry commander in South Africa, and he had little experience of trench warfare. He took over a plan for a combined English and French attack on the powerful German position on the Somme plateau, but in early 1916 this plan had to be reduced since the Germans attacked at Verdun first. Now the Somme battle was intended just to draw German troops away from their attacks on the French.

Should Haig have done better?

Though the German trenches were bombarded for a week before the battle, the Germans were safe in deep dug-outs, and the shelling just warned them to be ready. After a disastrous first day for Britain on 1st July, the battle lasted for a further five months, with enormous casualties on both sides. Just a few miles of territory, of no great worth, were won. Was the battle worth the cost?

Against Haig	For Haig
<ul><li>Neither Haig nor anyone else could think of a better way to attack than to send wave after wave of soldiers to their deaths in 'No-Man's Land. Even when attacks were hopeless, Haig persisted in them.</li><li>About 620,000 British casualties were sustained without breaking through the German lines to end the war.</li><li>Huge amounts of artillery were used, which alerted the enemy to attacks but did not destroy them. They churned up the ground, making attack even more difficult.</li></ul>	<ul><li>Pressure on Verdun was relieved and the French army survived to fight the war.</li><li>The tactics were not Haig's, but those of his more experienced juniors. Nobody could do better, so Haig should not be blamed alone.</li><li>To do nothing was impossible and Haig was trying to end the war as decisively as he could.</li></ul>

KEY POINT

Trench warfare was new to everyone and similarly huge casualty figures were sustained by others who challenged the full power of the German army. Don't be too hard on Haig.

2.3 The other fronts

LEARNING SUMMARY	After studying this section you should be able to understand:
	<ul><li>the strategic importance of war at sea</li><li>how other fronts failed to bring victory</li></ul>

The war at sea

AQA B	✓
EDEXCEL A	✗
OCR B	✓
WJEC A	✗
WJEC B	✗
CCEA	✗

Even before the war, naval rivalry had an important effect: the race to build **Dreadnought** battleships had been an important focus of competition. Unexpectedly there was only one major sea battle, but the war at sea was decisive:

- By keeping **control of the seas**, Britain was able to resupply herself (especially from the USA) while blockading enemy ports so that their supplies were cut off.
- Without control of the seas, the British coastline would have been open to German attack and communication with the Western Front would have been impossible.

It is important to understand the effects that the other fronts had on the war, which fronts were most decisive and why.

KEY POINT

Maintaining sea power was just as crucial as winning the war on land.

The Battle of Jutland

The only major sea battle was fought off Jutland in 1916. Neither side wished to risk losing their fleet, so the battle was confused and indecisive. The British lost more ships, but the German fleet went back to port and didn't threaten Britain again for the rest of the war. Winston Churchill remarked of Admiral Jellicoe, in charge of the British fleet, that he was 'the only man on either side who could lose the war in an afternoon'.

Blockades

Britain's supply lifeline stretched across the Atlantic from the USA. Deprived of the use of their fleet, Germany used submarines ('**U-boats**') from 1915 to sink the merchant ships and cut this lifeline. In 1917 Germany declared '**unrestricted submarine warfare**', sinking any ships thought to be supplying Britain. At this time, Britain only had six week's supply of food left, so it seemed she would be starved into defeat. However, this threat was overcome by...

- making merchant ships travel in **convoys** protected by warships
- using **depth charges** to sink submarines
- using **Q-ships** (warships disguised as merchant ships), which sank the U-boats when they surfaced.

Meanwhile, the British blockade of German ports was so successful that **Germany was starved of food and other essentials of war**. This shortage was one of the decisive factors in making the German people want peace in 1918.

The Eastern Front

AQA B	✓
EDEXCEL A	✗
OCR B	✓
WJEC A	✗
WJEC B	✗
CCEA	✗

The **early success** of the Russian army in East Prussia in 1914 was very important in defeating the Schlieffen Plan, but it did not continue. The huge Russian army (3 million men actually fought on the Eastern Front) was poorly equipped, badly led and disorganised. In 1914 they were defeated at the battles of **Tannenburg** and the **Masurian Lakes** and, by 1917, they had lost the whole of Poland and Romania. This was due to the following:

- In order to solve the supply problem for his huge army, Nicholas II (the Russian Tsar) focused all efforts on this, **neglecting the needs of the rest of the country** and forcing people to work very long hours for very poor pay, pushing his people towards revolution.
- The **winter of 1916** was very harsh and the transport system seized up. The towns could not be fed. When revolution broke out in March 1917, the Tsar was forced to abdicate.
- Though the new government (the Provisional Government) continued with the war, they were **unable to keep control**. Soldiers deserted or mutinied and the army disintegrated.
- By November, when the Bolsheviks (communists) had taken over, the **German army was advancing into Russia**.
- The Bolsheviks were forced to sign a peace treaty at **Brest-Litovsk in March 1918**, which gave Germany a huge section of the Russian Empire.

> **KEY POINT**
>
> Although the defeat of Russia was a victory for Germany, she was unable to move enough troops to the Western Front to defeat Britain and France in 1918 because about 1 million soldiers were tied down in Russia.

Gallipoli, 1915

AQA B	✓
EDEXCEL A	✗
OCR B	✓
WJEC A	✗
WJEC B	✗
CCEA	✗

The Plan

By 1915 when there was deadlock on the Western Front, **Winston Churchill**, as First Lord of the Admiralty, thought up a plan to attack Germany through Turkey. This would have the following advantages:

1 **Turkey could quickly be knocked out of the war**, ending conflict in the Middle East.

2 The capture of the Dardanelles would **open up a supply route** to Russia, through the Black Sea, which would be better than the ice-bound route via Murmansk or Archangel.

3 The defeat of Turkey would allow British troops to **threaten Bulgaria and Austria**, who were easier opponents than Germany.

The intention was to mount a naval attack on the Gallipoli peninsula, followed by landings by Australian and New Zealand troops – the ANZACS.

Figure 2.5 The Gallipoli Campaign

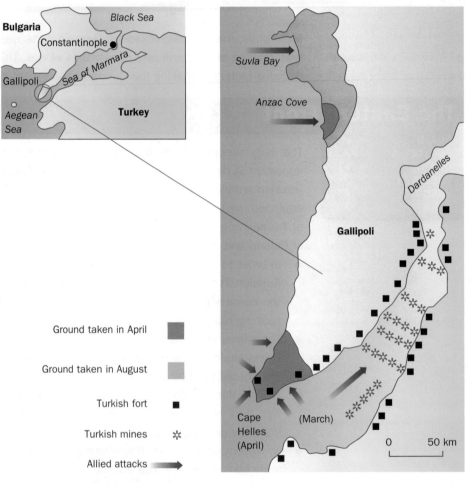

Reasons for failure

1 The **naval attack went wrong** when ships were sunk by mines. This alerted the Turks.

2 When the troops were landed, they found Gallipoli **strongly defended by Turkish artillery** and they were trapped on the beaches.

3 Casualties were high and 135,000 troops were only evacuated in December after **about 200,000 had already been killed**.

The war in the air

AQA B	✓
EDEXCEL A	✗
OCR B	✓
WJEC A	✗
WJEC B	✗
CCEA	✗

Airships

Airships were used by both sides and were **more important than aeroplanes** at first. The British used them to escort merchant ships because they could spot U-boats easily and warn the ships. The Germans used airships (**Zeppelins**) to bomb British cities, but by 1916 fighter planes had tracer shells and anti-aircraft guns had been developed, which made them very vulnerable.

Aeroplanes

At first aeroplanes were used just for **reconnaissance** and were extremely basic, built with wood, canvas, wire and a piston engine. They had no guns and were used to take photographs, to warn of enemy attack and to find the right range for artillery to hit their targets. During the war, aeroplanes were developed for the following uses:

- **Fighters** to shoot down reconnaissance planes. They became more efficient, with forward-firing machine guns so that dogfights and strafing began to develop.
- **Bombers** to travel long distances and to attack cities, even in enemy countries.

By the end of the war the RAF had been formed. It had 23,000 aeroplanes, compared to 37 at the beginning of the war.

2.4 How victory was achieved

LEARNING SUMMARY	After studying this section you should be able to understand:
	• how the war changed in favour of Britain and France
	• how Germany was defeated on the Western Front

New developments

AQA B	✓
EDEXCEL A	✓
OCR B	✓
WJEC A	✗
WJEC B	✗
CCEA	✗

The tank and other new weapons

Although the **tank was first used in the Battle of the Somme in 1916**, it had never lived up to its potential. Even at the Battle of Cambrai in 1917, when tanks broke through German lines, the ground won was speedily lost because tanks were **slow**, **unreliable** and **vulnerable** if they were used on their own. By 1918, smaller, lighter tanks had been developed, which were used in co-operation with the infantry. From the **Battle of Amiens** in August 1918, tanks became an important part of a 'triple alliance' between tanks, infantry and aircraft, which could take firepower forward into battle.

Alliance with the USA

The **USA entered the war in 1917**, but only about 300,000 troops had reached the Western Front before the end of the war. The American contribution was really significant in supplying Britain and France and in persuading Germany to try to bring the war to an end before the Americans arrived in force.

Attrition

While Britain and France benefited from American supplies, **the blockade was biting on Germany**, which was short of food and raw materials. Germany must either win the war quickly or fall into revolution and chaos.

The Ludendorff Offensive

The Ludendorff Offensive in 1918 was the first time that German troops had adopted an offensive strategy since 1914 and it proved their undoing. General Ludendorff ordered three great attacks, starting in March 1918. As the Allies were pushed back, there was alarm that the Germans might take Paris, but **General Foch**, the Allied Supreme Commander, had kept reinforcements back until the German advance had outrun its supplies. The counter-attack began an Allied advance that did not end until the Armistice.

Revolution in Germany

Sailors in Kiel mutinied on 29th October and eventually took over Berlin. **Bavaria** had a short-lived communist revolution in November, under **Kurt Eisner**. On 9th November, Kaiser Wilhelm II abdicated, handing the government over to Freidrich Ebert, leader of the Social Democrat Party so that an Armistice could be signed.

German isolation

Between September and November 1918 Germany's allies, **Bulgaria, Turkey and Austria–Hungary had all surrendered**, opening Germany to attack from all sides. She no longer had the resources to meet the threat of attack from the south.

PROGRESS CHECK

1. Why did the Austrian quarrel with Serbia cause Germany to attack France?
2. Where did the British Expeditionary Force hold up the German advance through Belgium?
3. What was the main battle during the 'race to the sea'?
4. On what date did the British Army lose 57,000 men?
5. Who could have lost the war 'in an afternoon'?
6. How did the British mainly use airships?
7. Where were tanks first used?
8. In which year did the USA enter the war?
9. Who was the Allied Supreme Commander in 1918?
10. Who led the communist revolution in Bavaria?

10. Kurt Eisner.
9. General Foch.
8. 1917
7. The Battle of the Somme 1916.
6. To protect convoys by spotting U-boats.
5. Admiral Jellicoe.
4. 1st July, 1916.
3. The First Battle of Ypres
2. Mons.
Germany did not want to be attacked on two fronts.
1. Russia would support Serbia and attack the Central Powers. France may support Russia.

Exam practice questions

1 Study Sources A, B, C and D and then answer all parts of the question.

Source A: A German description of a trench in 1915

We stayed where we were for three days. Then we were withdrawn behind Chailly for another three days, and then sent back into our trenches again. Our dug-out became more and more complete with wooden shelves for the dixies and nails in the roof to hang the bread and sausages on, so that the rats could not get at them. Since our dug-out completely blocked the main trench, we cut a loop line of trench behind it for the men to go round. We also began to make a latrine, so that we could relieve ourselves during the day.

Source B: A British description of 'No-Man's Land' in July 1916

It eventually became clear that the German line followed points of eminence, always giving a commanding view of No Man's Land. Immediately in front, and spreading left and right until hidden from sight, was clear evidence that the attack had been brutally repulsed. Hundreds of dead, many belonging to the 37th Brigade, were strung like wreckage washed up to a high-water mark. Quite as many died on the enemy wire as on the ground, like fish caught in a net. They hung there in grotesque postures... From the way the bodies were evenly spread out, whether on the wire or lying in front of it, it was clear that there were no gaps in the wire at the time of the attack.

Source C: An RAF pilot in action in 1918

Flying east for a couple of miles we turn back and I spray the area with both guns and let go two Coopers (bombs) at five-second intervals on two Archie (anti-aircraft) crews. It looks okay on one and a near miss on the other. Daley, 200 yards behind, is doing the same thing. I notice that about half the area is burnt-out and shot-up very thoroughly.

Source D: A British historian writes in 1966

Army officers in every country came from the conservative, privileged classes and had no contact with the scientific creative spirit of the age. When their first brutal onslaughts failed, they cried out for more men or, as most, for more shells. They did not cry out for new methods. No general consulted a civil engineer or the head of a great industrial concern... The generals had little interest in new weapons. They had accepted the rifle, though mainly in order to stick a bayonet on the end of it – a variant of the pike... They regarded the tank and aeroplane with suspicion... They sat in remote headquarters, working on railway timetables and accumulating an ever greater weight of men and shells.

Exam practice questions

(a) Look at Source A. Compare this German account of a trench in 1915 with your knowledge of British trenches.

....

....

.... **(3)**

(b) Look at Source B. How useful is this account in explaining the problems encountered on the first day of the Battle of the Somme?

....

....

....

....

....

.... **(6)**

(c) Use Source C to explain the growing importance of the aeroplane in warfare during the First World War.

....

....

....

....

....

....

.... **(8)**

(d) Is Source D a fair interpretation of the role of army officers and generals in the First World War? Use Source D and your own knowledge to answer the question.

....

....

....

....

....

....

.... **(8)**

You may need to continue your answers on a separate sheet of paper.

3 The failure of international peace 1919–1939

The following topics are covered in this chapter:

- The peace settlements 1919–1923
- The League of Nations 1919–1936
- Why international peace had collapsed by 1939

3.1 The peace settlements 1919–1923

LEARNING SUMMARY

After studying this section you should be able to understand:

- the differing aims of the victorious powers
- the need for compromise in creating a peace settlement
- how Germany and the other defeated countries were punished
- the issues left unresolved by the peace treaties

The intentions of the victorious powers

AQA B	✓
EDEXCEL A	✓
OCR B	✓
WJEC A	✗
WJEC B	✗
CCEA	✗

An **Armistice** or provisional peace had been agreed on 11th November 1918 after which the Allies called a peace conference in Paris in January 1919. There, the talks were dominated by the '**big three**': President Woodrow Wilson (USA), Prime Minister David Lloyd George (Britain) and Prime Minister Georges Clemenceau (France).

Germany sent representatives, but not to negotiate, just to accept the victors' decisions (a '**diktat**'). They expected a settlement based on President Wilson's '**Fourteen Points**' of 1917, which promised 'just peace' since many Germans did not accept that they had lost the war.

The victorious powers' main objective was to make a lasting peace, but their opinions differed on…

- how far Germany should be punished
- to what extent the victors should be repaid for the war
- how the peace should be enforced.

Make sure you can discuss how the victorious powers disagreed.

France: Prime Minister Georges Clemenceau

'Tiger' Clemenceau wanted three main gains for France:

1. **Revenge** (*revanchism*): In 1870 France had lost the provinces of Alsace and

Lorraine. It was a main aim that these two areas should be returned, but in every part of the settlement, Clemenceau wished to be as hard as possible on Germany.

2 Reparations (*repayments*): France had been invaded, her towns and industry destroyed and millions of her people killed or injured. Germany must pay for these damages and for the French war debt.

3 Security: France must be guaranteed that Germany would be weakened so that she could never invade France again. Clemenceau aimed to take both the Saar and the Rhineland to strengthen France's eastern border, while enforcing disarmament on Germany.

Britain: Prime Minister David Lloyd George

Lloyd George had been re-elected in 1918 to squeeze Germany 'as a lemon is squeezed, until the pips squeak' (Eric Geddes), but he knew that, as Britain's biggest trading partner before 1914, the destruction of Germany would not be in the British interest in the long term. He intended that Germany should…

- lose her **colonies** overseas to end rivalry with Britain and France
- lose her **naval power** to leave Britain in command of the seas
- repay Britain's **war debt**.

USA: President Woodrow Wilson

President Wilson thought that revenge would cause another war. Instead he wanted a just peace, based on lasting principles such as '**national self-determination**' and a **League of Nations**.

> **KEY POINT**
>
> National self-determination means that each nation should have its own country and govern itself.

Wilson's aims are found in his **Fourteen Points** (1917). However, these would demand US involvement in Europe for the future, when many Americans wanted to withdraw from World affairs (isolationism).

Wilson's Fourteen Points
1 No secret treaties between countries
2 Free access to the sea for all
3 Free trade between countries
4 Disarmament by all countries
5 Colonies to have a say in their own future
6 German troops to leave Russia
7 Belgium to be independent
8 France to regain Alsace–Lorraine
9 Frontier between Austria and Italy to be adjusted
10 Self-determination for people of Eastern Europe
11 Serbia to have access to the sea
12 Self-determination for people in the Turkish Empire
13 Poland to be independent with access to the sea
14 A League of Nations to settle disputes between countries

How far were these aims fulfilled in the final treaties?

The Paris Peace Treaties

AQA B	✓
EDEXCEL A	✓
OCR B	✓
WJEC A	✗
WJEC B	✗
CCEA	✗

Germany: The Treaty of Versailles 1919

1	Territory	In Europe Germany lost: • **Alsace–Lorraine** to France • The **Saar and Danzig** (under the League of Nations) • The '**Polish Corridor**' to Poland Elsewhere Germany lost all her **colonies** and they were put under the control of the League of Nations (administered by Britain and France) including: • Tanganyika • German South West Africa
2	Sovereignty (rights)	• **German armed forces** were strictly limited to 100,000 men in the army (with no conscription) with no tanks, the navy was limited to six battleships and no submarines, and the air force was disbanded. • The **Rhineland** remained German but German troops could not enter it (**demilitarised**). • Union with other Germans in Austria was prohibited (no **Anschluss**)
3	War guilt	• Germany had to accept guilt for starting the war (Clause 231) • Because it was guilty, Germany had to pay reparations to the Allies for the damage caused, set (in 1921) at **£6,600 million in gold.**
4	League of Nations	A **League of Nations** was set up, both to settle disputes and to enforce the Treaty, but Germany was not allowed at first to join.

> Decide to what extent these points would ensure peace for the future.

Rather than promoting a lasting peace, the Treaty of Versailles angered Germans to the extent that it formed the basis for the success of Hitler in Germany in 1932. Hitler argued the following points:

- That the Treaty was a 'diktat' – there could be no negotiation and only the threat of war.
- Wilson's Fourteen Points had promised self-determination, but now Germans were in Poland, Czechoslovakia, Austria, Denmark and France.
- German pride in their army and navy was destroyed: they became too small to protect Germans from invasion or civil war. Other nations were not forced to disarm.
- Nations other than Germany had also contributed to starting the war.
- Reparations were cruel and unfair, especially when some industrial areas were taken by France and Poland. The German economy was ruined, causing inflation and German failure to pay reparation payments. France and Belgium made matters worse by invading Germany in January 1923 to take the Ruhr to force payment. Workers in the Ruhr went on strike, paid by the German government with worthless currency. The Treaty of Versailles was blamed for hyperinflation (huge fall in the worth of money), injustice and bankruptcy.

Figure 3.1 German losses at Versailles.

- Owned by Germany before the First World War
- Taken by France
- Taken by Poland
- Taken by Lithuania
- Taken by Denmark
- Land owned by Russia before the First World War
- New Eastern Europe states taken from Russia
- Taken by Belgium

Austria: The Treaty of St. Germain 1919

1 Austria lost her empire including Hungary, Bohemia and Moravia, Transylvania and Croatia.

2 Hungary, Czechoslovakia and Yugoslavia became separate states; Czechoslovakia and Yugoslavia contained several races each.

3 Austria was forbidden to join with Germany (no Anschluss, although Austrians were German too).

4 Austrian armed forces were limited to 30,000.

Bulgaria: The Treaty of Neuilly 1919

1 Bulgaria lost some territory to Greece and Yugoslavia, but gained some from Turkey.

2 Her armed forces were limited to 20,000.

3 She was charged £100 million in reparations.

Hungary: The Treaty of Trianon 1920

1 Hungary had been co-head of the Austrian Empire and shared in Austrian territorial losses.

2 Three million Hungarians were lost to their country.

3 Reparations were expected, but Hungary's economy was too ruined for her to pay.

Turkey: Treaties of Sevres, 1920 and Lausanne 1923

At Sevres, Turkey lost the following:

1 Control of the straits running into the Black Sea and Smyrna to Greece.

2 Morocco, Tunisia, Syria and Lebanon to France and Iraq, Palestine and Transjordan to Britain (some under control of the League of Nations).

At Lausanne, Turkey regained Smyrna. Originally given to Greece at Sevres, Smyrna had been taken back by Mustapha Kemal. Now Turkey was allowed to keep it.

Were the Treaties fair or effective?

Most countries thought that the Treaties were unfair, but the reasons for unfairness contradicted each other. The Treaties were a compromise to achieve a short-term peace, but in the longer term, would the Powers be prepared to fight to maintain it, when each thought it so faulty?

- Obviously Germans would not think the Treaty of Versailles fair, but they had been equally unfair in the past to France (1871) and Russia (1918). What mattered was that the humiliation opened the door to Hitler's policies in the 1930s.
- In the short term, peace was made despite the compromise nature of the settlements.
- In the long term, neither Britain, France nor the USA liked the settlements enough to enforce them in the 1930s, because not one of the victors gained all that they wanted.
- The issue of national self-determination caused insoluble problems since millions of Germans were left outside the new Germany, millions of Hungarians outside Hungary and large minorities were included in Poland, Czechoslovakia and Yugoslavia.
- The only Powers to guarantee the peace, Britain and France, were in decline, whereas the rising Powers of the USA, the Soviet Union and Germany were missing from the League of Nations.

PROGRESS CHECK

1 How much did Germany have to pay in reparations?
2 Which countries were newly formed?
3 Which country was Germany not allowed to unite with?
4 Which country was blamed for causing the First World War?
5 Which empire lost land to Czechoslovakia and Yugoslavia?
6 Which country lost Alsace–Lorraine?
7 Which territories were lost by Turkey in 1920?
8 Which territory were German armed forces not allowed to enter?

8. Rhineland.
7. Morocco, Tunisia, Syria and Lebanon to France and Iraq, Palestine and Transjordan to Britain (some under control of the League of Nations).
6. Germany.
5. Austria and Hungary.
4. Germany.
3. Austria.
2. Czechoslovakia and Yugoslavia.
1. £6,600 million.

3.2 The League of Nations 1919–1936

LEARNING SUMMARY	After studying this section you should be able to understand:
	• the aims and structure of the League
	• why the League could be successful in the 1920s and yet fail in the 1930s
	• the crises of Manchuria and Abyssinia which directly caused the League's failure
	• the League's strengths and weaknesses

The creation of the League

AQA B	✓
EDEXCEL A	✓
OCR B	✓
WJEC A	✗
WJEC B	✗
CCEA	✗

The aims and purpose of the League

The idea of a League of Nations was President Wilson's, and had been included in his Fourteen Points. Another war was unthinkable, but it would certainly come unless nations adopted new methods of keeping the peace. The old way of relying on the 'Balance of Power' had allowed a powerful nation to bully others. Now Wilson suggested a new system of 'collective security'.

> **KEY POINT**
>
> Collective security meant that all countries should unite against an aggressor, if peace was threatened.

Wilson had made sure that the League was inserted as a condition in all the peace treaties, but he was eventually unsuccessful in ensuring that the USA would become a member.

The aims of the League were listed in its '**Covenant**' or foundation charter. They were...

Make sure that you know the aims so that you can use them to gauge the success of the League.

- to achieve international peace
- to encourage nations not to go to war but to solve disputes peacefully
- to encourage disarmament
- to improve working and living conditions throughout the world.

These aims were to be achieved by collective security, which meant that nations would combine to impose the following sanctions:
- **Diplomatic sanctions** (telling the aggressor that he was wrong).
- **Economic sanctions** (refusing trade with the aggressor).
- **Military sanctions** (as a last resort going to war together against the aggressor).

The organisation of the League

AQA B	✓
EDEXCEL A	✓
OCR B	✓
WJEC A	✗
WJEC B	✗
CCEA	✗

The Covenant set out the organisation of the League:

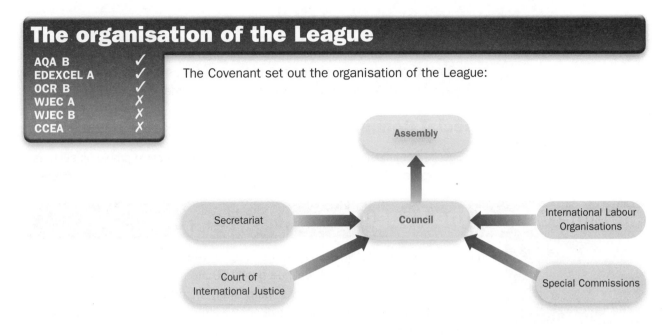

The Assembly

Could the Assembly ever reach a decision in a crisis?

- The Assembly consisted of delegations from every member country, each with one vote.
- Decisions had to be unanimous (no disagreeing).
- The Assembly could discuss any matter, either the organisation of the League itself or any crisis or problem.
- The Assembly could only recommend and not enforce its decision on the Council.
- With up to 60 nations, the Assembly was too big for useful discussion. Unanimous decisions were rarely agreed upon and, because the Assembly usually only met once a year, quick action was impossible. They therefore delegated their power to a caretaker Council.

The Council

What was to stop the permanent members from stopping decisions against them?

- The Council consisted of **four permanent members**: Britain, France, Italy and Japan. Germany was added in 1926.
- In addition there were **four temporary members** elected by the Assembly. Temporary members increased over the years, e.g. to six in 1922.
- Permanent members had a **veto**, i.e. they could stop the Council from reaching a decision.

The Secretariat

The Secretariat was set up to help the Assembly and the Council with their work. It kept records of discussions and decisions, and prepared reports to inform discussion. It was based in Geneva in Switzerland, which became the home of the League.

The Court of International Justice

The Court of International Justice was based in The Hague and was intended to judge international disputes. Judges were appointed from different member countries. It could not interfere unless it was asked to make a judgement and it had no way of enforcing its decision. Even so, it settled over 70 major cases in the 1920s and 1930s.

The International Labour Organisation

The League intended the International Labour Organisation to improve working conditions. Each country sent workers and employers as well as its own representatives. Information was collected and recommendations were made.

Special Commissions

The Special Commissions were set up where necessary to solve problems such as drugs, refugees, slavery and health, and to oversee the rule of mandated territories.

Membership of the League

AQA B	✓
EDEXCEL A	✓
OCR B	✓
WJEC A	✗
WJEC B	✗
CCEA	✗

In order to exert collective pressure, the League needed a large membership. It started with 42 countries and reached nearly 60 members by 1930. While this seemed impressive, there were three particularly important absentees as first:

- The **USA** never joined, despite President Wilson's wishes. Many Republicans (majority party) wanted to keep the USA out of European affairs. This isolationist policy was partly due to the high human cost of the First World War and partly because of the self-sufficiency of the USA. America would have had to pay to keep the peace in Europe. The Senate (the upper house of Congress) refused to confirm the Treaty of Versailles and kept the USA out of the League.
- **Germany** was not allowed at first to join the League. Having proved itself responsible, it joined in 1926, but Hitler withdrew in 1933 over disarmament.
- The **USSR** had become communist in 1917 and intended to promote revolution in other states. Other powers were afraid of communism and did not trust Russia to fulfil her promises. The USSR did not join the League until 1934, leaving again in 1939.

Figure 3.2 A British cartoon commenting on US importance to the League

THE GAP IN THE BRIDGE.

KEY POINT

When major powers were not members of the League, the League's sanctions would not work. What good would economic sanctions do, if the USA or USSR would carry on trading at the expense of members' own workers?

The League's weaknesses and strengths

AQA B	✓
EDEXCEL A	✓
OCR B	✓
WJEC A	✗
WJEC B	✗
CCEA	✗

Weaknesses	Strengths
<ul><li>The absence of important powers weakened the League and forced reliance on Britain and France, both of which were severely weakened by the First World War.</li><li>Collective action, on which the League depended, would only work if members put the League's interests first. Selfishness was much too common.</li><li>The Assembly could not usually come to quick or unanimous decisions, and could not enforce these on the Council, where decisions could be prevented by the veto. Individual states were able to prevent any action at all.</li><li>The League could not rely on member states to provide armed force, when they were not obliged to. Members were reluctant to spend the money, or pay the cost in casualties. Without effective economic or military sanctions, the League was powerless.</li><li>The League was bound to enforce the increasingly impossible Treaty of Versailles, but lacked the force to do so.</li></ul>	<ul><li>Over 42 countries did join.</li><li>Members did support the aims and most were determined to avoid another war.</li><li>In times without crises members were prepared to co-operate with each other, especially to aid the work of the Commissions.</li></ul>

Search for useful examples of the strengths and weaknesses in action from the following pages. Without examples your argument will not be convincing.

The League in the 1920s

AQA B	✓
EDEXCEL A	✓
OCR B	✓
WJEC A	✗
WJEC B	✗
CCEA	✗

Knowing its weaknesses, it is perhaps surprising how successful the League was during the 1920s. This is more because nations were still stunned by the slaughter of the First World War and were intent on rebuilding, rather than on aggression.

Was the League successful in international disputes during the 1920s?

There are various factors to consider when deciding if the League was a success or failure during the 1920s:

1 **Vilna 1920–1923**: The city of Vilna was given to Poland in 1919, but Lithuania was given the city by her allies, the Russians, in 1920. Poland appealed to the League and attacked Vilna. The League appointed a Commission, and suggested a vote, but was unable to enforce a settlement. In 1923 the **Conference of Ambassadors** awarded Vilna to Poland without consulting the

League. The Conference of Ambassadors included representatives from Britain, France, Italy and Japan and was intended to supervise the action of the peace settlement. Should it have been used in place of the League?

2 **The Aaland Islands 1920–1921**: The Swedish population of these Finnish islands declared their loyalty to Sweden in 1917. Finland sent troops to regain them and the dispute was referred to the League, which set up a Commission of Enquiry in 1920. This Commission recommended a compromise in 1921, allowing the population to remain Swedish, while the islands remained formally Finnish. Guarantees were exchanged and both sides agreed.

3 **Corfu 1923**: Mussolini blamed Greece when an Italian general on League business was shot dead. He claimed compensation within 24 hours, then bombarded and invaded the island of Corfu, which was Greek. Greece appealed both to the League and to the Conference of Ambassadors. **Mussolini denied the League's jurisdiction** and threatened to leave. The League left the problem to the Conference of Ambassadors, who forced Italy out of Corfu but insisted that Greece should compensate Italy.

4 **The French invasion of the Ruhr 1923**: Germany was late with her first instalments of reparations to France. French and Belgian troops then occupied the Ruhr (a very important industrial area) intending to take German coal and steel. Deadlock occurred when the Germans went on strike and was only solved by the **Locarno Pact** in 1925, which was sponsored by the League.

5 **Greece and Bulgaria 1925**: A border dispute flared into an invasion of Bulgaria by Greece. Within a month, the League had stopped the fighting and Greece had agreed to withdraw. A League Commission of Enquiry forced Greece to pay compensation to Bulgaria.

KEY POINT

Usually, powerful nations gained what they wanted but smaller countries were effectively policed by the League.

Figure 3.3 The first meeting of the League of Nations, 1920

Other successes and failures in the 1920s

Many of the League's successes during the 1920s were not to do with international crises. The work of the League with social and economic agencies or to promote international agreements is often ignored:

- **The Refugees Commission** gave refugees passports, which helped settle over 3 million into new lives in new countries. About 400,000 prisoners of war were returned to their homes.
- The League's **Health Organisation** trained officers, set up clinics for children and distributed medicines. It started a worldwide campaign to exterminate malaria-carrying mosquitoes while it virtually ran the public health system in China. It was less successful in controlling the international drugs trade.
- The League outlawed the **slave trade** freeing over 200,000 slaves in Sierra Leone. However, it failed to stop the trade completely.
- **Women and Children** were protected, as far as possible, from sexual abuse.
- **The International Labour Organisation** was particularly successful:
  - Countries agreed to **reduce working hours**.
  - **Trade Union membership** became a right.
  - A **minimum working age** was set at 15.
- **Disarmament** was less successful. At first, navies actually grew in size while only Germany was forced to disarm. However, at the Washington Conference 1921–1922 the large navies were reduced in size. This was the only move towards disarmament during the 1920s.
- **The Locarno Treaties, 1925** allowed Europe to move towards peace, even if disarmament was failing. Germany and France negotiated as equals, guaranteeing each other's borders as laid down at the Treaty of Versailles. Germany accepted that the Rhineland should remain demilitarised and France withdrew her troops from the Ruhr. All disputes were to be taken to the League, which Germany would join in 1926. Britain and Italy promised to enforce these agreements.
- **The Kellogg–Briand Pact, 1928** was initially signed by 15 countries, but gradually most, even the USA, joined in. All agreed that they would not use war to settle disputes, so that a peaceful future seemed assured. Unfortunately this could not be enforced.

> Members did not always enforce these reforms.

> These agreements were made outside the League. Did this reduce the League's importance?

The failure of the League in the 1930s

AQA B	✓
EDEXCEL A	✓
OCR B	✓
WJEC A	✗
WJEC B	✗
CCEA	✗

The effects of the Great Depression

The Wall Street Crash and the onset of the Great Depression seemed to herald the downfall of the League. However, this does not mean that the Depression was the main cause of its failure. You should also consider…

- the structure and membership of the League
- the faults of the Treaty of Versailles, which the League had to uphold
- the selfishness of all the members
- the impossibility of seeking disarmament at the same time as needing armies to enforce the League's decisions
- the growing threat from dictatorships in Germany and Russia, as well as in Japan and Italy.

For the Wall Street Crash see page 187

The **effects of the Great Depression**, beginning with the Wall Street Crash in 1929 and worsening over the next four years, affected the whole world, making international co-operation more difficult:

- Countries tried to save their own industries by putting **import tariffs** on foreign goods, which led to the breaking down of international trade.
- Millions of people had been thrown out of work, so some countries like Britain concentrated on **solving their own economic problems**, ignoring international commitments.
- Other countries like Japan and Germany moved towards extremism: **Hitler was elected to destroy the Treaty of Versailles** and take back by force what Germany had lost; Japan invaded and conquered Manchuria.
- Mussolini invaded Abyssinia because no other power would stop her in these circumstances.

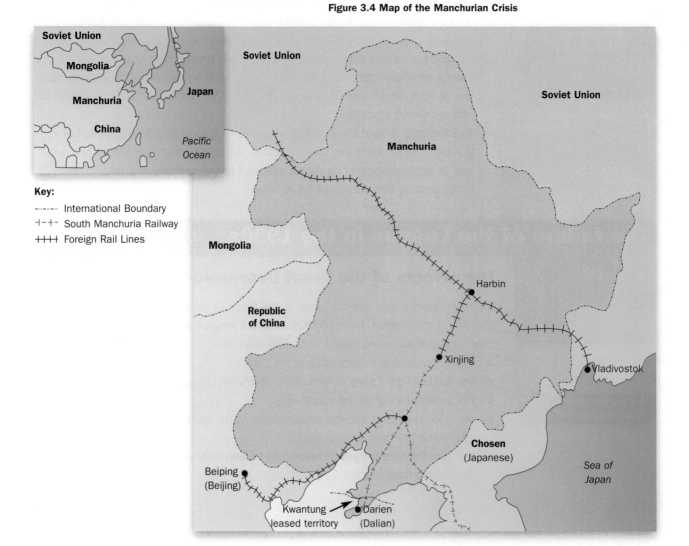

See below for the Manchurian and Abyssinian crises

The failure of the World Disarmament Conference

At Geneva, 1932–1933, 59 countries failed to reach agreement on disarmament:

- **France feared Germany's determination** to revise the Treaty of Versailles.
- **Germany withdrew** and began to rearm because Hitler refused to disarm further until other countries had reduced their armed forces to the same weak state as Germany's.

Failure in Manchuria 1931

Figure 3.4 Map of the Manchurian Crisis

Key:
- ------ International Boundary
- -+-+- South Manchuria Railway
- ++++ Foreign Rail Lines

Soviet Union
Mongolia
Manchuria
Japan
China
Pacific Ocean

Soviet Union

Manchuria

Mongolia

Republic of China

Harbin

Xinjing

Vladivostok

Beiping (Beijing)

Kwantung leased territory

Darien (Dalian)

Chosen (Japanese)

Sea of Japan

Japan invaded Manchuria in 1931 due to the following reasons:

- **The economic depression** had hit Japan very hard because it depended on exports, especially silk to the USA.
- **Japan wanted an empire** in Manchuria to control its trade and because it was rich in natural resources (coal and iron).
- **Japan's population was growing** fast and she needed living space.
- **The Japanese Army was intent on conquest** and out of control.
- An excuse was manufactured when **the Japanese Army blew up its own railway** in Manchuria and blamed this on the Chinese. They then began the invasion from bases they already held.

This is what then happened:

Which factor was most important?
- The absence of the USA
- Britain's lack of interest
- The need for decisions to be unanimous
- Slowness and indecision.

September 1931	**China appealed to the League.** The League tried to involve the USA in a Commission of Enquiry, but the USA refused to be involved, while Britain had no interest in the area. The League asked both sides to stop fighting and return to their own territory and did not even impose sanctions on Japan.
October 1931	**Japan vetoed a Council resolution** calling for the withdrawal of Japanese troops.
November 1931	The League set up a **Commission of Enquiry** under Lord Lytton, but Japan continued to attack undisturbed.
September 1932	The Lytton Commission condemned Japan in its report.
March 1933	**Japan walked out of the League** but kept control of Manchuria.

Failure in Abyssinia (Ethiopia) 1935

Figure 3.5 Map of the Abyssinian Crisis

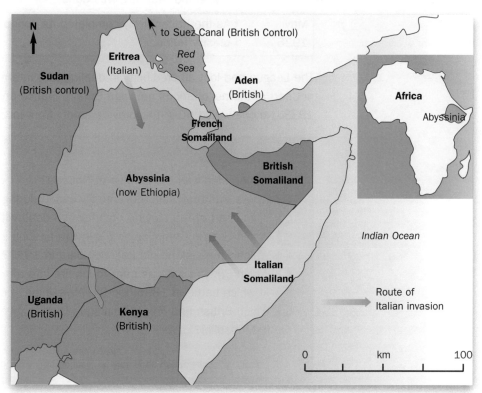

In 1935, **Mussolini decided to invade Abyssinia** due to the following reasons:

- As a Fascist dictator, he wanted to **rebuild Italy's pride in herself** as the successor to the ancient Roman Empire and to distract her from her economic problems.
- **Abyssinia was close to Italian land**, bordering the Italian colonies of Eritrea and Italian Somaliland, and it had coal and oil, which Italy lacked.
- The Italians had been defeated by the Abyssinians in 1896 at the Battle of Adowa. **Revenge was coupled with convenience**: Mussolini had seen Japan go unpunished over Manchuria, so he thought he would get away with it.
- Invasion was justified by a border incident at the end of 1934 and by Mussolini's excuse that **Abyssinia had still not abolished slavery**. He was invading to carry out League policy.

This is how Italy was allowed to succeed:

January 1935	**Haile Selassie** (Emperor of Abyssinia) asked for League support against Italian threats.
March 1935	Hitler announced the rearmament of Germany. Italy, France and Britain together formed the 'Stresa' Front against him. **Italy was too valuable an ally in Europe to be lost because of a colonial dispute.** Mussolini doubtless appreciated this.
October 1935	Having made sure that Britain would not intervene, **Mussolini sent his well-equipped army into Abyssinia. The League imposed economic sanctions, but not on oil.** Meanwhile non-League countries, e.g. USA, continued to trade with Italy.
December 1935	**Britain and France tried to give most of Abyssinia to Italy** (the 'Hoare Laval' Pact) but the plan was leaked so nothing happened because of the outcry.
March 1936	The League debated adding oil to the sanctions, but Britain and France opposed because Hitler had just remilitarised the Rhineland. **Nothing was done.**
May 1936	As the Italian Army completed its conquest, **the League had clearly failed**.

Reasons for failure are easy to find: the structure of the League; the absence of important powers, lack of military force, selfishness of Council members, etc. Do not try to argue them all, but concentrate on the best three arguments. How can you illustrate each argument? How can you compare the arguments to find the most convincing one?

The League had lost all credibility in dealing with international disputes and was not part of the negotiations between Britain, France and Germany at Munich in 1938. No one would trust it to provide safety from invasion.

PROGRESS CHECK

1. Whose idea was the League of Nations?
2. Where was the League eventually based during the 1920s?
3. Which part of the League organisation dealt with international crises?
4. Which League Commission dealt with prisoners of war?
5. Which Greek island did Italy bombard in 1923?
6. Which British Lord was sent to inquire into the Manchuria Crisis?
7. At which battle in 1896 had the Abyssinians beaten the Italians?
8. Which British and French ministers tried to give most of Abyssinia to Mussolini?

1. President Wilson's. 2. Geneva. 3. The Council. 4. Refugees Commission. 5. Corfu. 6. Lord Lytton. 7. Battle of Adowa. 8. Hoare and Laval.

3.3 Why international peace had collapsed by 1939

LEARNING SUMMARY

After studying this section you should be able to understand:

- the political effects of the Great Depression
- Hitler's foreign policy ambitions
- the reasons why other countries were slow to oppose Hitler
- the reasons for war

The political effects of the Great Depression

AQA B	✓
EDEXCEL A	✓
OCR B	✓
WJEC A	✗
WJEC B	✗
CCEA	✓

The economic effects of the Great Depression forced far-reaching political changes, both in Germany and in other countries.

The effects of the Great Depression on Germany

As the improvement of the German economy had been based on foreign loans (the Dawes and Young Plans) **the onset of depression had a huge effect** there. US and British bankers withdrew their support, causing a huge rise in unemployment coupled with a crisis in the democratic Weimar government. Moderate parties were seen to fail and so support moved towards extremists: the Nazi and Communist Parties became so powerful because they promised revolutionary solutions.

Communist revolution was attractive because, in the Soviet Union, Stalin was protecting his own industries from foreign competition and forcing restructuring of agriculture and industry at this time. Faced with the likelihood of a communist government in Germany, the professional and landed classes decided to join in support of the only alternative – Hitler and the Nazi Party. **Hitler did not preach class war**, but instead he promised decisive leadership and to recreate German power abroad.

Hitler's support grew in step with unemployment in Germany: the Nazis emerged as the major party in 1932, when unemployment briefly reached 6 million. Without a clear majority, Hitler was helped into power by the Nationalist Party and, once there, he consolidated his hold by exaggerating the fear of communism, promising social justice and full employment. It was his skill to channel the blame for poverty into a campaign for German rights in Europe, while abroad he posed as the only protection against Soviet communism.

The effects of the Great Depression on Britain and France

Britain and France were also hit hard by the effects of the Great Depression. **In Britain, a coalition government focused on the problem of 2.5 million unemployed** while supporting disarmament and trying to avoid entanglements abroad. In France, prosperity continued because they had benefited from reparation payments and they had a shortage of manpower because of the First World War. However, as the tourist trade and the markets for farm produce and luxury goods declined, France gradually followed Britain into crisis, appointing a Leftist government under Leon Blum in 1934, who failed to deal with the problems, then a radical Liberal government under Eduard Daladier in 1937. The emphasis in France was on economic survival, especially as other countries moved out of recession much faster than she did. Neither Britain nor France could afford to rearm, still less to contemplate war with Germany, which would mean real economic sacrifice, and which their governments would not survive. The consequence was the policy of appeasement, followed by both countries until 1939.

Hitler's foreign policy ambitions

AQA B	✓
EDEXCEL A	✓
OCR B	✓
WJEC A	✗
WJEC B	✗
CCEA	✓

Hitler's ambitions abroad were always quite clear – he had stated them in the Twenty-five Point Programme of the Nazi Party in 1921 and again in '*Mein Kampf*' in 1924. They included...

- the destruction of the Treaty of Versailles
- the rearmament of Germany
- the expansion of Germany to include all people of German race
- the conquest of Living Space (Lebensraum) to give land and resources sufficient for Germans at the expense of Slavs and Jews
- competition with the USA for world dominance (through control in Europe).

> **KEY POINT**
>
> Hitler made no secret of his ambitions to use war to force change in Europe, but while he intended disruption, he did not expect that all other countries would combine against him at once.

Hitler's steps towards war

Figure 3.6 German aggression up to September 1939

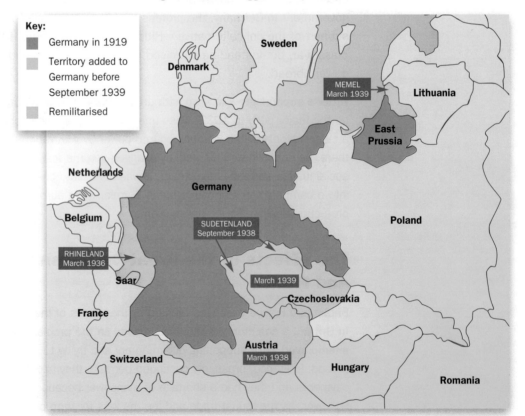

Key:
- Germany in 1919
- Territory added to Germany before September 1939
- Remilitarised

The following steps led to war in 1939:

- In 1933 **Hitler walked out of the World Disarmament Conference**, arguing that Germany should not be the only country who had been disarmed. He refused to be bound by the restrictions imposed by the Treaty of Versailles unless others were too. He followed this by withdrawing from the League of Nations.

- In 1935 90% of the population of **the Saar voted to return to Germany**. It had been administered by the League under the Treaty of Versailles, but now its valuable coal deposits returned to Germany.

- **Hitler began rearmament in 1935**, reintroducing conscription and rebuilding the air force and navy. In the **Anglo–German Naval Treaty** Britain allowed Germany's fleet to grow to 35% of the size of Britain's, in contravention of the Treaty of Versailles. This was the first clear act of appeasement.

- In 1936 **Hitler sent troops into the Rhineland**, which had been demilitarised by the Treaty of Versailles. He was clearly breaking the terms of the Treaty, threatening France's security and taking a big risk that Britain and France would not object. In the middle of the Abyssinian Crisis, Britain decided to agree to Hitler's move because France had just signed a Mutual Assistance Treaty with the USSR. Perhaps the influence of communism seemed a greater threat than Hitler to the Conservative Government in Britain. France, meanwhile, was preparing for a general election. While Hitler was weak at this time, Britain and France had neither the armies nor the cohesion to stop him.

Figure 3.7 A British cartoon about the occupation of the Rhineland in 1936

THE GOOSE-STEP

- With a mostly German population, Austria had fared badly during the 1930s. Her economy was slow to improve, while in Germany prosperity was returning. Hitler, as an Austrian German, appreciated this. He also knew that his own position had strengthened with rearmament, the destruction of the League's influence and the disinterest shown by Britain, so he contemplated **Anschluss** (the joining of Austria to Germany). In February 1938, after complaints that Nazis were being mistreated, Hitler forced Schuschnigg (Chancellor of Austria) to appoint two Nazis to government posts. Schuschnigg called a referendum in which Austrians would vote whether to join Germany. Hitler pre-empted this by ordering the Wehrmacht to invade on 11th March. **The peaceful invasion resulted in the integration of Austria into the Reich**. In the Nazi-organised referendum, 99% of Austrians voted in favour. Britain and France protested but did nothing, justifying this by saying that it was natural for Germans to wish to be united.

Fear of the Soviet Union was much greater than fear of Germany: a stronger Germany was to the benefit of Britain and France.

- **Czechoslovakia** had been created from part of the Austrian Empire at the end of the First World War. On her western fringes lived a large German minority which, with Nazi money from Germany and under the leadership of Konrad Henlein, had started to protest that they were mistreated by the Czech government. Hitler was ready to invade in 1938, but Neville Chamberlain, the British Prime Minister, tried to broker an agreement, firstly with Eduard Benes, the Czech President, who he persuaded to let the Germans have self-government as the '**Sudetenland**'. Hitler demanded that they must join Germany, gradually increasing his demand to send German troops in. Chamberlain, determined to avoid war, had a total of three meetings with Hitler. The third meeting was at **Munich** in September 1938. Chamberlain, Mussolini, and Daladier (French Prime Minister) persuaded Hitler to limit his invasion to a peaceful takeover (**The Munich Pact**). The Soviet Union and Czechoslovakia were not invited to the conference. The following morning, in a private meeting with Hitler, Chamberlain got his signature to a declaration that Germany would make no further demands. Returning to Britain, waving this '**Munich Agreement**' Chamberlain declared, 'I believe it is peace for our time'.

- After Munich, Czechoslovakia could not be defended: she was set upon by Poland, Hungary and Germany. **In March 1939 the German army marched in**, making their first non-German conquest, breaking the Munich Agreement and setting off a flurry of diplomatic activity as Britain and France hastily allied themselves with Poland and Romania.

- Stalin had never forgiven Britain and France for leaving him out of the Munich meeting. His army was weak because of the 'Purges' so it was imperative to postpone war. He negotiated with Britain and France to join them against Germany without enthusiasm. When Hitler offered him all the Baltic states and half of Poland he realised the advantages this would bring – recovering Russia's lost provinces from 1917 and postponing serious war for the moment. In August 1939 the **Nazi–Soviet Pact** was signed, despite the competition from British and French delegations. Hitler by this masterly stroke avoided war on two fronts.

> Britain and France had always backed off when Hitler declared war. Work out why they did not continue to do so.

Figure 3.8 A British cartoon about the Nazi–Soviet Pact of 1939. It shows Hitler and Stalin greeting each other over the body of Poland

RENDEZVOUS

- **On 1st September 1939 the German army invaded Poland**, ignoring the ultimatum issued by Britain and France. On 3rd September Britain and France declared war on Germany. On 17th September the Soviet Union invaded eastern Poland.

Should Britain and France have appeased Germany?

For appeasement	Against appeasement
• Britain and France were determined not to fight another World War. • The spread of communism from the Soviet Union appeared a more important threat to Britain and France. They saw Hitler as a strong ally. • Strengthening Germany would make it a more effective bulwark against the Soviet Union, while the Treaty of Versailles now looked very unfair. • Britain had reduced her armed forces and was too weak to fight Germany, but at the same time she was too poor to afford quick rearmament. Chamberlain was rearming as fast as the economy could support it.	• Every time Britain and France appeased Hitler he was strengthened in men and resources and was more certain that no one would stand up to him. • In appeasing Hitler, Britain and France undermined any chance of an alliance with the Soviet Union. Stalin suspected that he would get no support against Germany. • Britain and France hoped that Hitler's newest demand would be his last. Leaders were forced to sound hopeful, and perhaps they were fooled by Hitler.

Reasons why war broke out in 1939

War broke out due to a combination of factors:
- Certainly the 1919 Treaties were flawed in that they fostered resentment without producing enough agreement to enforce them.
- The League of Nations had failed to show that aggressors would be punished.
- The Great Depression fostered aggressive dictatorships, whilst weakening moderate governments.
- Hitler intended war (though probably not a World War). He broke the Treaty of Versailles and threatened war. Italy, Japan and the Soviet Union also weakened the resolve of the moderate powers.
- The policy of appeasement by Britain and France was to blame in that it encouraged Hitler to believe that he could get away with anything, whilst giving him time to increase his resources.
- Britain and France were reluctant to ally with the communist Soviet Union. This made the Nazi–Soviet Pact possible, opening Poland to invasion.

> Together these form a 'web of causation', each reason being interdependent, though it is fair to point out that only Hitler wanted war and that everyone else was trying to avoid it.

PROGRESS CHECK

1. Who controlled the Saar from 1919 until 1935?
2. Why did Britain allow Germany to remilitarise the Rhineland?
3. Which Austrian Chancellor opposed Anschluss?
4. Which nations should have been at the Munich Conference but were not?

1. The League of Nations. 2. Fear of communism; lack of armed force; the Abyssinian crisis diverted their attention. 3. Schuschnigg. 4. Czechoslovakia, Soviet Union

Sample GCSE questions

(a) Which countries did Hitler invade due to his policy of German Nationalism?

- Austria, most Austrians were of German race
- Sudetenland, Sudeten Germans were a German minority
- Poland, many Germans lived in the Polish Corridor. **(4)**

> You could give three countries, but if you give a good reason you will be given an extra mark.

(b) Why did Britain and France avoid declaring war with Hitler over Czechoslovakia?

- Britain regretted that the Treaty of Versailles had spread the German population into several different countries and thought that a united Germany would be a stronger bulwark against the Soviet Union.
- France was in deep financial trouble and unable to afford war.
- Czechoslovakia was a far distant country to whom Britain was not directly allied.
- Neither Britain nor France had the resources to rearm fast enough to be protected from German aggression.
- The policy of appeasement allowed them to put off war until they were better prepared. **(6)**

> Be careful to give answers as reasons. If you develop them with extra supporting facts you may gain extra marks so that you do not need six reasons.

(c) What was the main cause of war in 1939?

There were many causes which worked together, e.g. the Treaty of Versailles failed to satisfy the great powers enough for them to enforce it, yet it caused continuing resentment in Germany. Even so, war would not have followed without the collapse of the League of Nations, which was intended to ensure peace. Without the Great Depression, the League may not have collapsed, Hitler probably wouldn't have come to power and Britain and France would not have become so weakened that they could not police Europe.

However, there are some causes that are more important than others: some blame the appeasement of Germany by Britain and France for allowing Hitler to grow so strong, though Britain could not afford to rearm and so could not go to war before 1939. More convincing is the argument that German foreign policy was the only one that threatened war: everyone else was working against it. By repeatedly threatening and expanding, Hitler began to consolidate alliances against him, which ensured an eventual confrontation.

Therefore, while all the reasons were interdependent, Hitler's aggressive policies were more responsible than the others for the outbreak of war in 1939. He made one gamble too many, forcing Britain and France to honour their agreements to oppose him. **(10)**

> You need to discuss several causes to show that it was not just Hitler's foreign policy that was responsible.
> Try to evaluate each point. What makes Hitler's policies more responsible than appeasement? Write a conclusion to pull the argument together.

Exam practice questions

1 **(a)** What principles had President Wilson outlined in his Fourteen Points, which he thought should guide the peacemakers?

....

....

....

.... **(4)**

(b) Why was Germany treated more harshly than other losing powers by the victors at the Treaty of Versailles?

....

....

....

....

....

....

....

....

....

.... **(6)**

(c) To what extent was the unfairness of the Treaty of Versailles to Germany the main reason for its failure?

....

....

....

....

....

....

....

....

....

.... **(10)**

You may need to continue your answers on a separate sheet of paper.

4 The Second World War 1939–1945

The following topics are covered in this chapter:

- **The early years in Europe and Africa**
- **The entry of the superpowers: victory in Europe and Asia**
- **The war at home**

4.1 The early years in Europe and Africa

LEARNING SUMMARY

After studying this section you should be able to understand:

- how Germany quickly expanded into both Eastern and Western Europe
- how Britain was able to survive
- how a turning point was reached in Africa

German victory in Europe by 1941

AQA B	✓
EDEXCEL A	✓
OCR B	✗
WJEC A	✗
WJEC B	✗
CCEA	✗

Blitzkrieg against Poland

Germany attacked Poland on 1st September 1939 from the west, and on 17th September Russia invaded from the east, as agreed in the Nazi–Soviet Pact. Since Britain and France could not help, Poland was swiftly defeated when Germany attacked with overwhelming force and speed – **'Blitzkrieg'** ('Lightning War'). Poland surrendered on 3rd October.

There was now a pause, the **'Phoney War'** during the winter of 1939–1940, while each side prepared and waited for the other to move first.

For the reasons for the German invasion of Poland and the Nazi–Soviet Pact, see Chapter 3.

Germany turns west

The invasion of Denmark and Norway by Germany was so quick in April 1940 that a British expedition to Norway was unable to establish itself. Norwegian forces had not been mobilised, while the German invasion was helped by Norwegian Nazis, led by Vidkun Quisling. Defeat there led to the replacement of British Prime Minister Neville Chamberlain by Winston Churchill in May 1940.

Holland, Belgium and France were attacked on 10th May. The decisive German advance through the Ardennes and round the north of the Maginot Line cut off British and French forces, forcing the retreat of 340,000 soldiers to **Dunkirk**. There, by a miracle, 300,000 troops were evacuated to Britain by the Royal Navy, with the help of about 700 small merchant ships and pleasure craft ('the

Be ready to make a balanced argument about Dunkirk: both a defeat and a triumph.

little ships') of Dunkirk. The rescue was organised by Vice Admiral Bertram Ramsay in **Operation Dynamo**. Dunkirk was a defeat because the British Expeditionary Force was prevented from helping the French army against the German advance, but Winston Churchill created a propaganda victory, rallying Britain to show the 'Dunkirk Spirit'.

France surrendered in June 1940, leaving Britain isolated in Western Europe (Spain remained neutral).

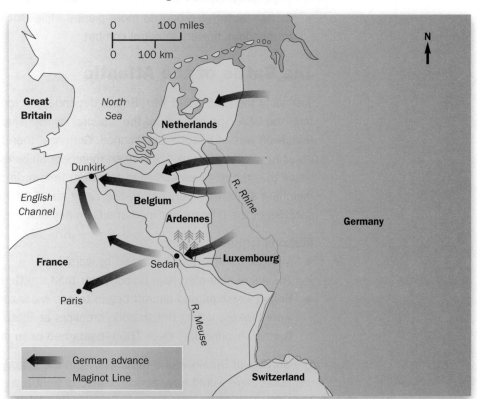

Figure 4.1 German invasion of France

The success of Blitzkrieg

'Blitzkrieg' was a development of British tactics at the end of the First World War in which **armour and troops advanced together, with air cover**. German generals refined the method, both by taking infantry forward in **troop carriers** and by using **paratroops** to take objectives from the air. The result was such a fast advance that resistance could not be successfully organised.

The significance of British survival

AQA B	✓
EDEXCEL A	✓
OCR B	✗
WJEC A	✗
WJEC B	✗
CCEA	✗

The Battle of Britain, July–September 1940

In order to invade Britain, Hitler needed to send a fleet of barges across the Channel (**Operation Sealion**). First he had to win **air power**.

The Battle of Britain was fought for air dominance, as the Luftwaffe changed its focus from attacking convoys in the Channel to attacking airfields and then factories. Although German losses were heavier than British, Hitler did not realise the seriousness of the damage inflicted on **airfields in South-East England** and the **shortage of planes and pilots**. He switched tactics to bombing London and other large cities, allowing the RAF to recover its effectiveness. By the time the German plans for invasion were abandoned, Germany had lost 1,389 planes; Britain had lost 792.

Reasons for British victory:
- Spitfires and Hurricanes were more manoeuvrable than German Messerschmidts. **German fighters only had fuel for a few minutes over Britain**, whereas British fighters could spend as long as they needed in the air.
- Britain used **radar** to concentrate defenders onto attacking German planes. The Germans failed to target the vital radar stations.
- **Hitler and Goering failed to push home the attack** on the RAF. If they had not changed their focus, they would have succeeded.
- **British factories** produced more planes while **British pilots** showed tremendous bravery in aerial combat.

The Battle of the Atlantic

Just as in the First World War, Britain depended on food, raw materials and oil from the USA. The creation of the 'special relationship' in 1940 by Churchill and Roosevelt was of historic significance. Germany, therefore, focused her efforts on using U-boats to sink 150 British merchant ships every month for a year, which they thought was sufficient to defeat Britain. In 1942 losses of British merchant ships were very heavy, averaging about 140 each month, but later the success of the U-boats declined and Germany lost the Battle of the Atlantic.

Reasons for British victory:
- Merchant ships were **convoyed** by warships.
- The Allies built merchant ships faster than the Germans could sink them.
- British warships and aircraft began to use **radar** while **German Enigma codes** were broken, letting British code breakers at **Bletchley Park** track the German 'wolfpacks'. Over 750 U-boats had been sunk by the end of the war.

The survival of Britain was a turning-point in the history of the Second World War: without it there would have been no second front against Hitler, the USA could not have entered the war in Europe and Germany could have concentrated her efforts against the Soviet Union.

Victory in Africa: a turning point in the War

AQA B	✓
EDEXCEL A	✗
OCR B	✗
WJEC A	✗
WJEC B	✗
CCEA	✗

Yugoslavia and Greece 1940

Hitler had attacked Yugoslavia in 1940 and, when an Italian attack on Greece was repulsed, he sent in German troops. British and Allied troops were overrun, making a last stand at Crete, which was captured by German parachutists in June 1940.

The significance of the campaign was that it delayed the German invasion of Russia, which would now take place in the winter.

North Africa 1940–1943

Mussolini invaded Egypt from Libya in 1940 but was repulsed by British and Empire troops. Hitler then sent **General Erwin Rommel**, whose Panzer Army pushed the British army deep into Egypt, threatening the Suez Canal and the Gulf oilfields.

Under a new commander, **General Montgomery**, and with new equipment from the USA, the 8th Army turned the tide at the **Battle of El Alamein**, pushing the Germans deep into Libya. An Allied landing in Algeria then led to complete victory in Africa.

In 1943 British and US forces invaded Italy from North Africa: El Alamein had been an important turning point.

4.2 The entry of the superpowers: victory in Europe and Asia

LEARNING SUMMARY

After studying this section you should be able to understand:

- how the Soviet Union was invaded and the defeat of the Germans there
- how the USA entered the war to defeat Japan
- how Germany was defeated

Invasion of the Soviet Union: the decisive turning point in Europe

AQA B	✓
EDEXCEL A	✗
OCR B	✗
WJEC A	✗
WJEC B	✗
CCEA	✓

Operation Barbarossa

Hitler had always intended to invade the Soviet Union in order to gain 'Living Space' for the German people, to destroy communism and to take resources such as wheat, coal and oil.*

*For more information on Hitler's intentions, see Chapter 3.

Hitler launched **Operation Barbarossa** in June 1941, taking Russian forces by surprise and striking deep into Soviet territory. But when the winter of 1941–1942 struck, German troops were ill-equipped for sub-zero. They only had **summer clothing** and were without the fuel additives to keep tanks and lorries moving. Their advance ground to a halt at **Leningrad** and **Moscow**. In 1943 they failed to take **Stalingrad**, where they had to endure another winter. The 100,000 men of von Paulus's army at Stalingrad surrendered to Soviet forces in January 1943. **This decisive victory was the real turning-point of the war in Europe**.

Soviet forces then began their long advance, beating the German Panzer Army at the **Battle of Kursk** in July 1943, and driving German forces out of Russia by June 1944 (at the cost of over 20 million Soviet deaths).

Reasons for German defeat:
- The **fatal delay** in launching Operation Barbarossa occurred because of the resistance to the invasion of Greece. The **harsh winters** halted German advances allowing Soviet resistance to regroup.

- The Soviet 'scorched earth' policy, destroying everything in the path of the advancing Germans, put huge strain on German supplies, which had to be transported over immense distances.
- Soviet armies and the Soviet people showed **heroic resistance**, especially at the sieges of Leningrad and Stalingrad.
- **Concentration on the Soviet Union** by Germany was a fatal error. Three quarters of German forces were used there, which gave the chance for the Allies to regroup for invasion of Europe in the west.

The USA and the war with Japan

AQA B	✓
EDEXCEL A	✗
OCR B	✗
WJEC A	✓
WJEC B	✗
CCEA	✗

*For the Japanese invasion of Manchuria, see Chapter 3.

Japanese rivalry with the USA

Japan started her expansion into China in 1931 and had taken the coastline by 1940.* In 1941 she invaded **Indo-China** seeking coal, oil, tin and other supplies. At home the Japanese army was virtually in control, and Japan had allied with Germany in 1936.

The USA had important links with China and in 1941 demanded that Japan should withdraw from China and Indo-China. She also imposed **sanctions on Japan**, the most damaging of which was a ban on oil exports, on which Japan depended.

Figure 4.2 The expansion of the Japanese empire, 1931–1942

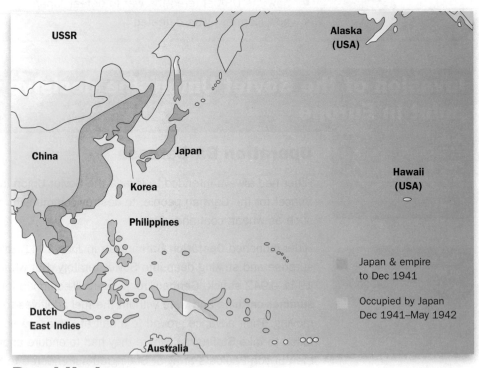

Pearl Harbor

Japan was not prepared to agree to US demands and instead planned a pre-emptive strike on **Pearl Harbor** in Hawaii. This attack, in December 1941, sank most of the US Pacific Fleet, **destroyed 120 aircraft** and **killed 2,400 Americans**. The US aircraft carriers, however, had put to sea and were saved.

The results were decisive:

- The USA was forced into war with Japan.
- Germany and Italy declared war on the USA the following day, connecting the wars in Europe and the Pacific.

Turning point in the Pacific

At first, Japan continued to make advances in 1941, taking the **Philippines**, **Malaya**, **Singapore** and **parts of Burma**. In 1942 the tide turned when, at the **Battle of Midway Island**, the US fleet sank four Japanese aircraft carriers, leaving the Japanese position in the Pacific seriously weakened.

US victory over Japan

During 1943, US forces captured one Pacific island after another, despite heavy casualties. In June 1944 British and Indian troops defeated Japan in **Burma**. From 1944–1945, US forces retook the **Philippines**.

The next objective was Japan itself, but it was obvious that a land invasion would be very costly since Japanese resistance was expected to be particularly fierce. Instead, **Harry Truman**, the new American President, decided to use the **Atom Bomb**. In early August, bombs were dropped on **Hiroshima** and **Nagasaki**. The bomb on Hiroshima caused about 70,000 deaths within minutes of the blast and on **14th August 1945, Japan surrendered**.

Figure 4.3 Hiroshima after the bomb

The defeat of Germany

AQA B	✓
EDEXCEL A	✓
OCR B	✗
WJEC A	✗
WJEC B	✗
CCEA	✗

D-Day 6th June 1944

Germany was fully committed to the war in the Soviet Union and so had provided the chance for British, French and American forces to regroup in Britain. From July 1943 British and American troops were advancing north in Italy where German troops had taken over the defence: in April 1945 Italy would fall.

The Allies concentrated overwhelming force in southern Britain ready to invade France, with over 3 million British, Canadian and American troops and 5,000 ships. They were equipped with 'mulberry' harbours and the Pluto fuel pipeline to ensure supply across the Channel. Meanwhile control of the skies had been assured to protect the invasion. The landings were on five beaches on a 60-mile stretch of the Normandy coast. German resistance was strong and casualties high.

The advance on Germany

25th August 1944	Paris fell to the Allies
September 1944	France and Belgium were freed
December 1944	'The Battle of the Bulge': a German counter-attack which momentarily turned the tide at the cost of 240,000 German casualties and 600 tanks.
April 1945	While the Allies were entering Germany, Soviet troops attacked Berlin.
30th April	Hitler shot himself
7th May	VE Day

Reasons for victory over Germany

1. The continued resistance of **Britain** opened Germany to war on two fronts and allowed the USA to enter the war in Europe.
2. By attacking the **Soviet Union**, Hitler made a serious mistake. Most historians see the failure in Russia as the decisive turning point in Europe.
3. **Italian failure** in southern Europe and Africa further over-stretched German resources in Greece, Africa and Italy.
4. **The entry of the USA** into the war in Europe changed the balance of the war.
5. **The war continued too long**, exhausting German and Italian resources, while the Allies gained support from US resources.

> **PROGRESS CHECK**
>
> 1. In which decisive battle did the USA turn the tide in the Pacific?
> 2. Which battle delayed the Allied advance on Germany, after D-Day?
> 3. Which American President ordered the dropping of Atom Bombs on Hiroshima and Nagasaki?
>
> 1. Midway 1942. 2. The Battle of the Bulge. 3. President Truman.

4.3 The war at home

LEARNING SUMMARY	After studying this section you should be able to understand:
	• how the British Government met the challenges of war
	• evacuation and the Blitz
	• how life in Britain changed during the war

How the British Government met the challenges of war

AQA B	✓
EDEXCEL A	✓
OCR B	✓
WJEC A	✓
WJEC B	✓
CCEA	✗

Preparations

Fear of war had been one of the reasons for the policy of **appeasement** (see Chapter 3). This fear was worsened by the German bombing of **Guernica** during the Spanish Civil War, which had shown what damage mass bombing could do. Although war was not welcomed, as in 1914, the Government had prepared in the following ways:

- **The Air Raid Precaution Act 1937** organised the formation of ARP teams in towns.

- In 1938 the first **air raid shelters and slit trenches** were prepared and gas masks were issued to everyone.
- By 1939 1.5 million **Anderson shelters** had been distributed to be buried in back gardens.

Figure 4.4 An Anderson shelter

- From April 1939 men aged 20–21 could be **conscripted** for the armed services. In September this was extended to men aged 19–41, except those in essential jobs. In 1941 unmarried women had to join the auxiliary services or work in essential industries.
- From July 1939 '**black out**' instructions were issued and two days before war was declared all lights in cities were hidden.

Government during the war

The **Defence of the Realm Act** was renewed in 1939 (see page 18). **Emergency Powers Acts in 1939 and 1940** gave the Government huge powers, for example:
- German nationals and Nazi sympathisers could be imprisoned without trial.
- Newspapers were censored. Government propaganda used posters, films and radio.
- The Government took control of industry, transport and the docks.

A National Government under Winston Churchill

Winston Churchill became Prime Minister of a **National Government** in 1940. This contained representatives of each main party and elections were suspended until the end of the war. In overall control were twin Cabinets: a Home and a War Cabinet. **Churchill chaired the War Cabinet**.

Churchill supplied the **leadership** that was essential. His **brilliant speeches** on the radio and in Parliament raised the morale of the British people, keeping them as 'a whole nation fighting and suffering together' and showing that surrender was not an option. He spoke in terms that people could understand and convinced them that they were going to win.

Evacuation and the Blitz

AQA B	✓
EDEXCEL A	✓
OCR B	✓
WJEC A	✓
WJEC B	✓
CCEA	✗

Evacuation

The fear of German bombing persuaded the Government to order the **evacuation of children**, their **teachers** and **mothers with young children** on the first weekend of the war. Evacuees were moved from cities to reception areas (country areas), where it was thought they would be safer, but the expected bombing did not happen, and by the time the Blitz began in September 1940, about half had returned to their homes. About 827,000 schoolchildren, 524,000 mothers and young children and 103,000 teachers were evacuated during the war.

Figure 4.5 Evacuees

The Blitz 1940–1941

In September 1940 the 'Blitz' began, when wave after wave of aeroplanes bombed London, then other major cities including Liverpool, Glasgow, Coventry and Plymouth. London was bombed every night bar one for 11 weeks, around one third being destroyed. By now **Morrison shelters** had also been distributed. These were steel cages in which you could sleep on a double mattress inside your house and which could also be used as tables. These helped to protect people in cities without access to a shelter. Many also sheltered in **public shelters** or in **underground stations**.

By the time the Blitz ended, in May 1941, **43,000 people had been killed and 1.4 million had been made homeless**. If the Germans intended to destroy British resistance, they achieved the opposite effect. People became determined, volunteering as **air-raid wardens, auxiliary fire-fighters or members of the Women's Voluntary Service**. The **Local Defence Volunteers (Home Guard)** guarded the coast, protected important buildings and prepared to defend the country in case of invasion. In total 250,000 men volunteered for the Home Guard, which allowed the Army to concentrate on fighting the war elsewhere.

The 'Second Blitz'

In early June 1944, Hitler's **flying bomb** weapons began to rain down on London and the South East. In total, 9251 V1s were aimed at Britain, of which about 4,000 were destroyed by the RAF and Anti-Aircraft Command, but they caused over 6,000 deaths and nearly 18,000 injuries. From 8th September, over 1,000 **V2 rockets**, flying at supersonic speed killed another 2,800 people and injured a further 6,500 civilians.

How life in Britain changed during the war

AQA B	✓
EDEXCEL A	✓
OCR B	✓
WJEC A	✓
WJEC B	✓
CCEA	✗

The changing role of women in wartime

Figure 4.6 Women's part in the workforce in 1938 and 1944

As in the First World War, women's contribution to the Second World War was hugely important, and their role changed. From 1941 unmarried women aged 20 to 30 were conscripted into the **Auxiliary Territorial Service** (ATS), **Women's Royal Naval Service** (WRNS), **Women's Auxiliary Air Force** (WAAF) or the **Women's Transport Service** (FANY). Women also joined the **Women's Voluntary Service** (WVS) to supply emergency services at home, or the **Women's Land Army** to help on farms. By 1943 90% of single women and 80% of married women were involved in war work of one kind or another.

Rationing

The experiences gained during the First World War led to the early introduction of **rationing, for food in 1940 and for clothes in 1941**. Both were in short supply during the Battle of the Atlantic. This gained popular acceptance because people realised it was fairer to treat rich and poor alike. Many ate better and became healthier as a result. Rationing continued until 1953.

A **typical weekly food ration** would include: 6oz bacon, 4oz cheese, 4oz butter, 2 eggs, 1 pint milk, 3oz tea, 12oz sugar, 3oz sweets, 4 pints dried milk, with 12 dried eggs every eight weeks.

> **PROGRESS CHECK**
>
> 1. Which kind of air raid shelter was issued for use inside people's homes?
> 2. Which Act of Parliament allowed the arrest of German nationals?
> 3. What was the ration of sweets each week during the war?
>
> 1. The Morrison shelter. 2. Emergency Powers Act. 3. 3oz.

Sample GCSE questions

Study the following sources.

Source A: Prime Minister Winston Churchill speaks to the House of Commons, 20th August, 1940

'The gratitude of every home in our island, in our Empire, and indeed throughout the world, except in the abodes of the guilty, goes out to the British airmen who, undaunted by odds, unwearied in their constant challenge and mortal danger, are turning the tide of the World War by their prowess and by their devotion. Never in the field of human conflict was so much owed by so many to so few.'

Source B: Hitler, 4th September 1940

'...When the British Air Force drops two or three or four thousand kilograms of bombs, then we will in one night drop 150-, 230-, 300- or 400,000 kilograms. When they declare that they will increase their attacks on our cities, then we will raze their cities to the ground. We will stop the handiwork of those night air pirates, so help us God!'

Source C: London, 7th September 1940, showing the smoke over the Isle of Dogs

Source D: Chester Wilmot, an American author, about the Battle of Britain, 1952

Yet every German variation and manoeuvre could be plotted by radar or spotted by the Observer Corps, traced on the map tables of the control rooms, and passed by radio to the squadrons in the air. It was a battle of chance and force against science and skill. There was no shortage of courage on the German part, though their pilots lacked the zest of the British, but their confidence was undermined by the knowledge that in comparison with their opponents they were blind, deaf and dumb.

Source E: A modern historian explains the crisis, writing in 1975

On 7th September the Germans turned aside to bomb London. This began the third phase. It also began, though no one appreciated this, the indiscriminate bombing of cities that was to continue throughout the war. The British thought the crisis was upon them. On the night of 7th September the signal 'Cromwell' for 'invasion imminent' was sent out. The Home Guard stood to arms. In some districts the ringing of church bells announced that German parachutists had actually landed...

Sample GCSE questions

Source F: A government scientist explained the importance of the raid on 7th September, 1940, writing in 1978.

The fires in the docks were enormous: they could never be put out before nightfall. Even if we jammed the beams completely, the night bombers would have perfect markers, for the flames in the docks could be seen from the coast. All the Luftwaffe would then have to do was to keep the fires stoked up with successive raids, while its main force aimed a few miles to the west and so pulverised central London. As we watched from Richmond, it was clear that the fires were still raging, and the night attacks on London began. But they were put out in a few days, despite all the odds, by the gallantry of the Regular and Auxiliary Fire Services, who continued to work throughout the raids.

These questions are about German attacks on Britain in 1940. Look carefully at Sources A to F and then answer the questions.

(a) Study Source B. What can you learn from this source about the intention of Hitler's raids on Britain?

From this source I can learn that Hitler's intention was to bomb British cities in revenge for British raids on Germany and that he intended to do that disproportionately. `When they declare that they will increase their attacks on our cities, then we will raze their cities to the ground.´ **(6)**

> This needs to be a relatively short answer for six marks. There are actually two points here, both that he intended revenge and that he intended that revenge to be disproportionate.

(b) Study Source A and use your own knowledge. What was the purpose of this speech? Use details of the speech and your own knowledge to explain your answer.

Source A is largely intended to give credit to the airmen, at that point still engaged in the Battle of Britain. Had they not shown such courage in keeping control of the air, then their airfields would have been destroyed and Hitler would have been able to launch Operation Sealion, the invasion of Britain. Britain had a great deal to be thankful for. Behind that lay another intention: the Battle of Britain was hardly won and the Blitz was about to begin. Churchill knew that Britain was in terrible danger of invasion. In these circumstances it was necessary to rally the nation, and this speech was repeated on the radio. Churchill's method was to give full praise to those concerned in order to reassure the country that everyone was in this together, and to imply that the sacrifices made by one group would be demanded of others. **(8)**

> When dealing with a famous speech such as this, it is important to explain its original audience and context in the war situation. The intention may be explained as what it says clearly, and what it implies. Look for both these meanings.

(c) Study Sources A and D. How far do these sources agree about the reasons for victory in the Battle of Britain? Explain your answer.

At first glance these two sources do not agree about the cause of victory: in Source A Churchill paid tribute to the `airmen who, undaunted by odds, unwearied in their constant challenge and mortal

Sample GCSE questions

danger, are turning the tide of the world war by their prowess and by their devotion'. This seems to be all about courage, rather than technology. In Source D, Chester Wilmot pointed out that: 'There was no shortage of courage on the German part' (the wrong side) while he gave the chief credit to science, in the form of radar. However, when you look more carefully, he gave the British pilots some credit for 'skill', and for 'zest', which cannot be too different from 'prowess and devotion' (Source A). Certainly there is still some difference in approach, but Chester Wilmot was writing much later, when the secret of radar had been made public, while Churchill was still keeping it secret.

(8)

> You need to find at least two differences. Illustrate them by quotations and try to explain their importance. While there isn't any instruction to use your own knowledge, your answer would not mean much without some explanation.

(d) Study Sources C and E. Which of these two sources is the more useful to the historian in explaining the crisis on 7th September? Explain your answer, using the sources and your knowledge.

It would be easy to argue that, being more reliable, a contemporary photograph must be the more useful to the historian. In Source C, one can clearly see the docks burning, behind Tower Bridge. The photograph appears to have been taken in daytime, so this must be some time after the night raid, so it was clearly very severe, and yet the photograph does not explain the significance of the date: 7th September was the date on which the Government expected invasion. One would need to supplement this photograph with a second source, perhaps Source E or Source F to understand its significance.

Source E was written by a modern historian. Therefore, it will be using a number of different primary sources to give a complete picture. It succeeds in putting 7th September into its context, both at the beginning of the third phase of the Battle of Britain, and the likely date of invasion, the signal, 'Cromwell' being given. On its own it may not seem reliable, but it is corroborated by the photograph (Source C) and Source F in terms of the raid on the docks, and I know that the invasion signal was given.

> Reliability is obviously a crucial question, but you should use other sources and your own knowledge to establish this. To be useful, a source must explain something important: argue in terms of the strengths and the weaknesses of each source with regard to the question. Try to sum up the comparison in your conclusion.

Of the two sources, the photograph is too limited to be of great use, except to support another source, while Source E both describes more aspects of that day and gives an idea of the importance of the events, so it is more useful in explaining the crisis.

(10)

(e) Study all the sources and use your own knowledge.
'The courage of "the Few" in winning the Battle of Britain saved Britain from invasion in 1940'. Use details from the sources and your own knowledge to explain your answer.

In Source A, Churchill gave airmen the credit for 'turning the tide of the World War by their prowess', but he was speaking several weeks before

Sample GCSE questions

the most likely date of the invasion, according to Source E, while Source D suggests that the real credit should be given to radar. The need for Churchill to rally the country without giving away secrets probably explains the reason for Churchill's misdirection of the House of Commons, and of course he could not know what would happen later. Even so, Churchill's point-of-view could not be a complete answer.

In Source B, Hitler spoke of bombing, rather than of invasion. He was hardly likely to give away his invasion plans, in public, so this source cannot prove that he had already changed his mind to concentrate on Yugoslavia and later the Soviet Union, but it does not prove that he still intended to invade Britain either.

The other sources focus on the Blitz, rather than on invasion plans, and yet these can be made relevant by Source E, in which the modern historian explains that, on the night of 7th September the invasion was expected, so that the ferocious raid on the Isle of Dogs was seen as a preparation for invasion. Source C, the photograph, shows the destruction of docks and shipping, clearly a useful prelude if invasion was planned. The modern historian and the government scientist explained the kind of crisis that Britain was in at this point. Though they did not agree on the detail, the scientist clearly thought that central London was the likely focus: the paralysis of government, rather than either economic damage or even invasion, whereas the historian thought that invasion was most important. Perhaps both of these points-of-view could be right, as government paralysis would have aided a successful invasion.

The real significance of these later sources is to show that 'the Few' had not finally saved Britain from invasion. Britain remained in a fix, with bombers regularly getting through to blitz British cities for long after Churchill's speech. In Source F the government scientist seemed to think that the Luftwaffe could readily bomb British cities and survival depended on the Fire Brigade, rather than the RAF.
I know that the truth is still more complex, and that survival depended on many different types of people, not least Hitler and Goering, who changed the focus of their bombing from airfields to
cities too early to gain the air power on which invasion depended. (8)

This is rather a long answer to a complex problem because none of the sources explain when, exactly, Hitler gave up his plan to invade. So, while it is easy to show that 'the Few' were not solely responsible, it is difficult to explain which event really changed his mind. Was it the failure of bombing to produce paralysis, or was it events outside Britain that persuaded him? It is important to evaluate the sources: how far can they be used to prove this point? A conclusion is important too, which gives due weight to your own knowledge. Candidates too often focus only on the sources, whereas the question specifically asks for your own knowledge too.

5 The Cold War begins 1945–1960

The following topics are covered in this chapter:

- Who was to blame for the Cold War?
- How did the Cold War develop 1945–1960?

5.1 Who was to blame for the Cold War?

LEARNING SUMMARY	After studying this section you should be able to understand:
	- how the alliance between the USSR and the USA broke down in 1945
	- how the USSR gained control of Eastern Europe by 1948
	- how the USA reacted to Soviet expansionism
	- who was more to blame for the start of the Cold War – the USA or the USSR

Why did the alliance between the USA and the USSR begin to break down in 1945?

AQA B	✓
EDEXCEL A	✓
OCR B	✓
WJEC A	✓
WJEC B	✗
CCEA	✓

The ideological origins of the split

Since the 1917 Russian Revolution, which brought communist governments to power in Russia, the Soviet Union and the USA had been at **opposite ideological extremes**: communist and capitalist. US opposition to communism had been increased during the 1930s by their experience of the Depression and the risk of communist agitation within the USA. Meanwhile, inside the Soviet Union, Stalin had used fear of a supposed capitalist threat to create a permanent state of emergency to justify his dictatorship. To the Soviet government, the USA or Britain was hardly less fascist or threatening than the Nazi Third Reich.

The **alliance** between Russia and the USA during the Second World War had **never been one of friendship**, but was of necessity, and could not be expected to last longer than its cause: the destruction of the Nazi Third Reich.

People in the USA had never forgotten the **Nazi–Soviet Pact** of 1939, which meant that they distrusted the Soviet Union as much as Nazi Germany.

The Yalta Conference, February 1945

Churchill, Roosevelt and Stalin met for the last time at Yalta. Roosevelt was already ill and died later that year. At their meeting, they agreed the following:

- **Germany would be divided into four** demilitarised zones under Britain, France, Russia and the USA. Berlin, inside the Soviet sector, would also be divided into four. German war criminals would be punished.
- The Soviet Union would join the war against Japan.
- Countries in Eastern Europe would hold **free and fair elections** for new governments.
- A new **United Nations** would replace the League of Nations.

They did not really agree on how the Soviet Union would treat **Eastern Europe**. Stalin demanded land in Poland, while the expectation of free elections was unlikely to be met because Eastern Europe would be a Soviet 'sphere of influence'. These vague terms would cause trouble later.

Figure 5.1 'The Big Three' piece Europe back together

The Potsdam Conference, July–August 1945

By July 1945 the situation was deteriorating quite fast:

- **Truman**, who was more anti-communist than Roosevelt, had become US President. During the Conference, Churchill lost the general election in Britain, being replaced by **Clement Attlee** (Labour), who could not act as mediator as Churchill had done. Stalin and Truman became more and more suspicious of each other.
- **Soviet armies had by now occupied Eastern Europe** and had set up a communist government in Poland. Stalin obviously wanted to make Eastern Europe communist, which Truman was particularly unhappy about.
- **Stalin wanted to punish and weaken Germany**, while extracting huge reparations. Truman thought that this would just be repeating the mistakes of the Treaty of Versailles.
- Truman told Stalin about a new weapon, but the details of the **Atomic Bomb** were kept from Stalin, making him suspicious that it may be used against the Soviet Union.

There was very little agreed at Potsdam:

- Six million Germans in Eastern Europe would be resettled in Germany.
- Each of the Allies could take what they wanted from their zone of Germany.

So, the final division between Eastern and Western Europe was going to be an **ideological** division, based on the line where the Allies met in their conquest of Germany. There would be no future meetings, because the **USA and USSR now viewed each other with too much suspicion**. Britain and France had been so weakened by the Second World War that they now carried little authority. In 1946, Winston Churchill would sum up the new situation in a memorable speech: 'From Stettin in the Baltic to Trieste in the Adriatic, an iron curtain has descended across the continent.'

> Make sure that you know why relations between the USA and USSR had worsened between Yalta and Potsdam.

Figure 5.2 The 'Iron Curtain'

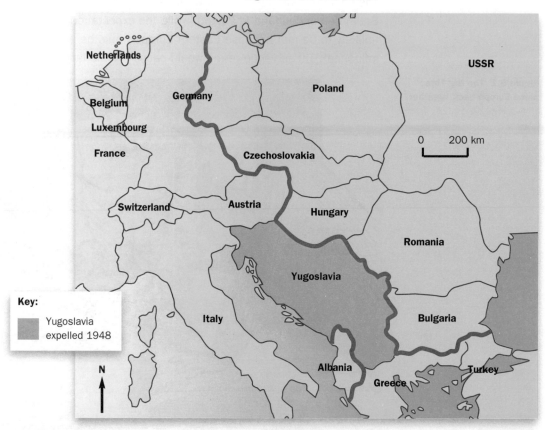

Key:

☐ Yugoslavia expelled 1948

How had the USSR gained control of Eastern Europe by 1948?

AQA B	✓
EDEXCEL A	✓
OCR B	✓
WJEC A	✓
WJEC B	✗
CCEA	✓

Soviet expansion in Eastern Europe

By 1946, **Poland**, **Hungary**, **Romania**, **Bulgaria**, **Yugoslavia** and **Albania** all had communist governments. Some came to power legally, as in Hungary, Romania, Albania and Yugoslavia, but some used democratic elections as a way to destroy democracy, by entering coalitions, then imprisoning or banning the other parties.

The **secret police** then imprisoned opponents of communism, or even those who may have opposed it in the future.

In October 1947, Stalin set up the Communist Information Bureau (**Cominform**) to co-ordinate Eastern European communist parties. He regularly brought leaders together to be briefed and removed those he thought may be too independent. **President Tito of Yugoslavia** resented such tactics and was **expelled** for his hostility in 1948.

'Iron Curtain' and Cold War

By 1948, Churchill's prediction in 1946 had become reality: there was an 'Iron Curtain'. Both Soviet and American leaders were regularly talking in public about the threat of war between them. Arms expenditures were increasing, rather than falling after the Second World War, while a propaganda war was developing, which people were calling a 'Cold War'.

How did the USA react to Soviet expansionism?

AQA B	✓
EDEXCEL A	✓
OCR B	✓
WJEC A	✓
WJEC B	✗
CCEA	✓

The collapse of British influence: The Truman Doctrine 1947

Historically, British sea power had controlled much of what had gone on in the Eastern Mediterranean, but **by 1947 Britain was in a deep financial crisis** and could not afford such commitments. They had become involved in a civil war between monarchists and communists in **Greece**, which they could not afford, and they decided to withdraw their troops, just as they did from **Palestine** in early 1948. Unless something was done, this would create a very worrying power vacuum, into which the Soviet Union would expand. The USA had quickly withdrawn their troops from Europe, except for Germany, in 1945. They preferred their normal peacetime policy of **isolationism**. However, this serious threat to European stability prompted action:

Was the USSR or the USA the aggressor?

- **President Truman paid for British troops to stay in Greece**, where royalists were soon in control.
- Truman promised to send money, equipment and advice to any country threatened by communist takeover. **The Truman Doctrine** made it quite clear that all nations could look to the United States for support to maintain freedom and showed that the USA would take a world role in opposition to the Soviet Union.

The Marshall Plan 1948

In 1947 Truman sent Secretary of State, **General George Marshall** to assess the economic state of Europe. There he found **ruined economies suffering extreme shortages** and continued rationing. In Britain in 1947, electricity was turned off for a period each day through lack of coal. European countries owed $11.5 billion to the USA. Marshall suggested that about **$17.5 billion would be needed** to rebuild Europe's prosperity. In December 1947 Truman attempted, at first unsuccessfully, to get the Marshall Plan passed by Congress.

> **KEY POINT**
>
> The US Congress thought that Truman was too involved in European affairs, and didn't see why they should pay.

But, in March 1948, anti-Soviet leaders were purged in **Czechoslovakia**, where the probable murder of pro-American Jan Masaryk persuaded the US Congress to accept the Marshall Plan and make $17 billion available over the following four years. Certainly the Marshall Plan would benefit the USA: Truman wanted to prevent a world slump, he wanted markets for American goods and wanted to ensure that a weakened Western Europe did not fall to communism, but the Marshall Plan was still a very well-timed and most generous gesture by the USA towards Europe.

Stalin considered Marshall Aid with suspicion, realising that it would strengthen the capitalist system and halt the spread of communism, making states dependent on dollars. He refused to allow any Eastern European state to benefit from it.

Marshall Aid was successful: by 1952 industrial output was 35% higher than it had been before the war. The return of European prosperity helped to fuel the American post-war boom.

Resistance to the Blockade of Berlin 1948 and the formation of NATO

It was clear to the Western Allies that Germany could not feed its own people unless it was allowed to **rebuild its industries**. In 1946 Britain, France and the USA had combined their zones in Germany. In 1948 they reformed the currency (the Deutschmark), and soon West Germany began to recover.

Stalin thought that the USA was using capitalism to **undermine Soviet policies** of keeping their side of Germany poor and weak. While he could do little about West German prosperity, he could control Berlin, which was linked to West Germany by roads, railways and canals that he could cut. In July 1948 Stalin blockaded the two million people in West Berlin, hoping to force the Western Allies out.

Truman was serious about his policy of containment, wanting West Berlin to remain as a beacon of freedom deep in the Soviet Zone. In June 1948 the Allies decided **to airlift supplies** to West Berlin, even though they realised that Stalin may interpret this as cause for war. The planes got through, and for ten months, West Berlin was supplied by air. Everything from food and fuel to building materials was ferried from three airports in West Germany, to three airports in West Berlin. 1.5 million tonnes of goods were supplied over 318 days. On 12th May 1949 Stalin reopened the roads and railways.

This was the first direct confrontation of the Cold War. In July 1948 American B29 bombers were deployed to bases in Britain which, the Soviets suspected, may carry nuclear weapons. During the Berlin Blockade, the Western Powers met in Washington, agreeing to set up a new organisation called **NATO** (North Atlantic Treaty Organisation) in April 1949 for their own defence. Germany was to remain divided into the Federal Republic (West Germany) and the German Democratic Republic (East Germany) for the next 41 years.

Figure 5.3 A divided Germany

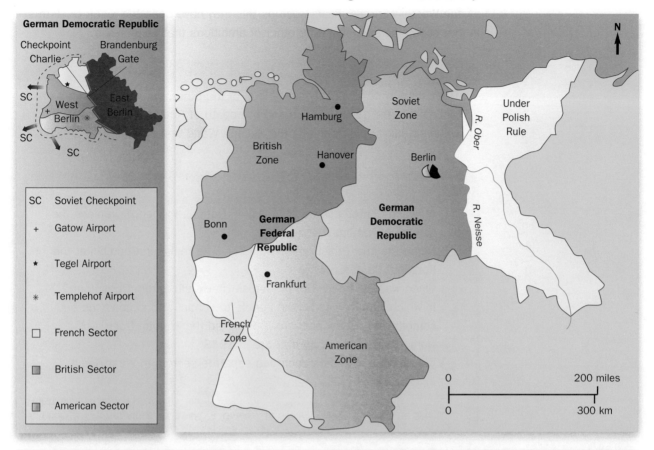

German Democratic Republic

Checkpoint Charlie
Brandenburg Gate
SC
West Berlin
East Berlin
SC
SC

SC   Soviet Checkpoint

\+   Gatow Airport

★   Tegel Airport

✳   Templehof Airport

☐   French Sector

▨   British Sector

▨   American Sector

Hamburg
British Zone
Hanover
Soviet Zone
Under Polish Rule
R. Ober
Berlin
R. Neisse
Bonn
German Federal Republic
German Democratic Republic
Frankfurt
French Zone
American Zone

N

0   200 miles
0   300 km

Who was more to blame for the Cold War – the USA or the USSR?

AQA B	✓
EDEXCEL A	✓
OCR B	✓
WJEC A	✓
WJEC B	✗
CCEA	✓

USA to blame	USSR to blame
• Churchill and Roosevelt had bribed Stalin with vague promises of a 'sphere of influence'. • Truman's suspicion of communism was important. He thought that the Soviet Union wanted to take over Western Europe. • The USA had kept knowledge of the Atom Bomb from the Russians. The existence of the Atom Bomb was a threat to Soviet security. • Truman had opposed Soviet expansionism with the Truman Doctrine, the Marshall Plan, the defence of Berlin and the formation of NATO, all of which the Soviet Union thought were aggressive acts. • Economic policies in Western Germany threatened the communist East through the return of prosperity.	• Stalin's suspicion of capitalism was important. • Russia had been invaded by Western Powers three times already in the 20th Century: Stalin was determined to create real security by controlling Eastern Europe. • Stalin had broken his promise of 'free and fair' elections in Eastern Europe. • Stalin had caused the Berlin Crisis by cutting off supplies. • The diplomatic posture of the Soviet Union was antagonistic to the West. • The large number of Soviet troops that remained in Eastern Europe seemed to threaten the West.

There is no evidence to suggest that the Soviet Union did have real plans to invade Western Europe. Fears such as this may have been the result of distrust in that each side suspected the other of ambitions that neither had.

KEY POINT

Both sides were justifiably suspicious of the other, but it was the loss of Churchill in the 1945 election and the death of Roosevelt that ended the understanding built up during the Second World War.

PROGRESS CHECK

1. At which Conference was the United Nations formed, to replace the League of Nations?
2. Name the new British Prime Minister, who replaced Churchill at the Potsdam Conference.
3. When was President Tito of Yugoslavia expelled from Cominform?
4. In which country was Britain unable to continue to support the anti-communist government, which provoked the Truman Doctrine?
5. Name the US Secretary of State in 1948.
6. Which three countries each had separate sectors in West Berlin in 1948?

1. Yalta. 2. Clement Attlee. 3. 1948. 4. Greece. 5. General George Marshall. 6. Britain, France and the USA.

5.2 How did the Cold War develop 1945–1960?

LEARNING SUMMARY	After studying this section you should be able to understand:
	• the rivalry in the nuclear arms race
	• the Korean War
	• the 'Thaw'

How did the nuclear arms race develop?

AQA B	✓
EDEXCEL A	✓
OCR B	✓
WJEC A	✓
WJEC B	✗
CCEA	✓

The nuclear threat

Ever since the dropping of Atomic Bombs on Hiroshima and Nagasaki, the **USSR felt under constant threat.** The USA had not shared her nuclear secrets, even though the Soviets were allies at the time. With 70,000 people being killed within minutes of the first bomb, and with huge destructive capabilities, the Atom Bomb destroyed the balance between conventional forces that would normally keep one power from invading the other.

The nuclear arms race

Date	USA	USSR
1945	Atom Bombs dropped on Hiroshima and Nagasaki.	Concern at the secrecy and implied threat to the USSR.
August 1949	Concern in the USA, since the early detonation was partly the result of spying.	USSR detonated its first Atomic Bomb.
1951	The US Strategic Air Command identified 6,000 potential targets in the USSR.	
1952	Detonation of the first Hydrogen Bomb, 1,000 times more powerful than the Atom Bomb	
1953		USSR detonated its own H-Bomb
March 1954	An H-Bomb small enough to be dropped from a bomber was developed.	
September 1954		An H-Bomb dropped from a bomber.
July 1956	U-2 spy plane developed to spy on USSR.	
May 1957		First Intercontinental Ballistic Missile developed.
October 1957		Sputnik satellite orbited the earth. Could be used to guide missiles.
January 1958	First US satellite orbited the earth.	
1959	Atlas and Minuteman ICBMs developed. Polaris missiles could be delivered from submarines. Public alarm at Soviet production of ICBMs not put to rest by President Eisenhower.	
April 1961		Cosmonaut Yuri Gagarin orbited the earth: the first man in space.
October 1961		Explosion of H-Bomb more powerful than all the explosives used in the Second World War.

The Korean War 1950–1953

AQA B	✓
EDEXCEL A	✓
OCR B	✓
WJEC A	✓
WJEC B	✗
CCEA	✓

Causes of the Korean War

Causes:

- North Korea was **communist** and supported by the Soviet Union; South Korea was **anti-communist** and was supported by the USA. Their border was on the 38th parallel, but both dictators claimed the whole peninsula.
- When, in 1950, **North Korea invaded the South**, the USA and 16 other nations sent troops in response to a United Nations request.
- **President Truman was determined to contain communism**, which was fast expanding in the Far East. In 1949 China had fallen to communism and the USA thought that Korea would be another domino falling: next may come Japan or Indo-China. The USA was aware that Malaya, Indonesia, Burma and the Philippines were also under threat.

The main events of the war

June 1950	North Koreans advanced to contain South Korean forces in the **Pusan** perimeter.
September 1950	General MacArthur's forces landed at Inchon, pushing North Koreans out of South Korea.
October 1950	UN **approved invasion of North Korea** leading to the unification of Korea and the advance towards the Korea–China border.
November 1950	**Chinese 'volunteers' poured into North Korea** to drive MacArthur back. MacArthur asked Truman to use the Atomic Bomb and to invade China.
April 1951	**MacArthur was sacked by Truman**, and replaced by General Ridgeway.
June 1951	Stalemate developed around the 38th parallel
1953	Armistice signed.

The UN army was made up of 50% US troops while 86% of the navy was American. MacArthur took orders from Truman, rather than the UN.

Figure 5.4 North and South Korea

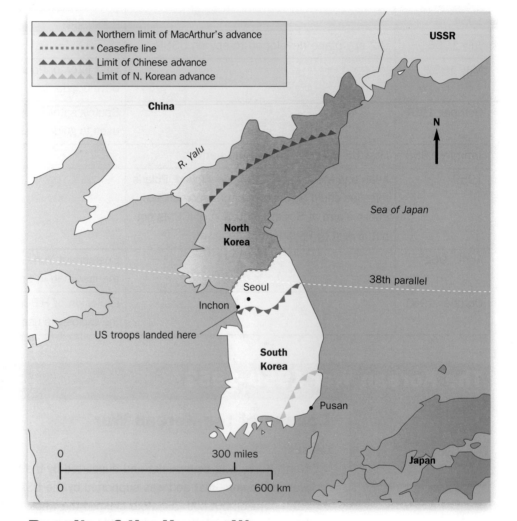

Results of the Korean War

The Korean War had the following results:

- America realised that, while **containment of communism** may be possible, it **could not defeat it**. Secretary of State, John Foster Dulles, set up a network of anti-communist alliances around the world: South East Asia Treaty Organisation (**SEATO**) 1954; Central Treaty Organisation (**CENTO**) 1955.

- The USSR responded with the **Warsaw Pact 1955**, which included all communist Eastern European states, with the exception of Yugoslavia.
- The war had demonstrated how easily a regional conflict could escalate to threaten world peace.
- The **UN was weakened**, since it seemed to be too dominated by the USA.

The 'Thaw'

AQA B	✓
EDEXCEL A	✓
OCR B	✓
WJEC A	✓
WJEC B	✗
CCEA	✓

The effects of the death of Stalin 1953

The death of Soviet dictator Joseph Stalin did appear to have the effect of lessening tensions for a while, but opinions differ as to whether this 'thaw' was real or just a matter of propaganda. Stalin's successor, **Nikita Khrushchev** denounced Stalin's policies, talked about peaceful co-existence, met with Western leaders in Summit Conferences in 1955 and 1960 and generally seemed to ease the tensions of the early 1950s.

However the reality was that Soviet policies had not changed:
- In 1956 (during the Suez Crisis) protests about rising food prices in **Poland** caused the Red Army to invade to impose order.
- In the same year, an anti-communist rising in **Hungary** was put down at the cost of 30,000 Hungarian lives by the Red Army.
- When the Soviet Union became alarmed at the economic success of Western Germany in 1961, they built the **Berlin Wall**, dividing Eastern and Western Berlin. Those wanting to emigrate illegally to Western Germany were shot by border guards.

Figure 5.5
Nikita Khrushchev

PROGRESS CHECK

1. In which year did the USSR detonate her own Atomic Bomb?
2. To which perimeter were South Korean forces forced to retreat in 1950 before receiving UN help?
3. In which year did the USSR form the Warsaw Pact?
4. Which Soviet President succeeded Joseph Stalin in 1953?

4. Nikita Khrushchev.
3. 1955.
2. Pusan.
1. 1949.

Sample GCSEs questions

(a) What was agreed at the Yalta Conference, 1945?

- Germany would be divided into four demilitarised zones under Britain, France, Russia and the USA. Berlin, inside the Soviet sector, would also be divided into four. German war criminals would be punished.
- The Soviet Union would join the war against Japan.
- Countries in Eastern Europe would hold free and fair elections for new governments.
- A new United Nations would replace the League of Nations. **(4)**

> Here are four clear points, though the first may merit more than one mark.

(b) Why was the Marshall Plan successful in Western Europe?

It was successful for the USA because Truman wanted to prevent a world slump, he wanted markets for American goods and wanted to ensure that a weakened Western Europe did not fall to communism, while the return of European prosperity helped to fuel the American post-war boom. It was successful for Western European nations because it allowed their economies to recover and international trade to re-start. Marshall Aid was successful: by 1952 industrial output was 35% higher than it had been before the war. **(6)**

> Only two reasons are given here, but they come with considerable supporting detail and explanation. They also show that success depended on who you were.

(c) How far was the Cold War caused by Stalin's intention to expand communism?

It was reasonable for the USSR to be very suspicious of American intentions. Churchill and Roosevelt had bribed Stalin with vague promises of a 'sphere of influence', but Truman was not prepared to honour that promise, thinking that the Soviet Union would take over Western Europe too. Meanwhile the secrecy in which the USA and Britain had developed the Atom Bomb suggested that it was intended for use against communists. Truman's later policies: the Truman Doctrine, the Marshall Plan, the defence of Berlin and the formation of NATO, all seemed aggressive to Stalin while economic policies in Western Germany threatened the communist East through the return of prosperity. However, the Western Powers did not intend to cause war with the USSR. On the other hand, Stalin's suspicion of capitalism was important. Russia had been invaded by Western Powers three times already in the 20th Century and Stalin was determined to create real security by controlling Eastern Europe. There, Stalin had broken his promise of 'free and fair' elections and then caused the Berlin Crisis by cutting off supplies. Throughout this time the diplomatic posture of the Soviet Union was antagonistic to the West while the large number of Soviet troops that remained in Eastern Europe seemed to threaten the West. Soviet expansionism in Europe and communist aggression in China and Korea seemed to give grounds for alarm. **(10)**

> It is more difficult to see the situation through Soviet eyes, but that is an important skill.

> The problem is mutual misunderstanding: your job is to explain this.

Exam practice questions

1 **(a)** What were the effects of Stalin's reopening of the roads and railways leading to Berlin in 1949?

....

....

....

.... **(4)**

(b) What were the causes of the Korean War in 1950?

....

....

....

....

....

.... **(6)**

(c) How far were the effects of the Korean War to the US advantage?

....

....

....

....

....

....

....

....

....

....

....

....

....

.... **(10)**

You may need to continue your answers on a separate sheet of paper.

6 Tension and détente 1960–1980

The following topics are covered in this chapter:

- **Who won the Cuban Missile Crisis?**
- **Why did the USA fail in Vietnam?**
- **Détente**

6.1 Who won the Cuban Missile Crisis?

LEARNING SUMMARY

After studying this section you should be able to understand:

- how the USA reacted to the Cuban Revolution
- why Khrushchev put missiles on Cuba
- why Kennedy reacted as he did
- who won the Cuban Missile Crisis and its effects.

The reaction of the USA to the Cuban Revolution

AQA B	✓
EDEXCEL A	✓
OCR B	✓
WJEC A	✓
WJEC B	✗
CCEA	✓

The Cuban Revolution

In 1959 communist leader **Fidel Castro overthrew the dictator Batista**, who had allowed American businessmen to make huge profits in Cuba and who had leased the site of the American base at **Guantanamo Bay** to the USA. Ordinary Cubans lived in great poverty under Batista's repressive rule, so that the moderate communism that Castro offered became very popular. Relations between the USA and Castro's Cuba rapidly deteriorated:

- Cubans fled to Miami where they plotted the downfall of Castro.
- Castro nationalised (confiscated) a lot of land.
- The USA refused to sell arms to Cuba.
- In 1960 the Soviet Union started to buy Cuban sugar, which the USA would no longer buy.
- President Eisenhower started to train Cuban exiles for the invasion of Cuba.
- Cuba began to buy arms from the Soviet Union.
- The USA tried to stop other countries selling oil to Cuba.
- August 1960: Castro nationalised hundreds of US companies in Cuba.
- October 1960: the USA stopped trading with Cuba.
- January 1961: the USA broke off diplomatic relations with Cuba.

> **KEY POINT**
>
> President Kennedy thought that US policy was responsible for the strength of communism in Cuba in the first place. The Bay of Pigs made this worse.

The Bay of Pigs Invasion, April 1961

In April 1961, 1,400 Cuban refugees, with CIA support, invaded Cuba. The new president, John Kennedy, had not been able to abort the plans, and the invasion was a disaster. The invaders lacked the support of the Cuban people and were easily defeated, but the real disaster was that this bullying by the USA pushed Castro further into the hands of the Soviet Union.

Why did Khrushchev put missiles on Cuba?

AQA B	✓
EDEXCEL A	✓
OCR B	✓
WJEC A	✓
WJEC B	✗
CCEA	✓

Cuba and the Soviet Union

The Soviet Union was feeling threatened by US **nuclear missiles in Turkey and Europe** and so she quickly responded to Castro's request for support. Conventional arms shipments were tolerated by the USA, while Kennedy's advisers were of the opinion that nuclear arms would not follow. On 11th September 1962, **Kennedy warned the Soviet Union** that he would prevent 'by whatever means necessary' Cuba being used as an offensive base to threaten the USA, and he received assurances that this would not be necessary.

On 14th October 1962, a **U-2 spy plane took photographs of Soviet missiles being installed on Cuba.** Some sites would be ready in about seven days, while 20 Soviet ships were on their way to Cuba. The missiles would be capable of reaching most big cities in the USA before they could be detected.

Figure 6.1 The missile threat from Cuba

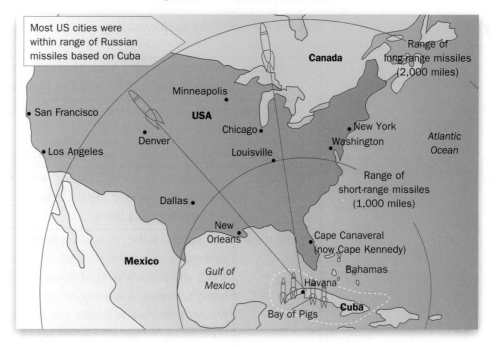

What prompted Khrushchev to take this risk with world peace?

Khrushchev was playing a complex game. He wanted…

- to defend Cuba against the USA
- to counter the threat of US missiles in Turkey and Europe and of ICBMs from the USA, which could all target the USSR
- to use Cuba as a bargaining chip: to demand US withdrawal of missiles from Turkey, or perhaps to force withdrawal from Berlin
- to test President Kennedy, whom he had met at Vienna and thought would be weak.

> Expect to be able to argue why Khrushchev put the missiles on Cuba and whether he was justified.

Why did Kennedy react as he did?

AQA B	✓
EDEXCEL A	✓
OCR B	✓
WJEC A	✓
WJEC B	✗
CCEA	✓

President Kennedy's decisions were crucial at this point, because the world was on the brink of nuclear war. He had the following options:

- **Do nothing**, which would make the USA seem weak and open her to permanent threat from the nuclear missiles.
- **Attack by air**, though the USSR might retaliate, especially as it would be difficult to destroy all the missiles.
- **Invade Cuba**, which would probably remove Castro and the missiles, but was likely to provoke war.
- **Blockade Cuba** – if he stopped more missiles arriving without using force he would show that the USA would not tolerate the missiles and give the USSR a way out of the crisis.

> Remember the advantages and disadvantages of each option.

Kennedy decided on the last option and announced on 22nd October that…

- there would be a naval blockade: Soviet ships would be stopped and searched, preventing more missiles getting to Cuba
- all missiles in Cuba must be removed.

This left the next move to Khrushchev:

23rd October	Kennedy received a letter from Khrushchev **refusing to observe the blockade** and not admitting that there were missiles on Cuba.
24th October	The first Soviet ships, accompanied by a submarine, **stopped and turned around**.
25th October	Work on missile bases in Cuba was **proceeding rapidly**.
26th October	Khrushchev, in a long personal letter to Kennedy, **offered to destroy the bases** if the US promised not to attack Cuba and if the blockade was lifted.
27th October	In a second letter, in a much harsher tone, Khrushchev **also demanded the removal of US missiles from Turkey**. A **U-2 spy plane was shot down** over Cuba, and Kennedy was urged to launch a reprisal attack. Kennedy decided **to ignore the second letter but to accept Khrushchev's first offer** while saying that, if the USSR did not withdraw, an attack would follow.
28th October	Khrushchev agreed, while Kennedy secretly promised to withdraw US missiles from Turkey in the future.

Results of the Cuban Missile Crisis

AQA B	✓
EDEXCEL A	✓
OCR B	✓
WJEC A	✓
WJEC B	✗
CCEA	✓

Who won?

USA	USSR
• Soviet missiles were withdrawn from Cuba under UN supervision. • Kennedy's reputation was strengthened: he had shown both that he could stand up to Khrushchev and that he was wise enough to avoid provocation.	• Cuban independence was guaranteed. • US missiles were eventually withdrawn from Turkey. • But Khrushchev's reputation was harmed: he had provoked the crisis, then he had backed down. In 1964 he was replaced.

Long-term results

The crisis had proved the importance of communication between the two sides. The teletype machine (which could not convey tone of voice) was replaced by the **telephone hotline**. This meant that leaders could communicate personally and build their relationship. This was important if a disagreement might have nuclear consequences.

In 1963 both sides signed a **Nuclear Test Ban Treaty**. This was the first move towards controlling the growth of nuclear weapons.

Critics of containment (Hawks) had wanted to attack Cuba, but the Cuban crisis had highlighted the unacceptable risks involved: while a communist Cuba was an inconvenience, a nuclear war would be the end of civilisation. **Moderate opinion in the USA** was strengthened.

> **PROGRESS CHECK**
>
> 1. Name the Cuban base leased to the USA by Batista.
> 2. Which US President trained the Cuban exiles for the invasion of Cuba?
> 3. Why was the USA particularly surprised and upset by the arrival of Soviet missiles on Cuba?
> 4. What kind of aeroplane took the photographs of Soviet missiles on Cuba?
> 5. From where were US missiles removed as a result of the Cuban crisis?
> 6. What was the advantage of the 'telephone hotline'?
>
> 6. US and Soviet presidents could hear each other and talk privately.
> 5. Turkey.
> 4. U-2 spy plane.
> 3. The missiles were capable of reaching most big cities in the USA.
> 2. President Eisenhower.
> 1. Guantanamo Bay.

6.2 Why did the USA fail in Vietnam?

LEARNING SUMMARY

After studying this section you should be able to understand:

- why the USA became involved in Vietnam
- how US and Vietcong methods differed
- which tactics were more effective
- why the USA eventually withdrew from Vietnam

Why the USA became involved in Vietnam

AQA B	✓
EDEXCEL A	✗
OCR B	✓
WJEC A	✓
WJEC B	✗
CCEA	✓

French failure in Vietnam

A fiercely nationalist and communist movement, the **Viet Minh**, under **Ho Chi Minh** had become established in opposition to the Japanese occupation of French Indo–China during the Second World War. When the French returned in 1945 they could not re-establish their control, while the Viet Minh were aided by **communist China**, after 1949. This then prompted the USA to help the French, who set up an anti-communist government in the South.

Despite $500 million aid each year from the USA, the French army of 190,000 was isolated in the towns, while Viet Minh **guerrilla tactics** made them impossible to beat. In 1954, at the decisive battle of Dien Bien Phu, French paratroopers lost 3000 dead and a further 8000 in captivity. Peace talks were held in Geneva and the country was divided into the communist North and pro-Western South Vietnam. Elections were promised, but US policy made sure they were never held, in case the communists won.

US involvement

President Eisenhower was convinced that the USSR and communist China intended to extend communism through Vietnam to Laos, Cambodia, Thailand, Burma and perhaps India (**Domino Theory**). He helped Ngo Dinh Diem (a South Vietnamese general) to set up the Republic of South Vietnam, which was pro-Christian, pro-landlord and extremely corrupt.

Although Diem was removed in 1963, he and his successors were all dependent on the USA, and their corruption helped to provoke the peasants into forming the National Front for the Liberation of South Vietnam (**Vietcong**) in 1960. With help from the Viet Minh, the Vietcong started a guerrilla war against the South Vietnam government and against US 'advisers' sent by **President Kennedy** in 1961.

While Kennedy was determined not to be sucked into a war which could not easily be won, his successor, **Lyndon Johnson**, was more optimistic. When, in August 1964, North Vietnamese patrol boats fired on US ships, US Congress gave Johnson the power to 'take all necessary measures' and 23,000 US troops were immediately committed. By 1967 there were 500,000 US troops in Vietnam.

Figure 6.2 The Vietnam War

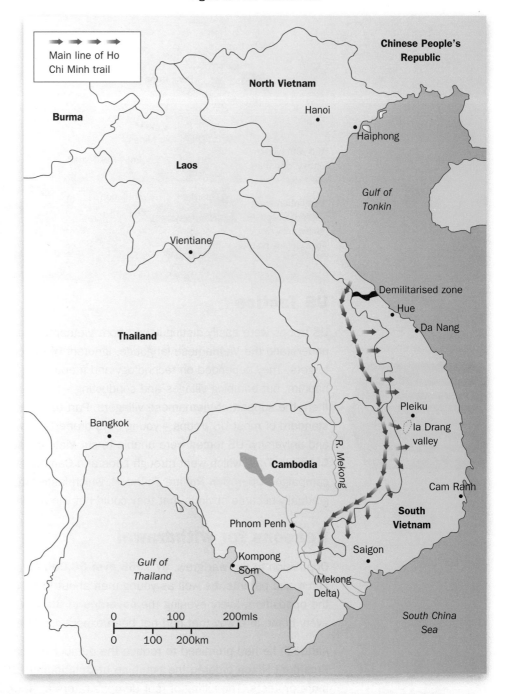

How the USA lost the war

AQA B	✓
EDEXCEL A	✗
OCR B	✓
WJEC A	✓
WJEC B	✗
CCEA	✓

Vietcong tactics

The Vietcong were masters of guerrilla tactics, avoiding large battles but using booby traps and ambushes, living off the land and disappearing among the ordinary people. They knew the country, they could melt away into it and they could rely on help from the peasantry. On the other hand, US forces could not tell Vietcong from the ordinary peasantry who hid them.

When the Vietcong did organise an offensive in 1968, they were driven back, but this **Tet Offensive** shocked the USA so much that it was a propaganda victory: people became convinced that the war could not be won, President Johnson did not seek re-election and peace talks began in Paris.

Figure 6.3 Vietcong tunnel system

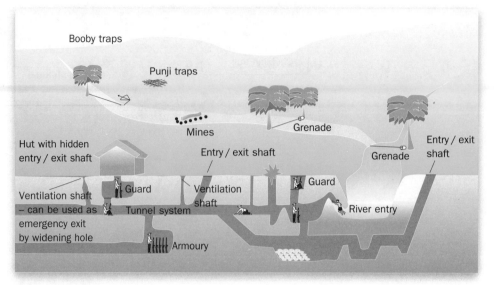

US Tactics

How had the Americans failed to win the 'hearts and minds' of the Vietnamese, and what other kind of victory could they seek?

US troops were easily distinguished from Vietnamese and most did not understand the Vietnamese language. Ignorant of the country, they were easy targets. They depended on technology and firepower, e.g. bombers, gunships and napalm, but bombing villages and conducting search and destroy missions lost them the support of Vietnamese villagers. Part of the problem was the low standard of most US troops – young boys drafted for two years between school and university. US forces were unable to cut Vietcong supply lines down the **Ho Chi Minh Trail**, which went through Laos and Cambodia, despite a huge bombing campaign, '**Operation Rolling Thunder**', which lasted from 1965–1968. It gradually became obvious that they could not win a military victory.

Reasons for withdrawal

Opposition to the war grew: **by 1968 over 36,000 US servicemen had been killed** and parents, as well as young men about to be drafted formed the core of the opposition. Every evening the **coverage of the war on the television** entered every home in a way that had not been experienced before.

Although he had promised to reduce the number of servicemen involved, **President Nixon** ordered the **bombing of Cambodia** in 1969, prompting even more protests. The killing of four demonstrators at **Kent State University** and the **Mai Lai massacre** in 1968 also stiffened opposition to continuing the war.

Nixon changed his policy to one of '**Vietnamisation**': making it possible for the South Vietnam army to continue the war on its own. The conclusion of a peace agreement in January 1973 allowed Nixon to proclaim 'peace with honour' and in **March 1973 the last US troops** were withdrawn. By 1975 North Vietnam and the Vietcong had conquered South Vietnam and reunited the country under communism.

PROGRESS CHECK

1. What was the name of communist forces in North Vietnam?
2. What was the name of the US bombing campaign in Vietnam?
3. What was the name of the North Vietnamese offensive in 1968?

1. Viet Minh. 2. Operation Rolling Thunder . 3. Tet Offensive.

6.3 Détente

LEARNING SUMMARY

After studying this section you should be able to understand:

- why détente became particularly necessary in the 1970s
- how détente had apparently ended by the late 1970s.

Peaceful co-existence

AQA B	✓
EDEXCEL A	✓
OCR B	✓
WJEC A	✓
WJEC B	✗
CCEA	✓

The need for détente

The desire to de-escalate tensions during the Cold War had always been there, e.g. the 'Thaw' during the 1950s, or the period after the Cuban crisis, but in the 1970s the need was much greater than before:

- **The arms race seemed to have reached stalemate**, with both the USA and the USSR able to destroy the other several times over. This nuclear balance was termed 'Mutual Assured Destruction' (**MAD**).
- By the 1970s, the huge amounts of money necessary for armaments were causing inflation in the USA and were lowering standards of living in the USSR. Both countries realised that the arms race was a **pointless waste of money**.
- **President Nixon wanted to get out of Vietnam** and needed the USSR to stop supporting North Vietnam.

Détente in action

Détente continued during the 1970s:

- In 1969 Soviet President Brezhnev announced the '**Brezhnev Doctrine**' in which he welcomed closer links with the West so long as there was no criticism of human rights within the Soviet Union.
- Strategic Arms Limitation Talks were begun immediately and, in 1972, the **SALT I Agreement** was signed. Both countries agreed to limit some types of missiles and to hold discussions about further limitations.
- In 1972 Brezhnev agreed to **artistic and sporting links** with the USA.
- In 1975 American and Soviet **astronauts** linked their spacecraft together.
- In 1975, at the **Helsinki Conference**, 35 countries agreed to exchange information about military manoeuvres; **Soviet domination of Eastern Europe was recognised** and the USSR agreed to sell oil to the West.

The end of détente

In 1977 **Jimmy Carter**, the new President of the USA criticised human rights violations in the Soviet Union. In 1979, when the **USSR invaded Afghanistan**, Carter called for a boycott of the Moscow Olympics in 1980 and **refused to sign SALT II**.

Détente was finally buried by **US President Reagan** who, in 1981, increased spending on arms and developed the **Strategic Defence Initiative** (Star Wars), designed to destroy any missiles aimed at the USA. This outpaced the technological resources of the USSR, while promising a release from MAD for the USA, which finally upset the nuclear balance.

Sample GCSE questions

Study Sources A and B and then answer the following questions.

Source A: Reasons for the escalation of US forces in Vietnam, 1964, by Robert McNamara, US Defence Secretary.

First is the simple fact that South Vietnam, a member of the free world family, is striving to preserve its independence from communist attack. Second, South East Asia has great significance in the forward defence of the USA. For Hanoi, the immediate object is limited conquest of the South and national unification. For Beijing, however, Hanoi's victory would only be a first step towards eventual Chinese dominance of the two Vietnams and South East Asia and towards the exploitation of the new strategy in other parts of the world.

Source B: A ten-year-old Vietnamese girl has torn her burning clothes off following a napalm attack by US forces, June 1972.

(a) How reliable is Source A to a historian writing about the reasons for US involvement in Vietnam?

Secretary McNamara was explaining US aims, which he should know well, quite effectively. This is useful for a historian. While US politicians, speaking in public, do not necessarily tell the whole truth, this appears to be quite reliable because it explains the `Domino Theory´, which was an important cause of the Vietnam War. `Secondly, South East Asia has great significance in the forward defence of the USA.´ i.e. communism must be fought in Saigon, or it will threaten San Francisco. The first sentence is also evidence of the South East Asia Treaty Organisation, of which South Vietnam was a member: `a member of the free world family´. Lastly, in seeing `Peking´ (Beijing) behind Hanoi, this is evidence that the USA saw a direct threat by a major power to stability in Asia.

(6)

> This answer begins by explaining who the source was spoken by and what his possible purpose was. Full marks are then gained because the answer uses knowledge to test the reliability of what Secretary McNamara was saying.

Sample GCSE questions

(b) What can you learn from Source B about the reasons for US failure in the Vietnam War?

This well-known photograph shows the aftermath of a napalm attack, and was fairly typical of the way that US high-tech warfare alienated the Vietnamese. We can see the cloud of burning napalm behind soldiers, away from whom the children seem to be running in terror. The soldiers have clearly not protected the children. Also, this is a press photograph, typical of the anti-war media coverage, which destroyed US support for the war at home. **(4)**

> Try to keep this short for four marks. Try to make just four points from the source.

(c) To what extent was the Vietnam War lost at home in the USA?

Certainly the media coverage of the war was important in provoking the riots and demonstrations of 1968 and after, e.g. at Kent State University, Seattle and San Francisco. The loss of popularity by President Lyndon Johnson opened the way for President Nixon, who promised to reduce US involvement. On the other hand, the lack of clear objectives in the war caused its loss of popularity while even Nixon thought that there could be a military solution through bombing Cambodia.

The real reason why the war was lost was that it could not be won without persuading the people of Vietnam that the South Vietnamese government was more attractive than communism. This was probably impossible, since the South Vietnamese government was corrupt, dictatorial and dependent on foreign aid for its very existence. It had never been democratically elected, even though there was a treaty commitment to hold democratic elections in 1956: the Americans had stopped this. Certainly the North Vietnamese government was also dependent on Chinese aid, but it was a Vietnamese, and not a foreign-imposed, government and it was neither corrupt nor dependent on bombs and napalm. The effect of losing the trust of the South Vietnamese people was increased by the presence of over 35,000 young, different coloured and very alien boys who could not understand or see much in common with the people they thought they were protecting. In these circumstances, military victories would be of momentary importance.

The media coverage showed the American people what was already too obvious on the ground: that you could not impose democratic values by force in spite of the wishes of the people. **(10)**

> This explores several reasons why media coverage was important, and several reasons why it was not. Always try to give a balanced answer. Each 'case' is ended by a quick evaluation: how convincing is this argument? There is a conclusion to give a final judgement at the end.

7 New World 1945–2000

The following topics are covered in this chapter:

- **Opposition to Soviet control in Eastern Europe**
- **Gorbachev and the collapse of the Soviet Union**
- **Northern Ireland 1968–2000**
- **Arab–Israeli conflict 1948–1995**
- **The Iraq War, 2003**
- **Terrorist or freedom fighter?**

7.1 Opposition to Soviet control in Eastern Europe

LEARNING SUMMARY

After studying this section you should be able to understand:

- how Soviet control was re-imposed in Hungary in 1956
- why the Soviet Union built the Berlin Wall in 1961 and its effects
- how 'Prague Spring' was suppressed in Czechoslovakia in 1968
- the success of Solidarity in Poland by 1989

The Hungarian Rising 1956

AQA B	✓
EDEXCEL A	✓
OCR B	✓
WJEC A	✗
WJEC B	✗
CCEA	✓

Reasons for opposition to Soviet control

The USSR had imposed communist governments on the countries of Eastern Europe by 1948 and tightly controlled them through **Cominform** (see page 74). Those who disagreed were harshly treated, while standards of living were low, consumer goods taking second place to the rebuilding of heavy industry inside the Soviet Union.

Opposition arose in Hungary in 1956 due to the following reasons:

- **Stalin had died in 1953** and **Khrushchev**, his successor, had denounced his methods in a speech in 1956 saying that the USSR could live peacefully with the West. He had reassured Yugoslavia that he believed in non-interference and national independence.

> **KEY POINT**
>
> Khrushchev had made the speech in secret, denouncing the use of terror: he had no intention of weakening the USSR's grip on Eastern Europe.

- When there were **demonstrations in Poland** in 1956, Khrushchev sent in Soviet troops, but he also made concessions, giving the Poles more freedom and raising hopes for concessions in Hungary.

Make sure that you know reasons inside and outside Hungary.

- Hungary was certain that the USA would help them: its radio station, '**Voice of America**', was sending a constant stream of reassurance that the USA would help people towards freedom.
- Inside Hungary there was a chance of change when the dictatorial communist, **Matyas Rakosi**, died. Rakosi had ruled through terror, imposed by secret police and censorship. His replacement, Erno Gero, allowed a state funeral for the dissident **Laszlo Rajik**, who had opposed Soviet rule and had been executed. This gave Hungarians an opportunity to show their opposition and thousands demonstrated against Soviet control.

What happened during the rising?

In the huge demonstration on **23rd October 1956** a statue of Stalin in Budapest was torn down while the demonstrators demanded the replacement of Erno Gero. The following morning Khrushchev agreed to a new government under **Imre Nagy** and Soviet troops were to be withdrawn.

Figure 7.1 Demonstrators destroying a statue of Stalin in Budapest

However, the demonstrations continued:
- Local councils replaced Soviet Power.
- Thousands of soldiers deserted to join the demonstrations.
- Farmland was to be returned to private ownership.
- Hungary was to **become neutral** between East and West in the Cold War.
- **Hungary was to leave the Warsaw Pact**.

Khrushchev could not accept Hungary's defection from the Warsaw Pact and, on 4th November, he sent 200,000 Soviet troops with 2,500 tanks into Budapest. In two weeks of fierce fighting, 3,000 Hungarians and 7,000–8,000 Russians were killed, while 200,000 Hungarians fled to Austria.

Nagy appealed to President Eisenhower for help but, though the USA protested, they were too preoccupied with the Suez Crisis to help at all. Nagy was arrested and shot in the Soviet Union, and was replaced by **Janos Kadar**, who spent several months crushing resistance, imprisoning 35,000 opponents and executing 300 people. **Khrushchev had acted harshly to set an example to other states**: he was not prepared to see the USSR's buffer states in the West disappear.

Many Hungarians lost faith in the West, since they realised that the US policy of containment meant that there would be no help for states already within the communist 'sphere of influence'. Equally, the UN was discredited because it did nothing to help when Hungary was invaded.

Do you think that keeping Hungary communist, or keeping it within the Warsaw Pact was most important to Khrushchev?

The Berlin Wall 1961

AQA B	✓
EDEXCEL A	✓
OCR B	✓
WJEC A	✓
WJEC B	✗
CCEA	✓

The problem

The effect of the **Hungarian Rising** was to convince people in Eastern Europe that there would be no improvement and that emigration was the only way to achieve freedom. In East Berlin this effect was particularly important because Eastern **living standards** contrasted so abruptly with Western, just a few metres away. The **Western Powers had invested massive amounts** in Berlin, while **Western television** was available in East Berlin.

During the 1950s it was **easy for East Germans to travel freely to West Berlin** and from there to West Germany and, therefore, thousands emigrated. East Germany **could not afford to lose the highly-skilled people** that tended to emigrate, while their defection reflected too badly on life in the East to be allowed to continue.

> Was this an admission of the failure of communism?

The Berlin Wall and its effects

On **13th August 1961** East German soldiers erected a **barbed-wire barrier** along the entire frontier between East and West Berlin, which was quickly converted to a wall. All the crossing points were sealed except one, Checkpoint Charlie.

Figure 7.2 The newly erected Berlin Wall

This had the following effects:

- **Families were divided**, Berliners were unable to go to work and hundreds were killed trying to cross over the next 30 years.
- **Access to East Berlin**, guaranteed to the Western Allies since 1945, **was cut off** on 27th October, when Soviet tanks sealed Checkpoint Charlie. There was a **confrontation between US and Soviet tanks**, which lasted 18 hours and which was only resolved as the tanks were gradually withdrawn, metre by metre, one at a time.
- Keen to avoid confrontation, Khrushchev ordered Herr Ulbricht, leader of Eastern Germany, to avoid actions that would increase tension. Kennedy thought that a wall was better than a war, so he accepted it.
- In a memorable visit to West Berlin on June 27th 1963, **President Kennedy** reaffirmed the West's support for West Berlin, using the phrase, '**Ich bin ein Berliner**'. This was a great morale booster for West Germany, which was now seen at the forefront of the free world. It was clear that further Soviet encroachments would not be tolerated.

> Why didn't the West do more at this point? Would Berlin have an effect on Cuba?

Czechoslovakia 1968

AQA B	✓
EDEXCEL A	✓
OCR B	✓
WJEC A	✗
WJEC B	✗
CCEA	✓

Prague Spring

There was opposition to the Stalinist government in Czechoslovakia due to the following reasons:

- There was **no freedom of speech**, of the press or of politics.
- People's **standards of living were poor**. Industries were under Soviet control and run for Soviet benefit.
- A new leader in 1968, **Alexander Dubcek**, introduced reforms known as '**socialism with a human face**' in which...
  - more control was given to managers and workers in industry
  - trades unions were given some freedom
  - press censorship was abolished and people were allowed to say what they thought
  - criticism of the government was allowed
  - foreign travel was possible.

> What was Dubcek doing wrong from the Soviet point-of-view?

This unleashed a torrent of criticism, both in the press and on television. New ideas seemed to be appearing everywhere. The Spring of 1968 became known as 'Prague Spring'. Dubcek had no intention of going too far: he was **both communist and committed to the Warsaw Pact**. However, he defended the reforms when they were criticised by other communist leaders.

The Soviet response

At first the Soviet response to the reforms was muted: Soviet, Polish and East German troops engaged in very obvious manoeuvres on the Czech frontier. A summit conference was held, at which Dubcek promised not to create a new Social Democratic Party. The **Warsaw Pact countries called on him to maintain stability**.

Brezhnev, the new Soviet leader, feared that chaos in Czechoslovakia would spread elsewhere, especially Yugoslavia. He thought that Czechoslovakia would become a democracy, leave the Warsaw Pact and join the West, providing an invasion route to Russia.

On **20th August 1968** Soviet, East German, Polish and Bulgarian tanks moved into Czechoslovakia. Dubcek did not resist, although there was a lot of peaceful resistance and some street fighting. Dubcek was removed and thousands of Czechs were arrested as Czechoslovakia was once more under Soviet control.

Figure 7.3 Soviet tank in Prague 1968 invasion

Results of Prague Spring

The Prague Spring had the following results:

- A **hard-line communist regime** was set up and new ideas were stifled.
- The **Brezhnev Doctrine** was published: states under Soviet control must maintain a one-party system and remain within the Warsaw Pact.
- **Dubcek was not executed**, but was **demoted** to become an ambassador before being expelled from the Communist Party.

> Compare Prague Spring with the Hungarian Rising: what were the similarities and differences?

Poland and Solidarity 1980–1989

AQA B	✓
EDEXCEL A	✓
OCR B	✓
WJEC A	✗
WJEC B	✗
CCEA	✓

The growth of opposition in Poland

There were several reasons why opposition in Poland grew:

- There was **a very long history of opposition** to Russian domination in Poland, which started with its original conquest in the 18th Century. After 1945 there were protests in 1949, 1956 and 1970, after which the Polish government had made concessions.
- Most Poles were Catholic, but the communist government was atheist (anti-religious). The Catholic Church acted as a focus for dissent.
- For a long time Poland had been the most prosperous of the Eastern European countries, but by 1980 **the standard of living there was falling sharply** as prices of food, clothing and fuel rose. Opposition arose in the trade union movement.
- **Solidarity**, the union of the Gdansk shipyards, was the most prominent trade union. **Lech Walesa** was a brilliant speaker and supplied crucial leadership so that there were soon 9 million members demanding better wages and better working conditions. Demands for political freedom soon followed.
- **Soviet control was not decisively imposed**, because Walesa was too popular, both in Poland and in the West.

Figure 7.4 Lech Walesa during a strike at Gdansk shipyard, 1980

> **KEY POINT**
>
> The existence of Solidarity would not have been tolerated earlier, but the USSR was already involved in war in Afghanistan.

The failure of repression

February 1981	The USSR appointed **General Jaruzelski**, the new leader of the Polish government. He was told that, unless he dealt with Solidarity, Soviet forces would invade.
March 1981	Walesa called off a strike at Bydgoszcz against some opposition.
May 1981	'Rural Solidarity' was formed.
September 1981	Lech Walesa was elected Chairman of Solidarity. Their Congress wrote an open letter promising that they were campaigning for workers' rights throughout the communist bloc.
November 1981	Negotiations between Walesa and the Polish Government to form a government of national unity broke down and Poland lurched towards chaos.
December 1981	**Solidarity was banned** and Walesa was arrested with thousands of supporters. Soviet troops massed on the Polish border. Military law was imposed.
1982	Jaruzelski tried to form a Patriotic Movement for National Regeneration to replace Solidarity, but it was ignored. Walesa became an international hero.
1983	Solidarity leaders were released from prison but were harassed and some were murdered. **Walesa was awarded the Nobel Peace Prize.** Jaruzelski started a campaign against the Roman Catholic Church, beating and murdering priests.
1984	**Father Jerzy Popieluszko** was battered to death by the secret police. **The USA and other Western states imposed economic sanctions** on Poland and economic chaos followed: the currency was devalued and inflation hit 70%.
1986	Solidarity was re-forming, operating almost openly and declaring a nationwide strike against price rises. The government stopped raising prices. Solidarity co-operated with the Catholic Church and openly broadcast from its own radio station.
1988	**Solidarity organised a boycott** of government elections. Foreign governments consulted Walesa as to whether to lift sanctions.
1989	**Jaruzelski was forced to hold free elections**, which Solidarity won with a massive majority. Poland had a non-communist government, with **Walesa as president**.

Reasons for the success of Solidarity

There were several reasons for the success of Solidarity:
- Solidarity had such **massive support** in Poland that the Soviet Union dare not try to destroy it.
- Solidarity used **strikes, rather than armed resistance**.
- There was **support from Western Powers**, e.g. they imposed sanctions and encouraged Walesa.
- While this was going on, **Gorbachev was beginning reforms in the USSR** parallel to those demanded in Poland. Jaruzelski was undermined by this and could not impose control without Soviet help.

> **KEY POINT**
>
> Walesa's links with the West were very important. The USSR were being very careful not to give more of an opportunity for Western involvement.

> **PROGRESS CHECK**
>
> 1 What was Cominform?
> 2 What was the name of the Czechoslovakian premier who began 'Prague Spring'?
> 3 Who did the USSR appoint to oppose Solidarity?

1. The Soviet organisation that kept Eastern European states loyal to the Soviet Union.
2. Alexander Dubcek. 3. General Jaruzelski

7.2 Gorbachev and the collapse of the Soviet Union

LEARNING SUMMARY

After studying this section you should be able to understand:
- the impact on the Soviet Union of failure in Afghanistan
- how Soviet foreign policy led to a second Cold War
- the reasons for Gorbachev's changing attitudes
- the collapse of Soviet control in Eastern Europe
- the dissolution of the USSR

The impact on the Soviet Union of the failure in Afghanistan

AQA B	✓
EDEXCEL A	✓
OCR B	✓
WJEC A	✓
WJEC B	✗
CCEA	✓

The invasion of Afghanistan 1979

Afghanistan had been ruled by a pro-Soviet regime, but by 1979 it was under threat from the Muslim **Mujahideen**. Soviet forces entered Afghanistan on **25th December 1979**, alarming Western Powers as the invasion brought the Soviets to within a short distance of Western oil supplies.

The USA began to send very large shipments of money, arms and equipment to Pakistan for the Mujahideen, turning Afghanistan into the Soviet Union's own Vietnam. The unwinnable campaign dragged on until the early 1990s.

The effects on the Soviet Union

While it didn't cause the decline of the Soviet Union, the Afghanistan war showed that **decline was already well-advanced**. By the time that **Mikhail Gorbachev** became the leader, in 1985, the Soviet economy was very weak because there had been almost no modernisation since the Second World War. **Leaders had ignored the warning signals**, guaranteeing workers a home and a job for life irrespective of how hard they worked. Laziness, cynicism and low standards had replaced the hard work of the days of Stalin. **Alcoholism** was rife to the extent that it was reducing the life expectancy of men during the 1980s. Citizens often had no loyalty to the government and neither believed nor cared what it said.

These weaknesses had particular effects:
- The **standard of living** of Soviet people was falling.
- The **Communist Party was corrupt**, with bosses living in luxury.
- **Farming was so inefficient** that the USSR had to import grain.
- The **arms race** was costing a huge proportion of national income, which had been heightened by the war in Afghanistan (costing $8 billion a year).
- The Soviet Union had fallen behind in the use of **information technology.**
- The **war in Afghanistan** was showing the weakness and low standards of the USSR, but especially of the Red Army.

Gorbachev's reforms

AQA B	✓
EDEXCEL A	✓
OCR B	✓
WJEC A	✓
WJEC B	✗
CCEA	✓

Glasnost and Perestroika

Gorbachev remained a convinced communist, but he was determined to make communism work again in the Soviet Union, despite the opposition to change from hardliners. He organised his policies around…

- 'glasnost': openness to new ideas, meaning both free speech and learning from the West
- 'perestroika': restructuring the economy to make it more efficient.

> **KEY POINT**
>
> Gorbachev was a convinced communist trying to find a new future for communism by moving it away from Stalinism. He never intended to destroy it.

Reforms inside the Soviet Union

Gorbachev made several reforms in the Soviet Union:

- **Market forces were reintroduced** to Soviet commerce: people were allowed to buy and sell for profit.
- He **cut spending on defence**.
- **Political prisoners were released**.
- **Farmers** were allowed to **sell their produce freely**.
- **Managers in industry were allowed to make decisions** to run their businesses better.

> **KEY POINT**
>
> Lenin had also used the free market, when a similar crisis occurred after the Russian Civil War (see page 153).

Changes to foreign policy

Gorbachev made several reforms to foreign policy:

- The admission that the USSR could not hope to rival the **US Strategic Defence Initiative** (Star Wars) and the reduction in armament expenditure opened the way for a **disarmament treaty** with the USA in 1987.
- The reduction in the Red Army meant that Eastern Europe could no longer be controlled: in 1988 the **Brezhnev Doctrine was abandoned**. The USSR would no longer interfere in Eastern Europe.
- In 1989 Gorbachev began to **withdraw troops from Afghanistan**.

> **PROGRESS CHECK**
>
> 1. Why were Western Powers particularly alarmed by the Soviet invasion of Afghanistan?
> 2. What was 'glasnost'?
> 3. By what name is the US Strategic Defence Initiative popularly known?
>
> 1. It took Soviet forces too close to the West's sources of oil.
> 2. Openness to new ideas 3. 'Star Wars'.

The collapse of the Soviet Empire

Without the Brezhnev Doctrine, communism in Eastern Europe simply collapsed:

1	May 1989	**Hungary** opened its border with Austria.
2	June 1989	Free elections took place in **Poland**.
3	October 1989	Gorbachev told **East Germany** to reform.
4	November 1989	Crowds tore down the **Berlin Wall**.
5	December 1989	Demonstrations in **Czechoslovakia** led to the fall of the communist government in the 'velvet revolution'.
6	December 1989	**Romania** overthrew the hated Ceausescu and his communist government.
7	December 1989	Demonstrations in **Bulgaria** forced the resignation of the government in Bulgaria.
8	December 1989	Free elections were announced in **Hungary**.
9	1990	**Germany** was reunited.
10	1991	The Soviet republics declared their independence and the **Soviet Union** ceased to exist.

7.3 Northern Ireland 1968–2000

LEARNING SUMMARY

After studying this section you should be able to understand:

- the issues involved in the Northern Irish Conflict
- how attempts at conciliation and agreement failed
- how the Good Friday Agreement ended the conflict

The Northern Ireland Emergency

AQA B	✓
EDEXCEL A	✗
OCR B	✓
WJEC A	✗
WJEC B	✗
CCEA	✓

The origin of 'The Troubles'

In the 17th Century a large group of **Scottish Protestants** was settled by force in Northern Ireland, where they were given land from which Catholics were cleared. Over the next 300 years their power over Ireland increased, supported by the British Government. When Ireland was partitioned in 1922 the major part of it was Catholic, with a Protestant majority only in the four counties that made up **Northern Ireland**. These counties remained part of the United Kingdom. In Northern Ireland, Protestants continued to have **political and civil privileges** over the Catholic minority until the early 1970s. Arguments were made by both sides about the fairness of the situation there, and in the 1940s and 1950s there were several violent campaigns by the **Irish Republican Army** (**IRA**) fighting in the name of the Catholic minority to try to change it. During the 1960s, however, the IRA had ceased to be much of a threat, concentrating more on communist political agitation than on violent disruption.

Figure 7.5 Map showing the six counties in Northern Ireland

Causes of 'The Troubles'

From 1966 the **Ulster Volunteer Force** (**UVF**) began to victimise Roman Catholics in Belfast.

In 1968 the **Northern Ireland Civil Rights Association** (**NICRA**) began a campaign for equal civil rights for Protestants and Catholics in Northern Ireland. Catholics were discriminated against in housing, employment and political representation. While Terence O'Neil, the Northern Irish Prime Minister, was prepared to make concessions, the extreme Protestants, led by Rev. Ian Paisley and William Craig, saw NICRA as a front for the IRA. Violence grew as Civil Rights demonstrations were targeted by Protestant paramilitaries and Protestant police alike.

In 1969 **British troops** were sent to stop violence against Civil Rights marchers, but over the next three years violence hugely increased, peaking in 1972 when about 500 died. The increase in violence was caused by the following:

- The creation of the **Provisional IRA** (**PIRA**) in 1970, which was determined to wage 'armed struggle' against British rule. It took on the role of defenders of the Catholic community.
- The **disappointment of hopes for Civil Rights** in actions such as the Falls Road Curfew, the reintroduction of internment without trial and the fatal shooting of 14 Civil Rights demonstrators on '**Bloody Sunday**', January 1972.

> You need to decide whether the actions of the British Government were always fair.

Sectarian violence

By 1972 the PIRA campaign was of such intensity that they had already killed more than 100 soldiers, wounded 500 more and carried out 1,300 bombings. On 'Bloody Friday', 21st July 1972, 22 bombs were set off in the centre of Belfast and the **PIRA were determined to carry on until they had achieved a united Ireland**.

As well as the UVF, Protestant paramilitaries by now included the **Ulster Defence Association** (**UDA**), which targeted nationalists. Sometimes they tortured as well as killed their victims. Catholics and Protestants were now too scared to live together and families moved into their own districts and estates.

Direct rule from Westminster

By 1972 it was quite clear that the Stormont government was incapable of dealing with the situation, so the UK Government **suspended Stormont Home Rule government**, replacing it with '**Direct Rule**' from London. This was intended to be short-term, until an agreed basis for a Northern Ireland Assembly could be reached, but it proved impossible to end over the next 25 years.

In 1973, the **Sunningdale Agreement** aimed to set up the first Protestant–Catholic power-sharing executive, but was brought down after Protestants, alarmed at the Irish Republic's role in the settlement, launched a general strike. The Agreement was very similar to the final Good Friday Agreement, but at this stage the extremists on both sides could not be persuaded to consider power-sharing so the violence continued.

> **KEY POINT**
>
> The Sunningdale Agreement could have been successful except that extremists on both sides were determined to wreck it.

Terrorism continues

Boosted by large donations of arms from Libya in the 1980s, the PIRA used bombs as well as shootings:

27th August 1979	**Lord Mountbatten** was blown up on his boat with three other people. The same afternoon 18 members of the Parachute Regiment were killed by bombs at **Warrenpoint**, County Down.
12th October 1984	The **Brighton Hotel Bombing** at the Grand Hotel where Prime Minister Margaret Thatcher was holding the Conservative Party Conference: five people were killed.

In **1985 the Anglo–Irish Agreement** was signed between Irish and British governments. The Irish government was to gain an advisory role on Northern Ireland, which was confirmed as a part of the United Kingdom, unless a majority voted for reunification. Both sides in Northern Ireland rejected it.

In response, the Loyalist paramilitaries **imported arms from South Africa** and stepped up their assassinations of Catholics. So PIRA and Protestant paramilitaries both continued assassinations and bombings.

The Peace Process begins

In **1994 the Downing Street Declaration** confirmed Northern Ireland's right to self-determination, but added that the people of the whole island had the right to solve problems on the island without interference from outside. Protestant and Catholic paramilitaries declared ceasefires. However, **Ian Paisley**, leader of the **Democratic Unionist Party** (**DUP**), rejected it as a 'sell-out.'

9th February 1996	The PIRA revoked its ceasefire with the **Docklands Bombing**, killing two people and causing £85 million worth of damage in London's Docklands.
15th June 1996	The **Manchester Bombing** destroyed a large area in the centre of the city. It was the largest bomb attack in Britain since the Second World War and it caused £411 million worth of damage.
August 1998	The Real IRA killed 29 civilians in the **Omagh Bombing**.

> **KEY POINT**
>
> By now there was a general revulsion at the scale of violence and the extremists had become discredited.

Figure 7.6 The habit of violence was hard to break

In **1998 the Belfast, or Good Friday, Agreement** was signed between British and Irish governments with the aim of restoring a devolved power-sharing executive in Belfast. Ireland dropped its territorial claim to Northern Ireland after an overwhelming majority endorsed the Agreement in referendums north and south of the border. The newly elected assembly met on 1st July 1998.

In **1999 the first power-sharing executive** was formed with David Trimble, leader of the Ulster Unionist Party (UUP), as First Minister.

> **PROGRESS CHECK**
>
> 1 Who led the extreme Protestants against the Northern Ireland Civil Rights Association?
> 2 Why did the Sunningdale Agreement fail in 1973?
> 3 Which prominent figure was killed in August 1979?
>
> 3. Lord Mountbatten.
> 2. Neither side was prepared to accept power sharing at that time.
> 1. Ian Paisley and William Craig.

7.4 Arab–Israeli conflict 1948–1995

LEARNING SUMMARY	**After studying this section you should be able to understand:** ● how the conflict began ● how the Six Day War extended Israeli territory ● why the conflict has been so difficult to settle

How the conflict began

AQA B	✓
EDEXCEL A	✗
OCR B	✓
WJEC A	✓
WJEC B	✗
CCEA	✗

The British Mandate

Palestine was populated by Arabs in the 19th Century, though there was an increasing trickle of **Jewish immigrants** under the Turkish Empire. During the First World War the area was taken by the British 'Arab Legion' and in 1919 it became a **League of Nations Mandate, ruled by Britain**. Britain began to encourage Jewish immigration, especially during the Nazi regime in Germany, resulting in such an increase that they had to restrict numbers from 1939 onwards, in the face of Arab protests. The Nazi Holocaust in Europe increased tensions since illegal immigration could not be prevented.

Partition derailed by the 1948 Arab–Israeli War

A United Nations committee recommended the partition of Palestine, which was agreed by the United Nations Assembly in November 1947, and 24 hours before the British Mandate ended on 15th May 1948, Israel declared its independence. On the following day, the **Arab League of Egypt, Syria, Lebanon, Jordan and Iraq, declared their opposition to the UN Resolution**, and attacked Israel in the First Arab–Israeli War. By December the Israeli Defence Force had recovered and had taken most of the ex-Mandate of Palestine with the exception of Gaza, the West Bank and Jordan itself. Many Palestinian Arabs had been displaced and became refugees at this point. The 1949 Armistice Agreements created the official borders of Israel today – the so-called 'Green Line', which lasted until 1967.

> **KEY POINT**
>
> Even from this early point, the survival of Israel depended on its friendship with the USA.

Further Jewish immigration then occurred, as Arab states discriminated against their own Jewish populations.

Figure 7.7 Israel in 1949

The Suez Crisis, 1956

In 1956 Egypt had closed the Gulf of Aqaba and Straits of Tiran to Israeli shipping, during the nationalisation of the Suez Canal. With British and French support the Israeli Army took the Gaza Strip and the Sinai Peninsula during the Suez Crisis, but relinquished them on assurances of free passage along the Suez Canal. The **United Nations Emergency Force** (UNEF) was deployed to police the demilitarisation of Sinai.

The Six Day War 1967

AQA B	✓
EDEXCEL A	✗
OCR B	✓
WJEC A	✓
WJEC B	✗
CCEA	✗

Threatening moves by Egypt

On 19th May 1967 the **Egyptian Government expelled UNEF** from Sinai and deployed 100,000 troops there. They then **closed the Straits of Tiran**, against the agreement of 1956. On 30th May Jordan joined a **Mutual Defence Pact** with Egypt and Syria.

The Israeli response

On 5th June 1967 Israel sent almost its entire air force to **destroy the Egyptian air force** on the ground and then they turned on the Syrian, Jordanian and Iraqi air forces. Within the next few days Israeli forces took the Sinai Peninsula, Gaza Strip, Golan Heights, East Jerusalem and the West Bank.

> There is huge disagreement between Israel and Arab nations about the details of the war and its origins. You need to decide which group was right.

As a result, at a conference at **Khartoum** in 1967, Arab leaders agreed not to recognise the State of Israel, and not to negotiate or make peace with it. In 1969, General Nasser of Egypt began a War of Attrition with Israel, which only ended at his death in 1970.

Figure 7.8 Israeli guns in action in Sinai, 1967

Terrorist attacks

> For details on the foundation of the PLO see pages 117–118

Groups attached to the **Palestine Liberation Organisation** (PLO) kept up the pressure on Israel through terrorist attacks:

- In September 1970 **three airliners were hijacked** in Jordan. The passengers were eventually released, though it is uncertain whether PLO prisoners in Israel were released in exchange.
- In 1976 Palestinians hijacked another aircraft with 100 Israeli passengers and flew it to Entebbe in Uganda.
- Most famously, the PLO organisation 'Black September' took 11 Israeli

athletes hostage at the **Munich Olympics**, killing them when German police intervened. Black September was a deniable part of the PLO, which was set up to take violent actions that Yasser Arafat thought were justifiable, but these actions horrified the general public, and lost rather than gained support.

The Yom Kippur War 1973

On October 6th 1973, Egypt and Syria staged a surprise attack on Israel, at first overwhelming the Israeli Army. Eventually the Israelis regrouped and began to fight back onto Egyptian and Syrian territory, but the war ended in a truce. This was negotiated by the USA and USSR through the United Nations, and was motivated by their own exposure to nuclear war.

Why the conflict has been so difficult to settle

AQA B	✓
EDEXCEL A	✗
OCR B	✓
WJEC A	✓
WJEC B	✗
CCEA	✗

Reluctance of the superpowers

Neither the USA nor the USSR were prepared to allow a war in the Middle East to resolve the conflict, since a war would imperil their own populations, exposing them to nuclear war.

> **KEY POINT**
>
> As well as the issues over the existence of Israel, the region has huge strategic significance as it is so close to the oil reserves in Iraq and Saudi Arabia.

Instability of the whole region

There was no easy solution to the Israeli–Palestinian dispute:
- After the Camp David Accords (signed by President Sadat and Prime Minister Begin), Israel and Egypt signed a **peace agreement** in March 1979, returning Sinai to Egypt. There was **no settlement of the Palestinian problem** though. Gaza remained under Israeli control.
- King Hussein of Jordan had expelled the Palestine Liberation Army from Jordan after a Civil War in 1970. They had **regrouped in Lebanon** where they staged raids into Israel. In 1981 **Syria allied with the PLO** and sited missiles in Lebanon to attack Israel. In June 1982 **Israel invaded Lebanon, expelling the Palestine Liberation Army**. There was a ceasefire agreement, but in March 1984 President Gemayel of Syria pressured the Lebanon government into breaking it. Israeli forces withdrew to a 10km strip along the border with Israel, which they kept until their final withdrawal in 2000.
- Hostilities resumed with Iraq: Israel had destroyed Iraqi nuclear facilities in Operation Opera in 1981. During the Gulf War 1990–91 **Iraq sent 30 missiles into Israel**, hoping to provoke other Arab states into joining the war against Israel. US diplomacy stopped the situation escalating, and Israel did not respond.
- In October 1994 **Israel and Jordan signed a treaty** of mutual co-operation, ending hostilities and resolving other issues.

> **KEY POINT**
>
> The trend has been towards Israel forming links with its Arab neighbours.

Continuing problem of Palestinians

In December 1987, the **First Intifada** began. It was a Palestinian campaign of civil disobedience, strikes, stone throwing and terrorist attacks. The PLO was excluded from peace negotiations until it **recognised Israel** and **renounced terrorism** the following year.

In September 1993, Israel and the PLO signed the **Oslo Accords**, known as the 'Declaration of Principles' or Oslo I. In this agreement...

- **Israel recognised the PLO** as the legitimate representative of the Palestinian people
- the **PLO recognised the right of the state of Israel to exist** and renounced terrorism, violence and its desire for the destruction of Israel.

The Oslo II agreement was signed in 1995 agreeing **an area which was to be under full Palestinian civilian control**, including internal security. The Oslo agreements remain the basis of Israeli–Palestinian relations today.

PROGRESS CHECK

1. What are the official borders of Israel created in 1949 still called today?
2. In 1979, what was the name of the agreement in which Israel agreed to return Sinai to Egypt?
3. What was / is an 'Intifada'?

1. The Green Line.
2. The Camp David Accords.
3. An Arab campaign of civil disobedience.

7.5 The Iraq War, 2003

LEARNING SUMMARY

After studying this section you should be able to understand:

- why the multi-national force invaded Iraq in 2003
- whether the invasion was legal and why there was opposition in many countries to the invasion
- how the invasion was completed so quickly
- what the consequences of the invasion were inside Iraq and internationally
- whether the invasion of Iraq was a success

Why did the multi-national force invade Iraq in 2003?

AQA B	X
EDEXCEL A	X
OCR B	✓
WJEC A	X
WJEC B	X
CCEA	X

British influence and the rise of Saddam Hussein

British policy had played a major role in destabilising Iraq:

- Britain had encouraged the nationalism of Kurds, Arabs, Sunni and Shi'ah elements during the First World War.
- In 1919, Britain set up a Mandate in Iraq, replacing Turkish with direct British rule, which ignored the different wishes of the population.
- By the time the country became independent in 1932, Britain had acquired a huge stake in the oil industry there.
- Britain left Iraq in the charge of an Iraqi monarchy, which continued to ignore the wishes of the different sections of the Iraqi community. In 1958 the monarchy fell, and was replaced by a republic, led by the Ba'ath party. By

1979 Saddam Hussein, a peasant's son, had taken control in a bloody coup, in which he had murdered 500 Ba'ath party members.

The Iran–Iraq War, 1980–1988

In 1979, when the Shah of Iran was overthrown, Iran was taken over by the militant Muslim Shi'ah sect under Ayatollah Khomeini. Saddam Hussein was worried that the Shi'ah majority in Iraq would support the religious revolution in Iran, threatening the power of his own Sunni group. Other states, such as Kuwait, Saudi Arabia, the USSR and the USA shared his concern and were prepared to support him.

In September 1980 Saddam Hussein launched a simultaneous air and ground offensive against Iran, expecting that it would be an easy target and that a quick victory would be possible. This disastrous miscalculation involved Iraq in a brutal struggle that lasted eight years and cost Iraq 250,000 dead, leaving her with debts of over $80 billion. The war opened up the rivalry of different groups within Iraq, as Saddam Hussein turned on his Shi'ah and Kurd populations, using cyanide and poison gas against separatist Kurds in March 1988.

The First Gulf War, 1990–1991

The only way for Saddam Hussein to pay off the debt was to **increase oil production**, but the other members of OPEC (a cartel of Oil Producing and Exporting Countries), notably Kuwait and Saudi Arabia, opposed the increase in production, because it would bring down the price of oil. In retaliation, Saddam Hussein decided to **invade Kuwait in order to take control of her oil**. This was a huge mistake, as he was instantly **condemned by the United Nations**, led by the USA under George Bush Senior, which was a major importer of Kuwaiti oil.

In January 1991 a US-led coalition removed Iraqi troops from Kuwait and inflicted a devastating **defeat on Saddam Hussein** in little over one month. Bush did not invade Iraq because he had no plans as to what to do with Iraq afterwards and he expected the Kurds and Shi'ah to take control themselves. However, the Kurds and Shi'ah were cruelly suppressed so Saddam Hussein was left in power.

Figure 7.9 Map showing Iraqi nations and religions

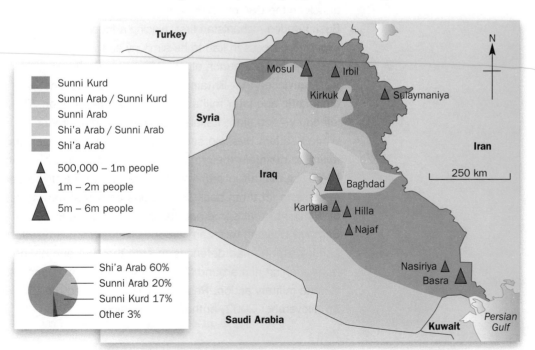

An insoluble problem, 1991–2003

The USA and her allies were left with an insoluble problem:

- If Iraq was given democratic government, she would break up, which would weaken her against Iran. Therefore, to remove Saddam Hussein would be disastrous. As a compromise the UN passed **Resolution 688**, which called on Saddam Hussein to **stop oppressing his own people and allowed no-fly zones** over Kurdish and Shi'ah territory to stop him using his air force against his own people.
- Leaving Saddam Hussein in power also ran the risk that he would renew his threats to neighbouring states. To combat this, the UN passed **Resolution 678**, which demanded the **destruction of all Saddam's Weapons of Mass Destruction** (WMDs). Saddam had to allow UN inspectors to search Iraq for supergun and nuclear sites and to destroy stocks of chemical weapons. This resolution also imposed reparations to Kuwait, enforced by tough economic sanctions, which restricted oil sales until these conditions were met. In this way the threats to Iraq's neighbours (and to oil supplies) was reduced.
- Through the next few years Saddam Hussein's power seemed to get stronger, rather than weaker. Neither he nor his followers suffered the deprivation of ordinary Iraqis, on whom malnutrition and disease had a devastating effect. Saddam sowed discord in the UN, promising to repay French and Chinese debts if sanctions were lifted. American-led UN reprisal attacks on Iraqi military installations were criticised by the UN and in the media. Meanwhile, Saddam was ruthlessly suppressing opposition, using bribery, threats and murder to maintain and strengthen his hold.

Immediate causes for the invasion of Iraq in 2003

The immediate causes of the invasion were:

- The impatience of the new President of the USA, **George W. Bush** with the compromises of President Clinton.
- The victory of the **neoconservatives** (neocons) within the Republican party in the USA, who favoured 'regime change'.
- President Bush thought that Saddam Hussein must have been involved in the attack on the USA on **11th September 2001** (9/11). In retaliation, George W. Bush invaded Afghanistan first, placing a friendly government in power, and they expected success in Iraq to be similarly easy.
- The USA had a staunch ally in Britain, under **Prime Minister Tony Blair**, who was convinced that Britain must support US actions. Blair provided political, diplomatic and later military support for the invasion. The coalition was also joined by Australian, Italian, Polish and Danish troops.
- While Saddam Hussein seemed to be getting stronger, as sanctions were failing to maintain their grip on the Iraqi economy, he continued to defy the UN, flying aircraft into the no-fly zones, removing UN weapons inspectors and refusing to let them back. Suspicions grew that he was resuming production of WMDs, or that some had never been destroyed. Now it seems that Saddam Hussein was carrying out a very effective disinformation campaign, bluffing that he had defences to stop the USA and his hostile neighbours from pushing him around. The USA was taken in. Congress authorised Bush to take military action. Resolution 1441 passed the UN Security Council on 8th November 2002, authorising invasion.

Was the invasion legal? Why was there opposition in many countries to the invasion?

AQA B	X
EDEXCEL A	X
OCR B	✓
WJEC A	X
WJEC B	X
CCEA	X

Why did people oppose the invasion of Iraq in 2003?

There were worldwide demonstrations against the invasion of Iraq:

- President George W. Bush seemed to be using **double standards** – ignoring the possession of nuclear weapons by Israel (who certainly did have them) but punishing Iraq (where possession of such weapons could not be proved).
- Most Arab nations would have supported the overthrow of Saddam Hussein by Iraqis, but thought it **illegal for the USA to interfere**. Turkey refused to let US troops invade over her border, even though she was an ally of the USA.
- Hans Blix, the UN's own weapons inspector, reported on the eve of invasion that he was **unable to find any WMDs** in Iraq. The US and British governments refused to believe him. He had not been given time to investigate fully, and France, China and Russia thought that he should have been. They suspected that Bush and Blair had inflated the threat of WMDs to justify an illegal invasion.

Was the invasion legal?

Bush and Blair argued that Resolution 1441 gave them the authority to invade Iraq. Many other states disagreed. Russia and China argued that the Resolution threatened 'serious consequences' but that this did not justify invasion. France, under President Jacques Chirac, refused to believe that Bush had proved Iraq's links with al-Qaeda and suspected that Bush and Blair refused to apply for a second, clearer resolution from the UN because they knew that they would not be successful. Even some British government advisers and ministers had doubts about the legality of the invasion.

Opposition in the USA and UK

Opposition continued after the invasion due to the following reasons:

- Media reports suggested that **Blair and Bush had 'hyped up' the intelligence on Iraq to justify invasion**. Blair had told Parliament that Saddam Hussein had the ability to deploy weapons in 45 minutes.
- Many in the USA and the UK suspected that the war was not about security but about the **control of oil supplies**.
- The war diverted attention away from the threat of terrorism. After the invasion there were more bombings in Istanbul, Madrid, London, Jordan, Algiers, the Danish Embassy in Pakistan and the attacks on Mumbai.
- Planning for the invasion was inadequate: too few troops were provided to maintain control and effective plans to restore the Iraqi economy were not made.

How was the invasion completed so quickly?

October 2002	The US Congress passed a law which allowed President Bush to use military force against Iraq.
November 2002	The USA and the UK jointly drafted Resolution 1441, which offered Iraq a final opportunity to comply with its obligations. It was passed unanimously, even with Iraqi support, and Hans Blix was enabled to revisit Iraq to search for WMDs.
March 2003	Most countries thought that a second resolution, enabling invasion, was unnecessary because Hans Blix had failed to find WMDs. The matter would return to the UN Security Council. On 10th March Jacques Chirac promised to veto any resolution that would lead to war. On 16th March, Bush, Blair and the Spanish Prime Minister, Jose Maria Aznar, gave the Iraqi government one day to provide evidence that they had disarmed. The war started a few days later. On 21st March 130,000 US troops and about 30,000 other coalition troops invaded Iraq.
April 2003	US forces took control of Saddam International Airport. On 7th April British forces took Basra. On 9th April Baghdad fell to US forces
May 2003	George W. Bush announced the end of major combat operations in Iraq.
July 2003	Saddam's sons, Uday and Qusay were killed in a shoot-out with US troops.
December 2003	Saddam Hussein was captured. He was executed in December 2006.

Reasons for success

Saddam Hussein's forces were no match for the coalition:
- The Iraqi air force had already been beaten, so the **coalition had complete air superiority**.
- The coalition used **satellite technology** both to co-ordinate attacks and to communicate.
- The **awesome firepower** of the coalition forces caused disproportionate casualties: about 7,000–12,000 Iraqi troops died compared to 140 US and 33 British. About 4,000–7,000 Iraqi civilians also died, mostly from bombing.

What were the consequences of the invasion inside Iraq and internationally?

AQA B	X
EDEXCEL A	X
OCR B	✓
WJEC A	X
WJEC B	X
CCEA	X

Breakdown in law and order

Invasion caused a breakdown in law and order inside Iraq as the **Iraqi army and police were disbanded**. In Baghdad and Basra, law and order broke down with huge amounts of looting and violence. Hospitals were targeted and stripped of supplies, while there were numerous rapes and murders. It was too dangerous for UN Relief Agencies to operate, so normal life became impossible. Coalition forces were blamed as water and electricity supplies collapsed and refugees fled into Jordan. Clearly life was worse under the coalition than under Saddam Hussein.

The rise of insurgency

Anarchy and chaos quickly resulted in **opposition to the coalition** as different groups sought to protect their interests. The following groups all fought against the coalition: Remaining members of the Ba'ath Party; Units of the disbanded Iraqi army; Islamic militants including al-Qaeda; Militant Shi'ah; Militant Sunni; Iraqi nationalists.

They used **roadside bombs, sniper attacks, kidnappings and executions**. They had the sympathy of the local population. They fought against each other as much as with coalition forces. They benefitted from the disbandment of the Iraqi army and police since coalition intelligence was very faulty at first. Even so, the coalition inflicted heavier casualties than it received. In the 2007 Qahtaniya and Jazeera bombings, 796 people died in one day. Abu Musab al-Zarqawi was killed by American laser-guided bombs in June 2006. The American and Iraqi offensive to retake Falluja from Sunni militants was called off in April 2004 because of the huge civilian death toll. When the offensive was later resumed, after civilians had been warned to leave, about 5,000 militants and civilians were killed and the town was devastated. The exposure of alleged atrocities at Abu Ghraib prison in 2004 helped to turn public opinion against the occupying force.

Was the invasion of Iraq a success?

AQA B	X
EDEXCEL A	X
OCR B	✓
WJEC A	X
WJEC B	X
CCEA	X

In military terms

The invasion took just **40 days to destroy Saddam Hussein's forces**, but the majority of casualties came after that. The insurgency took US and British resources away from Afghanistan, which were sorely needed there.

The invasion destroyed the Ba'ath party, paving the way for democratic government in Iraq, but it alienated the Sunni minority.

- US leadership failed by providing **too few troops**.
- US planning **failed to work out how Iraq would be run after the invasion**. The Coalition Provisional Authority at first had no offices, no telephone and no computers.
- The wrong assumptions were made: it was expected that Iraqi troops would surrender, but they 'melted' into the population. The **Americans were not seen as liberators but as an occupying force**.
- Mistakes were made when General Paul Bremer banned the Ba'ath party in March 2003 (losing 30,000 trained administrators) and disbanded the Iraqi army and security services (releasing 300,000 armed men into the community).

The impact on civilians

Educated Iraqis were targeted by the insurgency, because their help would be needed if the new administration was to reconstruct Iraq. Many of Iraq's most qualified people fled the country as almost 5 million people were displaced by violence. Meanwhile, unemployment varied between 30% and 60% of the workforce, while life expectancy, the annual average salary and access to fresh water all fell steeply. Infant and maternal mortality rates rose steeply showing that there had been no advantage for the Iraqi people in Bush and Blair's invasion. The democratic government has also failed to deliver expected women's rights.

The US administration too often seemed to work for its own advantage and ignore the needs of ordinary Iraqis. There was a real failure to reach out to Iraqis, to win their hearts and minds. With 10,000 interned without trial, US rule looked as repressive as that of Saddam Hussein to many Iraqis.

International consequences

The war also had international consequences:

- **Deep divisions** were created between factions in both the US and British governments.
- **Relations between the USA, France and Russia were soured.**
- **Support for militant Islam** around the world was increased, with the USA and UK becoming particular targets for terrorist attack.
- The insurgency proved that even the **USA was not invincible.**

PROGRESS CHECK

1. What form of Islamic belief became dominant in Iran after the victory of Ayatollah Khomeini?
2. Why did most Arab nations not support the American and coalition invasion of Iraq in 2003?

1. Shi'ah. 2. They thought it was illegal for them to interfere in Iraqi affairs.

7.6 Terrorist or freedom fighter?

LEARNING SUMMARY

After studying this section you should be able to understand:

- the roles that religion, nationalism and ideology play in terrorism
- how terrorist groups differ in their membership, aims, motives and methods
- how important the leaders of terrorist groups are
- how governments have reacted to terrorism
- how effective terrorist groups have been and what determines their success or failure

What roles do religion, nationalism and ideology play in terrorism?

AQA B	✓
EDEXCEL A	✗
OCR B	✓
WJEC A	✗
WJEC B	✗
CCEA	✗

What is 'terrorism'?

There is no generally accepted definition of the word 'terrorism'. The same person can be viewed by one group as a '**terrorist**' because he is working against them and by another group as a '**freedom fighter**' because they agree with him. In Northern Ireland we saw that this could apply to the **Provisional IRA (PIRA)** who, according to the British Government, were terrorists, while many in Ireland considered them to be 'freedom fighters'. Certainly a 'terrorist' would expect to use **physical violence to undermine the state in order to force it to change its policy**. Usually terrorism is, therefore, the policy of the small minority, trying to force its views on the majority, though there are exceptions to this rule.

In Northern Ireland, terrorist organisations included all the paramilitary forces, which intended to take the law into their own hands, from the Ulster Volunteer Force (UVF) to the Real IRA. In Israel, the **Palestine Liberation Organisation** (**PLO**) was called terrorist by the Israelis while in Iraq, President Bush suspected that the whole state had become terrorist, and then that **al-Qaeda** had infiltrated the insurgent groups.

Terrorism is not limited to one time, race or religion:

- There have always been terrorists in history (e.g. the Zealots, a Jewish group during Roman times and the Assassins, a Muslim group from the 7th Century).
- During the 1960s, there was a sudden resurgence of terrorism: in Germany (Red Army Faction); in Northern Ireland (PIRA and the UVF). Examples sprang up all over the world, so that now every continent has its 'terrorist' groups.

How different are terrorist groups in their membership, aims, motives and methods?

AQA B	✓
EDEXCEL A	X
OCR B	✓
WJEC A	X
WJEC B	X
CCEA	X

The following paragraphs compare three major terrorist groups of our time: the PIRA, the PLO and al-Qaeda.

Membership

The **PIRA was largely Catholic** in membership, dedicated to setting right the wrongful partition of Ireland under the Anglo-Irish Treaty, 1921. Many were also republican, some also communist, but all felt a historic grievance created by inequality and **lack of civil rights**. They felt that Irish territory had been unfairly given to Scottish protestant settlers in the 16th Century, so they felt deprived of their birthright. However, the movement was **fuelled by poverty and social problems** as much as by religion and historical folk memory.

The **PLO** was created because **Jewish settlers displaced the Palestinian population** of Israel during the 1920s and 1930s. Hard line Jewish settlers (Zionists) decided to set up a Jewish state in what they saw as their traditional land. Britain was forced to give up her mandate in 1947 so Palestine was handed back to the United Nations, who intended to partition it, but were forestalled when the state of Israel was declared. The Palestinians, therefore, **fled as refugees to Gaza or the Left Bank**, which became fertile recruiting grounds for the PLO.

> **KEY POINT**
>
> Poverty, deprivation, nationalism and religious differences were combined in Israel, as in Northern Ireland.

Al-Qaeda had its origins in the war between the **Afghanistan freedom fighters** (or mujahidin) and the Soviet Union, which had invaded Afghanistan in 1979 to prop up a communist government there. Afghan tribes were supported by neighbouring states, and even by the USA. The Saudi Arabian government saw the struggle as a **holy war** (jihad) and encouraged volunteers to fight. Osama bin Laden involved himself in fundraising and later in the fighting, coming under the influence of a radical preacher, Abdul Azzam, whose ideas formed the basis of al-Qaeda's actions. For them, the **American involvement** in the victory against the Soviet Union made the new Afghan government unacceptable. In this case, the combination of deprivation, loss of their homeland and idealist motivation is rather different from the previous cases.

Aims and motives

The aims of the PIRA were to defend their Nationalist communities, to **make the six counties of Ulster part of a united Ireland** and, in doing so, to **remove British troops and influence**. Many had Republican or communist aims, but not all did. The PIRA were hugely helped by the lack of civil rights for Catholics at first, but by the time these had been given, the fighting had taken on its own momentum.

The **PLO was created by Yasser Arafat** who, in 1969, pulled the various Palestinian organisations, including his own, Fatah, together into one organisation to create a Palestinian state. This meant the **destruction of Israel** which, by then, was not likely to be carried out through open warfare.

Methods

The PIRA attacked British troops and the Northern Ireland police force (Royal Ulster Constabulary). They planted bombs in Northern Ireland and mainland Britain (while they themselves were attacked by Loyalist terrorists).

The PLO carried out commando raids into Israeli territory during the 1970s, fired rockets at Israeli towns and carried out high-profile assassinations and hijackings.

Within al-Qaeda there are separate groups: a high-profile terrorist group, which carries out terrorist acts against those they see as opposed to Islam; an organisation that seeks to influence other groups and provides finance and training; a propaganda organisation to rally support for militant Islam and provide publicity. Al-Qaeda launched a series of attacks using suicide bombers against Western targets, or targets associated with the USA, including the World Trade Centre (9/11). Following this, the US action against their bases in Afghanistan destroyed their central organisation, but its splintered remnants survive.

How important are the leaders of terrorist groups?

AQA B	✓
EDEXCEL A	✗
OCR B	✓
WJEC A	✗
WJEC B	✗
CCEA	✗

KEY POINT

Terrorist leaders are very important: they are vital in defining the political reason for action and in aiming that action to do the most damage.

The PIRA were led by an Army Council and consisted of **small, tightly organised cells**. Chiefs of Staff included **Seán Mac Stíofáin** and **Martin McGuiness**. By 1975 it numbered only a few thousand active members, but their capability to plan and aim attacks led the British and Irish governments to take them very seriously.

The PLO with Yasser Arafat as leader was organised around the **Palestinian National Council** and relied on the support of the **Fatah Party**. Decisions were taken by an Executive Committee, but because **Arafat failed to control it**, the breakaway Rejectionist Front acted independently from 1974. Arafat's failure to take the membership with him in signing the Oslo Accords in 1991 led to the creation of the hard line group, Hamas. Arafat's leadership was weakened until his death in 2004.

Figure 7.10 Yasser Arafat in 1969

Al-Qaeda seems synonymous with **Osama bin Laden**, but in reality bin Laden does not run the organisation on his own. There is a close-knit group of advisers overseeing a loosely-knit group of cells. These can recruit from thousands of Muslim radicals throughout the world. The role of al-Qaeda is to inspire action in others. **Muslim extremists** commit terrorist acts, which al-Qaeda can claim credit for, without being closely enough connected to imperil itself.

Terrorist organisations, therefore, do not need high-profile leaders (the PIRA leaders were quite anonymous) but they need careful organisation – both the PIRA and al-Qaeda use the cell structure to reduce the impact of infiltration.

How have governments reacted to terrorism?

AQA B	X
EDEXCEL A	X
OCR B	✓
WJEC A	X
WJEC B	X
CCEA	X

Infiltration

In 1975, as the ceasefire collapsed in Northern Ireland, the British Government arrested many high-profile PIRA figures. Infiltration of the PIRA had given the British Government important information, which they used to break up the organisation. The PIRA retaliated by reducing numbers and resorting to the cell structure.

Negotiation

The Israeli government's resistance was worn down by the violence of the First Intifada so that, in 1993 when the PLO was suffering a funding crisis, they were prepared to sign the Oslo Accords, which recognised the PLO as the official Palestinian authority in exchange for Arafat's recognition of the state of Israel and pledge to reject violence.

War

The US government launched cruise missiles against Sudan and Afghanistan as a direct reaction to the embassy bombings in East Africa. In 2001, attacks on the World Trade Centre led the USA to offer Mullah Omar, the Taliban leader who was sheltering al-Qaeda, the chance to surrender bin Laden. When Mullah Omar refused, the USA and its allies invaded Afghanistan and, with the help of the Northern Alliance, they removed the Taliban government. Al-Qaeda's training camps were destroyed and its organisation destabilised but the leadership escaped.

7.11 The al-Qaeda attack on the World Trade Centre on 11th September 2001

How effective have terrorist groups been?

AQA B	X
EDEXCEL A	X
OCR B	✓
WJEC A	X
WJEC B	X
CCEA	X

Though terrorist organisations have never been completely effective, they can achieve a situation in which governments will make **concessions for peace**. Careful compromises can bring **important benefits for terrorists**. The terrorist organisation that has not compromised has not achieved any of its aims.

	Effective	Not very effective
PIRA	Has reduced British influence in Northern Ireland. Has helped to achieve equality for Catholics. Has won the concession that the future of Northern Ireland depends on a majority vote of its citizens.	Has not achieved the unification of Ireland.
PLO (to 1993)	Oslo Accords gave Gaza Strip and Jericho area self-rule.	Had not destroyed the state of Israel or created a viable Palestinian state. Many issues had been shelved rather than settled, e.g. the future of Jerusalem.
Al-Qaeda (to 2003)		Rather than reducing Western influence in Iraq and Afghanistan, Western influence has been extended. The state of Israel has not been destroyed.

PROGRESS CHECK

1. What is the alternative name for a 'terrorist', if you agree with his actions?
2. How did Yasser Arafat fail over the Oslo Accords in 1991?

2. He failed to take the membership of the PLO with him, leading to its fragmentation.
1. Freedom fighter.

Exam practice questions

1   Study the following sources and then answer the questions that follow.

Source A: Speech by Nikita Khrushchev to the 20th Party Congress, 1956

Stalin acted not through persuasion, explanation and patient co-operation with people, but by imposing his concepts and demanding absolute submission to his opinion. Whoever opposed this concept or tried to prove his viewpoint, and the correctness of his position, was doomed to removal from the leading collective and to subsequent moral and physical annihilation. This was especially true during the period following the 17th Party Congress, when many prominent Party leaders and rank-and-file Party workers, honest and dedicated to the cause of communism, fell victim to Stalin's despotism.

Source B: A cartoon from a British newspaper 23rd July 1968

© The Times, London, 1968

Source C: A modern communist view of the invasion of Czechoslovakia

A genuine Leninist leadership would have prepared the Czech people for the eventuality of an invasion, both politically and militarily. The confrontation of the Red Army by an armed working class, organised in Soviets, would have had a tremendous effect on the Russian workers in uniform. As it was, numerous eye-witness accounts tell of the bewilderment and demoralisation of the Warsaw Fact troops, as the realisation dawned on them that they had been duped by their leaders. There were instances of Russian troops breaking down and weeping in the streets, protesting that they didn't even know they were in Czechoslovakia...

Exam practice questions

(a) Study Source A. Why did Khrushchev's speech provoke uncertainty in Eastern Europe? Explain your answer, using details of the speech and your knowledge.

....

....

....

....

....

(6)

(b) Study Source B. What was the message the cartoonist intended to make? Explain your answer, using details of the cartoon and your knowledge.

....

....

....

....

....

....

....

(8)

(c) Study Source C. Do you believe that Dubcek would ever have considered cutting Czechoslovakia's ties with Eastern Europe? Explain your answer, using details of the source and your knowledge.

....

....

....

....

....

....

....

....

....

....

(8)

You may need to continue your answers on a separate sheet of paper.

8 Britain 1919–1978

The following topics are covered in this chapter:

- Depression and unrest in the 1920s and 1930s
- The reconstruction of Britain in the 1940s and 1950s
- The transformation of society between 1950 and 1980.

8.1 Depression and unrest in the 1920s and 1930s

LEARNING SUMMARY

After studying this section you should be able to understand:

- Britain's industrial problems after the First World War
- how the General Strike occurred and was ended

Britain's industries in decline after the First World War

AQA B	✓
EDEXCEL A	✓
OCR B	✗
WJEC A	✓
WJEC B	✓
CCEA	✗

In the Coupon Election, in December 1918, **Lloyd George was triumphantly returned at the head of a coalition government**, mostly made up of Conservatives. They enjoyed a short post-war boom in industry and, by late 1919 over 4 million troops were 'demobbed' (demobilised).

Inflation and strikes

The end of the war had seen a sudden inflation, as **prices rose uncontrollably**, but **wages lagged behind**. Trades Unions were determined to protect their workers and, between 1919 and 1920, there were **over 2,000 strikes**. Disillusionment from the trenches, and the success of Bolshevism in Russia both helped to inflame the situation.

There was a particularly serious strike of **Clydeside engineers and shipbuilders** in 1919, which resulted in the calling in of troops and tanks.

The **Miners' Federation** demanded a six-hour day and a 30% wage increase and continued government control of the mines. Lloyd George offered a seven-hour day and continued government control but appointed the **Sankey Commission** to investigate the problem.

Slump in 1921

In 1921, levels of unemployment in Britain reached a peak because of the following:

- **The slow decline of British industry since the 1870s**, reversed due to war production, now became evident again. Industrialists were losing the race towards greater mechanisation and investment in industry.
- **Foreign buyers**, unable to obtain British goods during the war, **had found alternative suppliers**. So demand for traditional British exports (ships, textiles, iron, steel, coal) never reached pre-war levels.
- While the government extended aid to the unemployed (the 'dole') they never attacked the seat of the problem – the declining profitability of industry.
- The Sankey Commission was unable to find a solution to the mining problems. **The entire industry came out on strike** but the mines and railways were handed back to private ownership on 1st April. Miners' wages were reduced because of the drop in exports. Betrayed by their friends in the railway and transport industries, the miners were unable to make the strike general, but they continued on strike for three months, after which they were forced to take wage reductions, followed by workers in the engineering, docks, shipbuilding, textiles, printing and railway industries. Lloyd George lost his popularity among the workers, losing the election in October 1922.
- **By the end of 1921, there were 2 million unemployed in Britain.** The figure would never fall below 1 million again until 1939.

The failure of the first Labour Government

After a short-lived Conservative government, **Ramsay MacDonald headed the first Labour ministry in January 1924**. This government failed to solve industrial problems because...

- they couldn't afford to be too radical because they relied on Liberal votes to stay in office
- they were seen as biased towards trade union interests, but the unions thought that the government was too independent of their wishes
- **Labour had no answers to the industrial problems** beyond nationalisation, which was impractical.

The Labour Government fell in October 1924. It was followed by Stanley Baldwin and the Conservatives with a huge majority of 200 MPs.

The General Strike

AQA B	✓
EDEXCEL A	✓
OCR B	✗
WJEC A	✓
WJEC B	✓
CCEA	✗

The background to the strike is one of continuing post-war depression and decline of important industries, the failure of Liberal and Labour attempts to solve the problems of the mining industry, falling exports and mass unemployment.

Causes

There are several factors that led to the General Strike:

- In April 1925, Winston Churchill, Conservative Chancellor of the Exchequer, took Britain back onto the gold standard. Economists have estimated that he overvalued the pound sterling by about 10%.

> **KEY POINT**
>
> The results of overvaluing the pound were that British wages seemed high compared to those abroad and British export prices were too high as well.

- Coal sales were worse hit than any other industry since, in June 1925, **cheap German coal** from the Ruhr coalfields became available. It **undersold British coal** at a time when competition was growing from gas, electricity and oil industries in any case.
- Germany and Poland could sell cheap coal partly because their mines were mechanised, whereas **only 20% of British mines used machines**. Most miners still used hand picks. In June 1925, mine owners announced that they would have to **reduce wages and increase hours** to be able to sell coal at an economic price. The miners protested, but Prime Minister Stanley Baldwin saved the situation by appointing the Samuel Commission to find a solution.
- The **Trade Union Congress** (TUC) made it clear that they would **support the miners** because a reduction in miners' wages would signal a further reduction in wages throughout industry.
- When the **Samuel Commission** reported, in April 1926, it recommended the following:
  1. Mine-owners should press ahead with **modernisation**.
  2. The government should **withdraw its subsidy**.
  3. Miners should accept a **temporary reduction in their wages**, though these should be restored when the crisis had passed.

Neither owners nor miners would accept this report. The government did not force them, and the TUC tried to keep negotiations going because they could not afford a General Strike.

- The mine-owners announced that **wages would be reduced** from 30th April. The miners decided to strike on 1st May, but were locked out by the mine-owners on 30th April. The TUC announced that a General Strike would begin on 3rd May if a settlement had not been reached.
- **Last minute negotiations** between the TUC and the Cabinet on 2nd May were hampered when the miners' leaders went home. Baldwin was enraged by the refusal of the *Daily Mail* compositors to print an article branding the strike as revolutionary, and abruptly ended the talks. The TUC went to Downing Street to protest, but found that the Cabinet had gone home and Baldwin was in bed.

The strike

In the industries called out by the TUC (road, rail, docks, printing, gas and electricity, building, iron, steel and chemicals) the response to the **strike was almost 100%**. By 11th May there was no sign of a climbdown on either side. Sir Herbert Samuel offered to mediate and the TUC accepted.

In the **Samuel Memorandum**, Sir Herbert Samuel suggested a short-term renewal of the subsidy to allow wages to be maintained during the reorganisation of the mining industry and a National Wages Board.

On 12th May the **TUC called off the General Strike**, hoping that the Memorandum would be accepted, though Baldwin had given no guarantees.

The strike was called off for the following reasons:

- There was no sign of the government giving ground.
- The TUC was completely unprepared for a General Strike and scared that it would escalate.
- In the House of Commons, Sir John Simon (a Liberal lawyer) had said that the strike was not an industrial dispute but an 'illegal proceeding' and thus strike leaders could be sued or gaoled.
- The TUC had already used £4 million of their £12 million strike fund.

The **strike lasted unofficially until 14th May**, but even then **the miners refused to return to work**. The mine-owners refused to compromise and the strike dragged on until December. The miners were forced to accept lower wages and longer hours and were bitter at their 'betrayal' by the TUC.

How well did Baldwin handle the strike?

Handled it well	Didn't handle it at all
<ul><li>Baldwin **played a waiting game**, knowing that the TUC could not hold out for long.</li><li>He saw the strike as an attack on the constitution so that no negotiations could begin until the strike ended.</li><li>The government had prepared months ahead and volunteers kept food supplies moving, protected convoys, etc.</li><li>Baldwin was conciliatory in tone when he appealed to the nation on 8th May, asking for a fair deal for everyone.</li></ul>	<ul><li>Baldwin allowed right-wingers (Churchill) to be aggressive in the *British Gazette*.</li><li>King George V had to tell Baldwin to restrain Churchill, who had suggested using armoured cars to protect convoys, though they were not needed and who used phrases such as, 'We are at war'.</li></ul>

Figure 8.1 Winston Churchill had called out the Army to protect supply convoys.

The results of the strike

The strike had the following effects:

- **Working-class disillusionment with the TUC** caused TUC membership to slump from over 8 million in 1926 to under 5 million in 1927.
- There was **no solution to the problems of the coal industry**, which continued to decline. In 1913 it exported 73 million tonnes; in 1932 just 39 million tonnes.
- The strike showed reasonable employers that wage reductions were not an easy solution to their difficulties.
- The **TUC realised that a General Strike would never succeed**. The working class turned to parliamentary action. This was partly responsible for the increase in Labour Party support in the 1929 General Election.
- The government introduced the **Trades Disputes Act 1927**, which made sympathetic strikes and intimidation illegal, and stopped trade unions from automatically contributing towards the Labour Party from members' subscriptions.

Were the 1930s years of depression or of recovery?

AQA B	✓
EDEXCEL A	✓
OCR B	✗
WJEC A	✓
WJEC B	✓
CCEA	✗

*For the Wall Street Crash see page 187

**For the Dawes Plan see page 167

The effects of the Wall Street Crash on Europe

Even before the Wall Street Crash*, the effects of American overproduction and protective tariffs were reducing Europe's ability to repay American loans. European prosperity was bound up with its ability to repay America, especially the Dawes Plan of 1924**.

German loans were used to pay reparations to Britain, France, Belgium and Italy, who then repaid their war debts to the USA. But in 1929 the USA...

- ceased to import goods from Europe
- stopped all future loans to Germany
- called in all short-term loans to Germany.

While Germany was hit most severely, Britain, as one of Germany's main creditors and trading partners, was also badly affected.

The Labour Government, 1929–1931

The second Labour Government had taken power under **Ramsay MacDonald** after a general election in 1929. They were confronted with an increase in unemployment from 1 million to 2.5 million by December 1930, yet they took no action to reduce it. Solutions suggested by radicals such as Sir Oswald Moseley and Lloyd George were ignored. Increasing unemployment was leading to financial crisis, so the government appointed Sir George May to investigate national expenditure.

Sir George May's Committee took until July 1931 to report. It proposed the following:

- **A general reduction of salaries in the public sector** (i.e. armed forces, civil servants, judges and police).
- Teachers were singled out for cuts of 20%.

The result was a sudden loss of confidence. **Foreign investors thought that Britain must be bankrupt** and withdrew their investments. Further reductions in government expenditure were demanded to restore confidence.

MacDonald and his Chancellor, Snowden, were prepared to go ahead with the May Committee proposals but they were thwarted when **ten out of 21 members of the cabinet refused to agree to any cut in unemployment benefit**.

MacDonald was forced to resign, but to everyone's surprise he emerged as the leader of a coalition National Government, consisting mostly of Conservatives and Liberals with only three Labour members.

The National Government, 1931–1935

Emergency measures were implemented in Snowden's budget on the lines of the May report:
- **Income tax was raised** from 4s.6d. to 5s. in the pound.
- **Salaries of public employees were reduced by 10%**. This did not restore confidence, and in September 1931 naval crews protested against salary cuts in the **Invergordon Mutiny**. This was only settled when the government promised not to cut further.

Further measures were taken by the government over the next five years:
- The government **took the pound off the gold standard**. Its value was allowed to fall by about 25%, but there was still no revival in exports. Unemployment continued to rise towards 3 million.
- Ramsay MacDonald called a surprise general election in October, asking for a 'doctor's mandate' (to let him do what was necessary to improve the economy). He won a majority with 521 MPs from different parties.
- In 1932 **Free Trade was finally abandoned** by Neville Chamberlain's Import Duties Act, which placed a 10% duty on most imports, except those from the Empire.
- Defence expenditure and interest on war loans were reduced.
- Attempts were made to **rationalise and modernise** iron, steel, coal, textiles and shipbuilding industries.
- The bank rate was reduced from 6% to 2% to reduce debt charges. Many local authorities took the opportunity to build council houses, relieving local unemployment to some degree.

Figure 8.2 Poverty in Wavertree, Liverpool in 1934.

- **The Unemployment Act, 1934** set up the National Unemployment Assistance Board. Through branches everywhere in the country it paid out benefit after an unemployed man ran out of the normal period of insurance benefit. It caused great bitterness because it was based on the **means test** introduced in 1931. This took into account the total family income and savings before paying out dole money. It, therefore, penalised the careful and thrifty.
- **The Special Areas Act, 1934**, provided £2 million to try to revive the depressed areas. It did not work effectively because employers could not be persuaded to move into the depressed areas.

Gradual recovery, 1932–1939

It is arguable that some measure of prosperity would have returned, even without the measures outlined above:

- **Prices had fallen faster than wages** because the world was suffering from oversupply. Therefore, there was an increase in real wages and people felt better off.
- People were able to spend their **extra cash on British consumer goods** and even luxuries, which in turn stimulated the economy and a return to prosperity. Unemployment had fallen to 2 million by 1935 and 1.4 million by 1937 (though there was an increase in 1938).

Some areas did better than others during this period:

- The Midlands and South did well because of increased population and modern industries such as automobile, aeronautical and electrical industries and commerce.
- Scotland, the North East, Cumberland, Lancashire and Northern Ireland did very badly because they were dependent on declining basic industries, such as coal, iron, steel, shipbuilding and textiles.
- **Jarrow** in 1934 had 68% unemployment. Merthyr Tydfil had 62%. In St. Albans the figure was only 3.9%.
- In **Stockton-on-Tees** the average income of families where the wage earner was unemployed was only £1.50 per week.
- The average **infant mortality** rate in the South was 42 per thousand live births; in South Wales it was 63; in Durham and Northumberland it was 76; in Jarrow it was 114.

Only the coming of war in 1939 solved long-term problems of unemployment and deprivation.

PROGRESS CHECK

1. What commission was appointed by Lloyd George to look into the problems in the mining industry?
2. How did Winston Churchill make the economic situation worse in 1925?
3. Why did Ramsay MacDonald's first Labour government fall in 1931?
4. Why, despite wages being reduced in 1932, did people seem better off by 1939?

1. The Sankey Commission. 2. He returned Britain to the gold standard. 3. Because they tried to reduce public sector salaries. 4. Because world prices were falling faster than wages.

8.2 The reconstruction of Britain in the 1940s and 1950s

LEARNING SUMMARY

After studying this section you should be able to understand:

- how the Second World War helped to destroy the British economy and change society
- how idealism during the Second World War led to the Welfare State
- how British society changed after the War

The impact of the Second World War

AQA B	✓
EDEXCEL A	✓
OCR B	✓
WJEC A	✓
WJEC B	✓
CCEA	✗

The effects of war on society and the economy

The civilian population was directly involved in the war from the beginning of the war through to the end:

- There was mass evacuation of children from the cities.
- Civilians were involved in digging shelters, piling sandbags and issuing gas masks.
- They maintained and enforced the blackout.
- They removed signposts, place names and station name-boards.
- There was rationing of bacon, butter, cheese and meat, and later clothes and fuel.
- Women were conscripted as well as men.
- Civilians volunteered for the Home Guard.
- German bombing, especially of London, Coventry, Liverpool, Manchester, Plymouth, Hull, Glasgow and Belfast killed about 60,000 civilians (half of which were in London) and seriously injured about 100,000.
- Hundreds of thousands of people were made homeless.

For details of the Home Front, see Chapter 4.

Changing attitudes

In more general terms the war caused **an acceleration of social change**. Many were appalled at the state of evacuee children and many were impressed at the co-operation of all classes of society in a truly national effort. **The poor, it was felt, had earned concessions**. There was a fear of revolution after the war if concessions were not made in good time. There were two immediate results of this:

- **The Beveridge Report 1942**: Churchill's National Government appointed a committee, under Sir William Beveridge, a Liberal, to investigate the problems of social insurance. In his report he wrote that the great evils to be overcome were **want, disease, ignorance, squalor and idleness**. These would be impacted upon by government insurance schemes, child allowances, a national health service and a policy of full employment. Churchill did not agree with the report and had only implemented child allowances before the end of his government in 1945.
- **The Butler Education Act 1944**: R.A. Butler, Conservative President of the Board of Education, made free secondary education available to all and raised the school leaving age to 15. Secondary schools were to be either grammar, technical or modern.

Economic crisis

Britain was impoverished, her gold reserves exhausted within the first two years of the war. In March 1941 the US Congress passed the **Lend Lease Act**, which allowed Britain to obtain crucial supplies from America, to be paid for later. By 1945 Britain's overseas debts had reached well over £3,000 million. On the defeat of Japan, President Truman abruptly ended Lend Lease and demanded repayment of the debt. The only way out was to agree a new loan from the USA on very unfavourable terms, which **reduced Britain to dependence**.

While initially the British Empire remained intact in 1945, within twenty years, most colonies had achieved independence. Nationalist feelings had been stirred by British defeats, especially in India and the Far East. **It was clear that Britain was now only a second-rate power**.

Labour in Power, 1945–1951

AQA B	✓
EDEXCEL A	✓
OCR B	✓
WJEC A	✓
WJEC B	✓
CCEA	✗

Attlee inherited a crisis

In May 1945, the Labour Party under **Clement Attlee** gained a massive victory over the Conservatives, with 393 seats to the Conservatives' 213. While Churchill had remained personally popular, the Conservative majority in the National Government was blamed for appeasement and for failing to implement the Beveridge Report. This was the first Labour Government with a real majority but it was hampered by huge economic problems:

- the premature ending of Lend Lease
- the loss of two-thirds of Britain's export trade
- the sinking of much of Britain's merchant fleet.

Labour created a 'mixed economy'

Against this background the Labour Government completed an astonishing list of measures, leaving Britain part socialist and part capitalist (the mixed economy). This created the **post-war consensus** that survived into the 1970s:

- **Nationalisation**: This was to give the **government control of Britain's most important industries**, to permit more efficient planning and co-operation between industries, and to ensure fair treatment and better working conditions for employees. Under the direction of Herbert Morrison (Leader of the House of Commons) the following industries were nationalised:
  - Bank of England (1946)
  - Coal Industry (1947)
  - Public transport (1948) including inland waterways, railways, docks, road haulage, road passenger transport and London Transport
  - Electricity (1948)
  - Gas (1949)
  - Iron and steel nationalisation was delayed by the House of Lords because these industries were reasonably efficient, but after the passing of the **Parliament Act 1949** they were finally nationalised in 1950.
- **Export or die**: The aim was to return exports to their pre-war level so that the balance of payments deficit would be removed. A loan was necessary to restore industry to peacetime production levels.

For details of Marshall Aid, see pages 75–76

> **KEY POINT**
>
> The balance of payments deficit: It is important that there should be a balance between the cost of goods exported and the cost of those imported, or that a country should export more than it imports. If imports are too high there is an outflow of wealth from the country.

- **J.M. Keynes**, the famous economist, was sent to the USA to negotiate an interest-free loan of 6,000 million dollars. The Americans drove a hard bargain. He returned with only 3750 million dollars, at 2% interest with repayments starting in 1951. By 1947 it had almost been used up, but industry was recovering and had reached **17% above the 1939 figure for exports**. However, the balance of payments deficit stood at £438 million.
- **Britain gratefully took a gift of £1263 million in Marshall Aid**. This enabled recovery to be completed so that, by 1950, exports had reached 75% above the 1938 level.

The Welfare State

The Labour party had been elected on a promise to put the **Beveridge Report** into action. In fact, the Labour party had its own plans for a comprehensive social security scheme, family allowances and a national health service.

The National Health Service Act 1946: The architect was **Aneurin Bevan**, Minister of Health, who faced strong opposition from the medical profession. Starting in 1948 the system gave everyone...

- free medical care from their own doctor
- free specialist care and hospital treatment in nationalised hospitals
- free eye tests, eye treatment and spectacles
- free dentistry, false teeth, drugs, midwifery, maternity and child welfare.

Figure 8.3 Aneurin Bevan, architect of the National Health Service

The scheme was financed partly from taxation and partly from National Insurance contributions. It was expensive, costing over £400 million in its first year of operation. This led Hugh Gaitskell, as Chancellor of the Exchequer, to begin charging adults for half the cost of false teeth and spectacles. Aneurin Bevan resigned, believing the principle of an entirely free health service had been violated.

National Insurance: A compulsory National Insurance scheme was begun in 1946, to which all workers contributed. It gave contributors sickness and unemployment benefit, old age pensions, widows' and orphans' pensions and maternity and death grants. In 1948 National Assistance Boards were set up to help those too old to be insured under the new scheme. Social services were to be provided by local authorities for the elderly and handicapped. The National Insurance Industrial Injuries Act, 1946, made employers and employees contribute to a state scheme to compensate workers and provide pensions for the disabled.

Education: The Butler Education Act of 1944 was put into action, with an 11-plus exam to select which secondary school children would enter. Ordinary Levels (O Levels) at 16 and Advanced Levels (A Levels) at 18 replaced the old School Certificate system.

Housing: There was already a housing shortage in 1939, but the war had destroyed a further 700,000 houses. Bevan launched a new housing drive. Despite the high cost of building materials at that time, considerable numbers were completed:

Year	Number of houses built
1946	55,400
1947	139,690
1948	284,230

He continued with over 200,000 a year until 1951. Although more houses were built than the number expected to be needed, the increase in marriages and rise in the birth rate after the war meant that housing remained short.

Two other measures helped to improve housing:
- **The New Towns Act 1946** gave the government the power to establish new towns, appoint development corporations and carry out projects. Healthy and pleasant new towns were created at Stevenage, Crawley, Hemel Hempstead and Harlow, East Kilbride, Peterlee and Glenrothes. A total of 14 new towns were established by the end of the government's time in office.
- **The Town and Country Planning Act 1947** gave the job of planning to the county councils, who were required to plan land development 20 years ahead. They were given powers of compulsory purchase; they could control advertisements and protect historic buildings.

PROGRESS CHECK

1. List the five great evils described in Sir William Beveridge's report.
2. Which Labour minister was the architect of the National Health Service?
3. What payments were made by workers to cover most of the costs of the Welfare State?

1. Want, disease, ignorance, squalor and idleness. 2. Aneurin Bevan.
3. National Insurance contributions.

8.3 The transformation of society between 1950 and 1980

LEARNING SUMMARY

After studying this section you should be able to understand:

- how the end of the Empire and economic change increased immigration
- how social changes affected both women and young people

Post-war immigration

AQA B	✓
EDEXCEL A	✗
OCR B	✓
WJEC A	✗
WJEC B	✗
CCEA	✗

The difference between perception and reality

In the 30 years after the Second World War, Britain changed very quickly: the end of the Empire, the growth of new industries and the decline of others, and the achievement of economic security by the vast majority of families in Britain all drove social change.

Official figures suggest that public perception of immigration and the reality have been quite different during the 20th Century:

Migration to and from the UK (to the nearest 100,000)

Decade	Outflow	Inflow
1900–09	4,404,000	2,287,000
1910–19	3,526,000	2,224,000
1920–29	3,960,000	2,590,000
1930–39	2,273,000	2,361,000
1940–49	590,000	240,000
1950–59	1,327,000	676,000
1960–69	1,916,000	1,243,000
1970–79	2,554,000	1,900,000

In reality, Britain has always received many immigrants but just as many have emigrated elsewhere from Britain. The perception of immigration has changed as a result of the kind of immigration: people of **different cultures and colours** replacing the less identifiable European immigrants of previous years. Waves of immigration in the early 20th Century had been of Irish, Jewish and other races from Eastern Europe. After 1948, the immigration continued from Poland and Eastern Europe, but was predominantly from the West Indies, India and Pakistan. The significance of immigration is, therefore, in the creation of a multi-racial and multi-cultural society in the later 20th Century.

Immigration in the 1950s

During the 1950s, West Indian immigration was officially welcomed. Newsreels commented enthusiastically on the arrival in 1948 of the first **Jamaican immigrants**

on board the ship Empire Windrush. Most were young men, who were all made British citizens and their success encouraged further emigration. The government appealed for Caribbean workers to fill vacancies, particularly in the hospital and transport services during Britain's acute post-war labour shortage. Soon, textile firms in London and the north of England were encouraging workers from the textile districts of **India** and **Pakistan**.

Figure 8.4 The pioneers on board the Empire Windrush

By the **late 1950s** a reaction was already apparent:
- **'No coloured' notices** appeared at factories and on boarding houses.
- **Complaints** were heard that immigrants were attracted as much by welfare benefits as by work.
- Friction was increased by the **housing shortage**, suggesting that this was the fault of immigration.

The reality was that emigration was consistently exceeding immigration, so immigration could not cause the housing shortage. Naturally, immigrants tended to congregate in particular areas and, with an average of 6% of immigrants being of non-European origin, this meant that immigrants became very noticeable in certain areas of cheaper accommodation. In 1958 **race riots** broke out in both **Nottingham and Notting Hill**, which shocked the government into action.

The **Commonwealth Immigrants Acts of 1962 and 1968** created a voucher scheme, which restricted the right of entry to those who actually had a job to go to. They were very controversial and were condemned by many as being racist, since they restricted immigration according to ethnic origins. The **Race Relations Acts in 1965 and 1968** prohibited discrimination, or incitement to discriminate and set up a Race Relations Board and Race Relations Commission.

Though well-intentioned, the Commonwealth Immigration Act in 1962 provoked a huge rise in immigration before it came into force, fuelling the anxieties of those who wanted a complete halt to immigration. **Enoch Powell** was the only prominent politician to take an openly anti-immigration stance. In 1968, in a notorious speech, he described a nightmare vision of Britain torn by racial conflict: 'As I look ahead, I am filled with foreboding. Like the Roman, I seem to see "the River Tiber foaming with much blood".' The speech was universally condemned and he lost his Cabinet post, but friction continued.

The impact of economic failure

The **economic failure** of the 1970s was most obvious in the immigrant areas, where disproportionately higher numbers of unemployed built up frustration. The continuous feeling among the black community was that they were subjected to unfair harassment by the police and there were serious riots in Bristol, Birmingham, Brixton and Liverpool in 1981.

Figure 8.5 Race riots in Brixton in 1981

The changing status of women

AQA B	✓
EDEXCEL A	✗
OCR B	✓
WJEC A	✗
WJEC B	✓
CCEA	✗

The status of women had changed quickly since 1918 when women over 30 had gained the vote.

1919	All the **professions** (except holy orders) were opened to women. Women could enter all **universities**.
1923	A woman could **divorce** her husband for adultery.
1926	Married and single women could **own and sell property** on the same terms as men.
1928	All women over 21 were given the **vote**.

After 1945 important events included:

1948	British women could retain their **nationality** on marriage to a foreigner.
1970	Women were to have **equal pay for equal work**.
1971	A husband and wife's earnings could be **taxed separately**.
1975	Women **could not be dismissed if they were pregnant**, but were to receive **paid maternity leave**. There was to be equality with regard to employment, education and training, housing, provision of services, banking, insurance and credit, and pensions. An Equal Opportunities Commission was set up.

Since the 1970s, the **feminist movement** has aimed to improve the circumstances of women and has pointed out social injustices beyond the scope of legislation. Targets have included: the nuclear family, the authoritarian role of men and sexual subservience.

An important development of the 1960s was the female **contraceptive pill**: for the first time in history women had genuine control over their own fertility. This was associated with the 'sexual revolution' of the 1960s when old sexual taboos were broken down. It was aided by the following:

- **The Lady Chatterley Case 1960**, in which Penguin Books were prosecuted for publishing *Lady Chatterley's Lover* by D.H. Lawrence, which contained four-letter words and sexual description. The not-guilty verdict began a more permissive age for the arts.
- **The Abortion Act 1967** permitted legal abortion if two doctors agreed that there was a serious mental or physical risk to the mother, or a strong possibility that the child would be seriously abnormal. This was controversial, but it gave women 'the right to choose'.
- **The Sexual Offences Act 1967** permitted male homosexual acts between consenting adults. Female homosexuality had never been illegal.

These changes in legislation allowed important changes in social practice:

- There was a rapid rise in **illegitimate births**, which rose from 3% in 1914 to 10% in 1970 and 25% in 1988.
- **Divorce rates** rose from 1 in every 10 marriages in 1960 to 1 in every 3 marriages by 1980.
- **Legal abortions rose** from 22,332 in 1968 to 128,600 in 1980.
- Whereas only 43% of married women worked in 1951, 59% did in 1970.

Yet, in 1984, a poll showed that 9 out of 10 women still did the washing and ironing, 7 out of 10 women still did the cleaning, 5 out of 10 women did the shopping and 1 out of 16 women did household repairs.

The evolution of the teenager

AQA B	✓
EDEXCEL A	✗
OCR B	✓
WJEC A	✗
WJEC B	✗
CCEA	✗

The **Second World War** had been an important influence on teenagers. Experiences of loss of parents, the absence of fathers, evacuation and disruption of homes all had an effect, as did the arrival of **American culture** and music. The creation of the Welfare State, and especially the health and educational reforms made very real improvements in the quality of people's lives and their aspirations for the future. Even so, during the 1950s, teenagers were in most respects seen as 'young adults', their sights set firmly on work and their opportunities restricted by the poverty of the times.

During the 1960s there were important changes:

1963	The **end of conscription** into the armed services, which had been for a term of two years.
1964	The beginning of the move towards **comprehensive schooling**. Previously, the 11-plus exam had sifted children into grammar, technical or secondary modern schools.
1972	The **school leaving age was raised from 15 to 16**, ensuring that most teenagers would sit examinations at 16.

This widened opportunities and encouraged an **expansion of university education**, evident in the large number of new universities and polytechnics founded in the 1960s and 1970s.

Consumerism had an important effect on teenage culture. During the 1950s and 1960s, teenagers in Britain were encouraged to be more individualistic. Individualism centred on not being the same as one's parents, so a distinct teenage culture evolved for the first time. Teenagers could dress differently, from Teddy Boys in the 1950s to Mods and Rockers in the 1960s and Punk in the 1970s. They could buy rock and roll or pop music and they could listen to more radio stations (e.g. Radio Caroline from 1964).

The '**generation gap**' was first noticed in the 1950s. Pop culture focused the aspirations of teenagers on their own idols, rather than on the idols of adults. In the 1960s hairstyles and clothes copied bands, such as the **Beatles**, while many girls copied the looks of **Dusty Springfield**.

Figure 8.6 The Beatles exploited the 'generation gap'

There was emphasis on personal gratification, leading to a rise in sexual activity among teenagers. The age of sexual activity lowered from 20 in the 1950s to 17 by the 1990s, by which time there were 90,000 teenage conceptions a year.

Protest Movements were a particular feature of youth culture in the 1960s and 1970s, partly because of movements elsewhere:

- The **Anti-Vietnam War** protests were very important, particularly at the Grosvenor Square demonstration against the American Embassy in 1969.
- **Campaign for Nuclear Disarmament** rallies were important, particularly the annual Aldermaston March.
- **Trotskyist and Anarchist** protests led to the closing of the London School of Economics in 1969. The youth movement particularly favoured Marxist groups such as the Young Socialists (or anything else with shock value).

PROGRESS CHECK

1. On which ship did the first large group of Jamaican immigrants travel in 1948?
2. In which year was a law passed to give women equal pay for equal work?
3. In which year did conscription end in Britain?

1. Empire Windrush. 2. 1970. 3. 1963.

Sample GCSE questions

(a) Give two examples of groups taking industrial action in 1919.

Clydeside engineers and shipbuilders; Miners. **(4)**

(b) Why was there a General Strike in 1926?

High wages and underinvestment in the mining industry meant that foreign coal was much cheaper than British coal. In 1926 the German coalfields were exporting cheap coal and the British mining industry decided it needed longer hours and lower wages to compete. Winston Churchill had just returned the pound to the gold standard, reducing the competitiveness of British exports and allowing imports to undercut British industries.

The mine-owners decided to reduce wages because the Samuel Commission had recommended that the government subsidy should be withdrawn. Neither the government nor the miners bothered to keep negotiations going, despite the efforts of the TUC. **(6)**

(c) 'It was only the level-headed attitude of Stanley Baldwin that prevented the General Strike from escalating towards real civil unrest' Do you agree with this statement? Explain your answer.

Baldwin did not see the urgency of the situation and actually went to bed rather than continue negotiations with the TUC, thus helping to cause the strike. His refusal to negotiate while the strike continued probably prolonged it, and Baldwin certainly did not restrain the rest of his Cabinet. The King had to tell Baldwin to control them, especially Winston Churchill, whose `British Gazette´ was inciting the middle classes to confront the strikers. He also called out the Army to guard food convoys, when volunteers were doing well. Really Baldwin was not level-headed so much as idle.

Baldwin had prepared the country some time in advance, and he realised that the TUC did not have the funds to continue the strike for long. He saw the strike as an attack on the constitution, but did not, himself, take sides. He was very conciliatory when he addressed the nation, asking for a fair deal for everyone. The government enforced the law irrespective of the political opinions of its individual members.
In any case, it is doubtful whether any group intended to push the dispute to the extent of civil war. The TUC had made every effort to settle even before the strike began and certainly took the first opportunity of calling it off, once Sir Herbert Samuel suggested a compromise.
It would not be fair to give the government the whole credit.
Even though Baldwin did on the whole act well, so did the TUC, while other members of the government did not. **(10)**

Exam practice questions

1 **(a)** What important groups of immigrants had come to Britain before the Second World War?

.... **(4)**

(b) Why did immigrants come to Britain during the 1940s and 1950s?

....

....

....

....

....

.... **(6)**

(c) To what extent were immigrants to Britain well received between the 1940s and 1970s?

....

....

....

....

....

....

....

....

....

....

....

....

....

....

....

....

....

.... **(10)**

You may need to continue your answers on a separate sheet of paper.

9 Russia and the Soviet Union 1914–1941

The following topics are covered in this chapter:

- Russia before the First World War
- The impact of the First World War on Russia
- March to November 1917
- The Bolshevik victory: October / November 1917
- Bolshevik rule and its impact 1918–1928
- The nature of Stalin's dictatorship

9.1 Russia before the First World War

LEARNING SUMMARY	After studying this section you should be able to understand:
	• why Russia was unstable before the First World War
	• the identity and aims of several important political parties in the Duma

Russian society before 1914

AQA B	✓
EDEXCEL A	✓
OCR B	✓
WJEC A	✓
WJEC B	✗
CCEA	✓

By 1914 Russian society was breaking apart, with each class following its own interests and none seeming very loyal to the Tsar. Indeed society seemed to be heading towards a crisis, which was put off by the patriotism of a nation suddenly at war.

Why society was breaking apart
Serfdom: Continued until 1861. It was ended by a compromise, which left neither the nobility nor the serfs satisfied. The peasants (freed serfs) suffered a 49-year indemnity (mortgage) on their land, and received less land than they expected.
Illiteracy: Only about 30% of peasants were literate by 1914. It had been the policy of the Tsars to keep them ignorant.
Nobility losing influence: The top few in society, the aristocracy, still had great power in the army, the civil service, local government and as landowners. They disliked their loss of authority since the freeing of the serfs. Money compensation was soon spent. They resented that Tsar Nicholas II shut himself and his family away at Tsarskoe Selo (Tsar's Village) outside St. Petersburg, and they preferred Grand Duke Michael, the Tsar's popular brother, who went about in society.

Poor urban conditions: The few industrial towns acted as magnets for the landless peasantry and were growing very fast, with a poor standard of buildings, hygiene and public amenities. Moscow and St. Petersburg (the capital) in particular were expanding hugely. There was a growing group of permanent urban workers, who resented their poor living and working conditions and who resorted to strikes and demonstrations to make their protests felt.

Middle classes dissatisfied: In towns, the middle class was small, but growing by 1914. Both professional people and industrialists thought that Tsardom ignored their needs and hoped for a constitutional government.

> **KEY POINT**
>
> A constitutional government is one that organises itself according to a set of rules (a constitution), which regulates the relationships between the ruler and the ruled. It usually implies some kind of democracy.

The economy before 1914

AQA B	✓
EDEXCEL A	✓
OCR B	✓
WJEC A	✓
WJEC B	✗
CCEA	✓

Russia was a poor country, with great resources locked inside by great distances and an extreme climate. She had produced cheap raw materials for other manufacturing countries, and a growing surplus of grain, but it was the policy of the Tsars, since 1855, to change this and to compete as a manufacturing power.

- **Even in 1914, 85% of the population were peasants.** There were some rich farms, mostly in the eastern 'black earth' regions, but most of these were noble owned.
- **Peasants couldn't usually afford to make farms pay,** so they had to be satisfied with subsistence farming (they produced what they needed, took little to market, did not use much money and could not easily be taxed). So, economically, the vast majority of the population contributed very little to Russian society.
- Under a succession of Tsarist ministers (Bunge, Witte and Stolypin) **railways** were being built, foreign investment was being attracted and landholdings were being reformed. Growth rates of the economy averaged 9% from 1894–1900 and 5% from 1900–1914. These were huge rates of change.
- **Industrial growth was centred on armaments** because Nicholas II intended to protect Russia's position as Great Power, so oil, textiles, minerals, iron and steel were the industries most affected.

By 1914, the Russian economy had grown relatively slower than those of Germany, the USA, France and Britain. But Russia put a huge army of 3 million troops onto the front against Germany and Austria. The huge size of the army meant that, given the still small economy, Russia was unable to equip her troops as well as her enemies could, and in a long, drawn-out conflict the strain of supplying them would be immense.

Politics under the Tsar

AQA B	✓
EDEXCEL A	✓
OCR B	✓
WJEC A	✓
WJEC B	✗
CCEA	✓

Tsar refused to change

In 1913 the Romanovs celebrated 300 years on the throne. Nicholas II was educated by his father (Alexander III) and his tutor (Pobedonostsev) to believe that no form of rule other than Tsardom was possible.

> **KEY POINT**
>
> Tsardom – The Tsar was an **autocrat**: he ruled without any check on his power from any other part of the government. He thought himself to be in a special relationship with God.

No Cabinet government	Repression	No democracy
Individual members of the Council of State were sworn to be loyal to the Tsar so the Council could not make decisions of its own, without the Tsar's agreement. The Civil Service was well known for time wasting, was open to bribery and treated the people badly.	The mounted Cossacks, who used knouts (rope clubs) and swords, the Okhrana (secret police) and the army backed up the police. In 1905 the army shot at a demonstration on Bloody Sunday and started a revolution. The Tsar only survived because the army stayed loyal and because he made concessions.	The Tsar's October Manifesto in 1905 promised a Duma (an assembly). This was never able to force the Tsar to change any policies. Four Dumas were called before 1917 and each had less power and represented a narrower band of society.

Opposition to Tsarist rule

AQA B	✓
EDEXCEL A	✓
OCR B	✓
WJEC A	✓
WJEC B	✗
CCEA	✓

Although the Dumas were powerless to change policies, debates could be printed, which overturned centuries of political censorship and popularised opposition parties.

Octobrists

The Octobrists were a **Conservative** group, who supported the October Manifesto. In 1913 they were led by Guchkov, who showed that even the Tsar's most loyal supporters thought that he had gone too far in removing the Duma's rights, given to them in 1905. Guchkov warned that there would be a catastrophe if the Tsar did not make the government more respected.

Kadets

The Kadet Party (Constitutional Democrats) was the **Liberal** group in the Duma. Led by Milyukov, they represented many of the middle-class professionals and businessmen, who wanted a constitutional monarchy in which the Tsar and his government would have to answer to a democratic Duma.

Social Democrats

> **KEY POINT**
>
> Communists called themselves Social Democrats at this stage, but were split into several different groups. All believed in the historical interpretation of politics pioneered by Karl Marx.

The Socialists had split, in 1903, into the **Mensheviks** (Men of the Minority), led by Martov, and the **Bolsheviks** (Men of the Majority), led by Lenin. They were mostly supported by industrial working classes, but their leadership was mostly middle class.

The **Mensheviks** represented the majority of Socialists and **concentrated on making life better for the working masses**. While they were not against revolution, they did not think it had to come before improving conditions.

The **Bolsheviks** were actually in the minority. Lenin often preached that **conditions should not be improved now because it would lessen support for revolution, which was the most important aim**. Revolution would be followed by a period of change in which society and the economy would be put right (socialism), followed by the communist future.

Socialist Revolutionaries

The Socialist Revolutionaries enjoyed **mass support from the peasantry** and were the **most popular Party** in Russia. They were led by Chernov. Some believed in using assassinations to weaken the government; many believed in revolution. What united the Party was their **determination to redistribute the land** so that everyone would have their fair share.

> **PROGRESS CHECK**
>
> **1** In what way did the Tsars try to change the Russian economy between 1855 and 1914?
>
> **2** Why was the Duma not a constitutional government?
>
> **3** What was the difference between the Bolsheviks and the Mensheviks?
>
> 1. They tried to industrialise it.
> 2. Because the Tsar did not take any notice of it.
> 3. The Bolsheviks didn't want to see improvements now; they wanted to speed up revolution.

9.2 The impact of the First World War on Russia

LEARNING SUMMARY	After studying this section you should be able to understand:
	• how the First World War was not the short war Russia expected
	• the ways in which the war showed up the weaknesses of the Russian state
	• how Nicholas II's efforts to improve Russia's effectiveness in battle were almost successful
	• why collapse occurred at home

The effects of the war

AQA B	✓
EDEXCEL A	✓
OCR B	✓
WJEC A	✓
WJEC B	✗
CCEA	✓

The war was not wholly successful

In August 1914 the Russian army mobilised much more quickly than the Germans had expected. Reinforcements had to be switched from the Western Front (the Schleiffen Plan) to the East, weakening the German thrust into France. However, at the battles of **Tannenburg** and the **Masurian Lakes**, the Russian army was beaten and forced to give up Poland.

In 1915 the Russian army suffered a severe **shell and rifle shortage**, partly as a result of the West's failure to supply as promised. Russia's efforts to put this right were immense and probably helped to account for the revolution.

By 1916 the Russian army was recovering and, under **Brusilov**, they fought the only successful offensive of the year. Unfortunately, Russia was greatly weakened by the capitulation of Romania later that year.

In early 1917, Russian generals were confident that their shortages were over and expected a successful year. But the **March Revolution** destroyed morale among the troops and the planned offensive against Austria–Hungary became a fiasco.

The strain of attrition

Russia had been expecting a short war and was not ready for the severe strain of a 'war of attrition'. It had the following effects:
- The government was forced to spend more money than it was taking in taxes, resulting in **inflation** (money was worth less). **Workers had fixed wages and peasants received fixed prices** for their produce, so they became rapidly poorer.
- **Nicholas II decided to go to the Army HQ at Mogilev in 1915**, where he took over from his uncle, Grand Duke Nicholas. He began to solve the supply difficulties, while leaving operational command to General Alexeev.

> **KEY POINT**
>
> The Tsar's concentration on the needs of the Eastern Front put undue strain on the rest of the country.

- In Petrograd (St. Petersburg) **the Tsarina, Alexandra, was left in charge of the government**. She was unpopular, partly because of her relationship with **Rasputin**, a holy man, thought to have miraculous powers of healing Prince Alexei, and partly because **she was German and suspected of being a spy**.
- The Tsarina was determined not to compromise in home policy but **chaos and economic dislocation increased** as transport broke down through the huge strain of supplying the Front.

Figure 9.1 Found in the archives of the Okhrana after the March Revolution, this cartoon shows the Tsar and Tsarina under the influence of Rasputin

- **Workers began to strike in protest** at the long hours necessary to supply the army. Food became short as peasants would not sell it at low government prices. The real cost of living shot up as food was only available on the black market.

PROGRESS CHECK

1. Name the two main battles lost by the Russians in 1914.
2. From whom did Tsar Nicholas II take over command of the army in 1915?
3. Which Russian general in 1916 fought the only successful offensive of that year?

1. The battles of Tannenburg and the Masurian Lakes. 2. From his uncle, Grand Duke Nicholas. 3. General Brusilov.

9.3 March to November 1917

LEARNING SUMMARY	After studying this section you should be able to understand:
	- why Russian society unexpectedly collapsed at home
	- why the Provisional Government was never likely to be successful
	- the mistakes the Provisional Government made

Reasons for revolution

AQA B	✓
EDEXCEL A	✓
OCR B	✓
WJEC A	✓
WJEC B	✗
CCEA	✓

Although increasingly successful in supplying the Front, **Russian society collapsed at home**:

- Poverty and hard conditions in industry created **fertile ground for socialist agitators**.

- The **peasants** could not survive the low prices for food and the high war taxation. **They wanted to take over land owned by the nobility**.
- The **professional and industrial middle classes** were upset by the defeats and shortages at the Front. They **wanted a hand in government to run the war more effectively**. Milyukov combined his Kadets with other moderate parties into a Progressive Bloc in the Duma. They demanded the right to help, but were refused by the Tsar, who realised that help would come at the price of constitutional concessions.
- The aristocracy disliked Alexandra's mismanagement and Nicholas's failures. In a plot, **Prince Yusupov murdered Rasputin in December 1916**, but the situation did not improve.

The March Revolution 1917

AQA B	✓
EDEXCEL A	✓
OCR B	✓
WJEC A	✓
WJEC B	✗
CCEA	✓

A winter of poverty and hunger was followed by several bright spring days. There were rumours of bread rationing in Petrograd. The huge Putilov engineering works had just shut down, leaving tens of thousands of workers unemployed.

8th March	<ul><li>An International Women's Day was taken over by marchers demanding bread.</li><li>The Duma had been recently dismissed by the Tsar. It carried on debating in the Tauride Palace, criticising the government.</li></ul>
9th March	<ul><li>The crowds grew more aggressive.</li><li>Nearly all the industrial plants in the city closed down.</li><li>There were violent clashes, in which some demonstrators and soldiers died, but the trouble was still contained.</li></ul>
10th March	<ul><li>Orders came from the Tsar at Mogilev to suppress the demonstrations by force.</li><li>Control of workers' quarters was lost.</li><li>Troops fired on demonstrators in Znamenski Square; 80 were killed or wounded.</li><li>That evening there was a mutiny among recruits from the Guard regiments, who were training to go to the Front.</li></ul>
12th March	<ul><li>By 12th March, Petrograd was in the hands of the 'peasants in uniform'.</li><li>By the following night Nicholas, marooned in the royal train at Pskov, had abdicated.</li></ul>

Nicholas expected the throne to pass to his brother Michael, who refused it.

The Provisional Government

AQA B	✓
EDEXCEL A	✓
OCR B	✓
WJEC A	✓
WJEC B	✗
CCEA	✓

Dual Power

In Petrograd, the **revolutionary parties** realised what was happening. They formed a Soviet (Council). This had the loyalty of the army, the navy and the industrial workers.

The **Provisional Government** (a small group of Liberal and Socialist politicians led by Prince George Lvov) declared themselves in control. From the beginning **they ruled only because the Soviet allowed them to**. The Provisional Government and the Soviet, therefore, agreed to shared power in an arrangement known as 'Dual Power'.

Problems the Provisional Government couldn't change

The Provisional Government had to deal with the following problems:

- **The economy was in crisis**. Inflation, a goods shortage and a food famine, the breakdown in transport and huge mounting public debt meant that a loan had to be negotiated from Russia's Western allies, but this would only come if Russia stayed in the war.
- **The Provisional Government didn't represent the people**. It wanted success in war whereas most of the country wanted peace. Members were Liberals with some Socialist Revolutionaries. They were unrepresentative of the country as a whole, but they did promise elections.
- **Dual Power with the Soviet**. This could only continue if the Provisional Government kept to its agreement with the Soviet. This weakened their control over the army, the police and political control in Petrograd. The city became a mix of conflicting political groups.

Problems the Provisional Government made for themselves

The Provisional Government then made the situation worse for themselves:

- They proclaimed **free speech, freedom of the press and an amnesty for political prisoners**.
- They **delayed the redistribution of land** until after a national election for a Constituent Assembly, but they **postponed the election** hoping to successfully win the war and increase their own political standing.
- **The Liberals were forced out of the government** when the Milyukov Note was leaked, which committed Russia to an offensive war. The Liberals were replaced by Socialist Revolutionaries led by Oleg Kerensky, who became Prime Minister.
- They **could not prevent the return** to Petrograd of the firebrand Vladimir Ilych **Lenin**. Lenin proclaimed total opposition to them in his April Theses. 'Bread, Peace and Land' was a powerful programme, which started to gain support. They could find no evidence that he was a German spy, and did not imprison him.
- **An offensive against Austria–Hungary in June was a fiasco**. It led to a retreat. Communist agitation and army desertions were already common.
- In the 'June Days' they put down Bolshevik anti-war demonstrations in Petrograd with force. This ruined their reputation as the upholders of liberty.
- **They did not provide any leadership after June**, allowing the army to begin to dissolve and support for the Bolshevik Party to grow.
- The Commander-in-Chief of the army, **General Kornilov**, attempted to take troops to Petrograd to take control in late August. The railway workers resisted his coup and it resulted in the arming of the Bolshevik Red Guards.

KEY POINT

The Kornilov Coup was the decisive point. Before it, Bolsheviks were unpopular. After it, they were the defenders of the revolution.

PROGRESS CHECK

1. What was 'Dual Power'?
2. Who led the Provisional Government from July until November 1917?
3. Which group resisted the troops sent to Petrograd by General Kornilov?

1. Sharing power between the Provisional Government and the Petrograd Soviet. 2. Oleg Kerensky. 3. The railway workers.

9.4 The Bolshevik victory: October / November 1917

LEARNING SUMMARY	**After studying this section you should be able to understand:**
	• the contributions of Lenin and Trotsky to success in the October Revolution
	• why the Bolshevik Party was able to profit from the collapse of the Provisional Government

The contributions of Lenin and Trotsky

AQA B	✓
EDEXCEL A	✓
OCR B	✓
WJEC A	✓
WJEC B	✗
CCEA	✓

Lenin

Lenin made the Bolshevik Party into the real opposition:

- In early April Lenin was the only leader to predict the failure of the Provisional Government and he disentangled the Bolsheviks from their associations with it.
- He provided them with a programme, 'Bread, Peace and Land'.
- He gave them a strategy to change people's minds.
- Even before Lenin was forced back into exile in July, support for Bolshevism was growing among the population, in the army and in the navy stationed nearby at Kronstadt.
- He remained the acknowledged leader of the Bolsheviks, while 'on the run'.
- He finally decided on the necessity of revolution in October, overcoming the opposition of Kamenev and Zinoviev.
- The communists believed that Lenin led the proletariat to victory in the October Revolution.

> **KEY POINT**
>
> In communist terms, the proletariat is the industrial working class, and does not include either the free peasantry or the bourgeoisie (the middle class).

Trotsky

Trotsky ran the October Revolution:

- He was already famous as a Menshevik before he joined the Bolsheviks in June.
- This made him **Lenin's second in command**, displacing Stalin.
- He played an important role as **Chairman of the Petrograd Soviet**.
- He **chaired the Military Revolutionary Committee**, which actually ran the revolution in November.

The October Revolution

AQA B	✓
EDEXCEL A	✓
OCR B	✓
WJEC A	✓
WJEC B	✗
CCEA	✓

By October the Bolsheviks had majorities in the Petrograd and Moscow Soviets. All they needed to do was to **withdraw their support from the Provisional Government** to make it fall. Power changed hands without a shot being fired.

Lenin timed this for the occasion of the meeting of the National Congress of Soviets on 7th November. There, **Menshevik deputies were encouraged to walk out**, leaving Lenin free to declare that the revolution was the will of the people. At the same time, Red Guards, who had taken strategic bridges, railway stations and telephone exchanges beforehand, **took the Winter Palace** and arrested the Provisional Government.

> **PROGRESS CHECK**
>
> 1. Which two Bolsheviks opposed Lenin's intention to run a revolution?
> 2. As chairman of which Soviet committee did Trotsky run the revolution?
>
> 1. Kemenev and Zinoviev. 2. The Military Revolutionary Committee.

9.5 Bolshevik rule and its impact 1918–1928

LEARNING SUMMARY

After studying this section you should be able to understand:

- how Lenin and the Bolsheviks secured their hold on Russia
- why the Red (Bolshevik) forces were in such a strong position in the Civil War
- how they compromised with the peasantry in the New Economic Policy
- why the New Economic Policy eventually failed

The growth of dictatorship

AQA B	✓
EDEXCEL A	✓
OCR B	✓
WJEC A	✓
WJEC B	✗
CCEA	✓

Lenin and the Bolsheviks did not gain real power immediately after the revolution:
- The new government was a coalition between the Bolsheviks and the Left Social Revolutionaries.
- They ruled in the name of the Soviets.
- They had no control over the rest of the country.

Declarations on taking power

Lenin immediately issued two decrees, which gave his supporters much of what they expected from the revolution:

- **The Decree on Peace** called for a just peace with Germany, without losing power or land, or reparations. Trotsky was unable to stop the war without Germany's agreement. As Commissar for Foreign Affairs he relied on a policy of '**no peace no war**' for the next few weeks. Then the Germans began to advance again and the Russian Government had to hastily call for peace negotiations. **This meant surrender**.
- **The Decree on Land** nationalised all land but **allowed it to be redistributed to the peasants**. Lenin had stolen the whole Social Revolutionary Land Programme in a bid to gain popularity with the peasants.

> **KEY POINT**
>
> Lenin expected a civil war and knew that he had to gain popularity quickly. These decrees gave the Bolsheviks a huge advantage.

The Cheka

In December 1917 Lenin established the Cheka (Secret Police), under Felix Dzerzhinsky. This forerunner of the KGB had **rights to investigate, try and execute enemies of the state outside normal courts**. It was used to terrorise and remove opponents, and marked the beginning of the Bolshevik move towards violence.

The Constituent Assembly

> Most groups in the Civil War were fighting to have the Constituent Assembly restored.

Lenin could not refuse to allow the elections to the Constituent Assembly. The Socialist Revolutionaries won the election. The Bolsheviks came second, with majorities in Petrograd and Moscow. Unless they did something about it, the Constituent Assembly would meet in January 1918 and deprive the Bolsheviks of their claim to represent the people.

Deputies were threatened with violence. Bolshevik deputies jeered and disrupted their speeches. When the Socialist Revolutionary majority refused to adopt the entire Bolshevik programme, Lenin walked out with the rest of the Bolshevik deputies. The assembly hall was shut and guarded. The deputies decided they would be safer at home in the provinces.

The Treaty of Brest–Litovsk, 3rd March 1918

The Soviet Government (Bolsheviks and Socialist Revolutionaries) was forced into agreeing to a peace that gave Germany all her demands:
- The Russian army was demobilised.
- Finland, Estonia, Latvia and the Ukraine became independent (the Ukraine under German domination).

> Foreign powers would support the 'Whites' to force Russia back into the war with Germany.

This angered many patriotic Russians and increased the anti-Soviet forces gathering throughout Russia. A more serious type of civil war replaced the feeble opposition of ex-Tsarist generals. 'White' (anti-communist) governments sprang up, which were backed by the foreign powers: Britain, France, Japan and the USA.

The Socialist Revolutionaries left the government. They reverted to old tactics, assassinating leading Bolsheviks and the German ambassador. The Soviet Government resorted to terror, imprisoning or shooting those it considered opponents.

The Civil War

AQA B	✓
EDEXCEL A	✓
OCR B	✓
WJEC A	✓
WJEC B	✗
CCEA	✓

During the Civil War the power of the Soviets was reduced, while that of the Bolshevik dictatorship increased:
- Soviet congresses became less frequent.
- The Soviets lost control of the government, which listened more to the Bolshevik Party.
- Elections to the Soviets gradually stopped.

The war

1918	The Soviet Government consolidated its control on the **western centre of the country**.
1919	The Red Soviet troops **beat back a three-pronged attack** by Kolchak from the east, Denikin from the south and Yudenich from the north-west. This was the Whites' best chance for victory, but at the end of the year all three armies were beaten back so their **Western allies abandoned them**. Only Ukrainian nationalists and the Volunteer Army remained in the Crimea while the Japanese remained in the Far East.
1920	**Poland**, under General Pilsudski, **attacked the Ukraine**. Soviet cavalry, under Tukhachevsky, pushed them back towards Warsaw, but overreached themselves and had to sign a truce giving Poland a thin slice of Russian territory. This was finalised in the **Treaty of Riga in 1921**. Wrangel's troops (Wrangel had replaced Denikin) were destroyed and forced to evacuate the Crimea. The centre of the war passed to the Far East.
1921	The Japanese evacuated the Far East. The Kronstadt and Tambov revolts were put down with force and the Soviet Government was finally left in control.

Why did the Reds win?

Geography was to the Red advantage. They defended a central area with cities (Moscow and Petrograd) and the main armaments industries against disunited White forces attacking from the Black Sea, across Siberia and from Latvia. The railway system was centred on Moscow. This allowed the Reds to switch troops from Front to Front, which the Whites could not do. Immense distances had to be crossed to attack this area from the south and east, signalling the threat early enough for the Reds to pick off their enemies one by one.

Leadership was shown by Trotsky. He established the Red Army, with Tsarist officers blackmailed into serving faithfully. Lenin ran the policy of War Communism: the Soviets took the resources they needed at the risk of alienating the peasantry. Trotsky's charismatic generalship (helped by his armoured train) meant that risky decisions were taken. For example, in 1919 the Red Army concentrated on destroying Kolchak in Siberia, ignoring Denikin's advance from the south until he was perilously close to Moscow.

White command was always disunited. White forces frequently fought each other, or stood by while the Reds destroyed them piecemeal, as in 1920, when Wrangel and Petliura failed to unite with the Poles.

Propaganda favoured the Reds. They used **agitprop** trains to show films, distribute posters and news sheets.

The Reds had the great advantage of having given the land to the peasants: the Whites would give it back to the landowners. The Reds were not anti-semitic: the Whites attacked Jewish settlements. The result was that most peasant guerrilla risings favoured the Reds and destabilised the rear of the White armies. The Reds were seen as patriotic, freeing Russia from foreign invaders.

> **KEY POINT**
>
> In 1918 the Soviet capital had moved from Petrograd to Moscow. In 1920 the Bolshevik Party changed its name to the Communist Party.

The New Economic Policy

AQA B	✓
EDEXCEL A	✓
OCR B	✓
WJEC A	✓
WJEC B	✗
CCEA	✓

The Communist Government crisis in 1921

The crisis occurred due to a mixture of economic, social and political factors:

Economic chaos: By 1921 the peasants were refusing to plant more than they could eat for fear of confiscation. Towns were shrinking: Petrograd had only one third of its former population. A famine would kill about 5 million Russians by 1922.

Peasant problem: The biggest problem was that peasants were alienated by the confiscations of War Communism, and had no real links with the Communist Party. Lenin viewed them as a separate group within the country, with whom his proletariat would have to make an agreement.

Political problems: The Communist Party itself seemed to be splitting up internally between…

- those who wanted increased Party democracy, but inside the Party structure (Democratic Centralists) and others
- those who wanted a swift transition to a planned economy and workers' armies (Trotsky, Preobrazhensky)
- those who wanted more democracy based on Trade Union power (Alexandra Kollontai and the Workers' Opposition).

These 'platforms' threatened the existence of the Party. Its membership was falling and it was isolated in the country as a whole.

10th Party Congress

The 10th Party Congress was held in Petrograd in March 1921 against the background of a crisis. The delegates were used to stiffen the morale of the troops in putting down the **Kronstadt revolt**. The peasant uprising in **Tambov** took place at the same time.

The Congress passed two major resolutions to deal with the discipline problems:

These decrees were blamed for the move towards dictatorship within the Party after Lenin's death.

- **The Syndicalist and Anarchist Deviation** within the Party: this directly criticised the Workers' Opposition.
- **On Party Unity**: defined fractions within the Party as 'groups with special platforms' and called for their immediate dissolution on pain of expulsion.

The New Economic Policy (NEP)

Lenin enforced a **truce with the peasantry** at the 10th Party Congress. This was very different from War Communism:

- Forced requisitioning of farm produce was replaced by a smaller, more predictable, '**tax in kind**' (i.e. tax paid in produce) allowing peasants to sell their surplus on the free market.
- **Small-scale businesses were denationalised**, freeing a large sector of the market to return to normal.
- '**The commanding heights of industry**' (coal, steel, transport, etc.) remained in government hands.
- **A purge of Party membership**, a reduction in persecution of 'class enemies' and the creation of law codes to allow a return to normal life.

Why would the Communist Party dislike the NEP?

Many in the Communist Party hated these measures. They thought they were compromises. Lenin justified them as 'one step backward in order to take two steps forward'.

During the NEP, communist organisation was hugely strengthened. This made the later move to real dictatorship and centralised control possible. The Communist Party survived in control and the economy began to recover, but the NEP was never regarded as a permanent feature.

The short-term success of the NEP

The NEP seemed to be a success at first. It returned the economy to pre-1914 levels and gave the Communist Party the breathing space it needed to survive.

These figures compare production as a percentage of the 1913 level.

	Index of Industrial Production	Index of Agricultural Production
1913	100	100
1921	31	60
1924	45	90
1926	98	118
1928	132	124

The long-term failure of the NEP

In the long-term, however, the NEP failed:

The Communist Party thought that the economic disease of capitalism would infect the proletariat.

- **Growth slackened after 1926** and it was clear that, once the spare capacity in the economy had been taken up, the NEP would fail to maximise industrial development. There could be no communist future without industrialisation.
- The **Communist Party could not contemplate relying on free enterprise for very long**. They thought that it was morally wrong.
- The **Soviet Government was worried about their external security**. The Treaty of Locarno, 1925, weakened the important friendship between Russia and Germany since Brest–Litovsk. The Soviet Union (the new name for Russia) was worried that capitalist powers would re-invade Russia, especially after Britain broke off relations in May 1927, and communism suffered reverses in China in 1927. There were inescapable connections between defence and industrialisation.
- There were **problems within the economy**, especially the '**scissors crisis**'. From 1923 until 1926 particularly, agriculture increased output faster than industry. There was a 'goods famine' during which the peasantry made large amounts of money, but could not spend it. It was difficult to move this money into the development of heavy industry, as the government wished.

PROGRESS CHECK

1. Which White general attacked from the south in 1919?
2. Which party was directly criticised by the Communist Party in the resolution against 'The Syndicalist and Anarchist Deviation'?
3. Why would the Treaty of Locarno weaken the important friendship between Russia and Germany?

1. General Denikin.
2. The Workers' Opposition.
3. Because Germany was entering the League of Nations. The price would be to protect Europe from the Soviet Union.

9.6 The nature of Stalin's dictatorship

LEARNING SUMMARY	After studying this section you should be able to understand:
	• how Stalin was able to take complete control
	• how far the Soviet Union benefited from industrialisation and collectivisation
	• how Stalin increased his hold on the Communist Party through the purges

The leadership struggle

AQA B	✓
EDEXCEL A	✓
OCR B	✓
WJEC A	✗
WJEC B	✗
CCEA	✓

Lenin's illness and death

In 1918, **Lenin was shot twice** by a Socialist Revolutionary, Dora Kaplan. He seemed to recover, but suffered a stroke in May 1922. He returned to work in October, suffered a second stroke in December, a third in March 1923 and died with a final stroke in January 1924. From 1923 to his death in 1924, Lenin was seriously disabled.

During the whole of this period, Lenin's personal well-being was in the hands of Joseph Stalin. He was deputed by the Politburo to provide for his recovery.

Stalin and the General Secretaryship

Stalin had made a serious political mistake when, as Commissar for Nationalities, he had used force to subdue the Georgian Communist Party in 1921. A new post was found for him in April 1922 as **General Secretary of the Communist Party**. This was not a promotion, but a step down to an administrative post.

> **KEY POINT**
>
> In the structure of the Communist Party, the Central Committee of the Communist Party was supposed to be most powerful, but in fact its important decisions were made in its committees: the Politburo for policy, the Orgburo for Party organisation and personnel, and the Secretariat for business organisation.

The strain of the Secretaryship had killed Yakov Sverdlov, the first Secretary. However, the General Secretary was crucial in the power struggles following Lenin's retirement:

• It brought membership of the three crucial organisations that ruled the Party: the Politburo, Orgburo and Secretariat.
• In charge of the Orgburo, Stalin directed personnel to carry out Politburo decisions and filled positions within the Party hierarchy.
• As Secretary, Stalin controlled the flow of information to the Politburo, wrote its agendas and minutes and controlled many other areas of Party organisation.

Figure 9.2 Lenin and Stalin in 1922, during Lenin's first illness. This picture was used by Stalin to demonstrate their 'closeness'. Its truthfulness has been questioned.

The struggle against Trotsky

Trotsky was the most able member of the leadership but he was disliked:

- He had only joined the Bolshevik Party in August 1917, when success was already likely.
- He had not served a long apprenticeship as others had within the Party.
- He was arrogant and insensitive.
- Many thought that he would take over and become a dictator when Lenin died.

Ranged against Trotsky in the Politburo in 1923, was a group known as the **Troika**: Stalin, Zinoviev and Kamenev.

There were two important disagreements between Trotsky and the Troika:

- **Bureaucratisation**: In a letter to the Central Committee in late 1923, Trotsky roundly criticised the lack of democracy within the Party, the practice of filling key posts through nomination by the Orgburo and the dominance of full time officials. This attack on Party bureaucracy was supported by the so-called 'Platform of the 46', a group of dissatisfied Congress members. It directly criticised the power of the Troika.
- **'Socialism in One Country'**: Lenin and Trotsky had always maintained that the victory of socialism (communism) in Russia would be accompanied by world revolution. However, by 1923 it was looking increasingly unlikely that communist revolution would sweep Europe. Stalin argued that communism could be achieved in Russia independently of international revolution. By showing his belief in the capacity of the Russian proletariat, Stalin was able to win most of the Communist Party onto his side.

On 17th January 1925, Trotsky was removed as War Commissar. He kept his membership of the Politburo for a short time longer.

The struggle against the Left opposition

In 1925 the Troika fell apart. Zinoviev and Kamenev recognised that Stalin, and not Trotsky was the greatest threat to their own leadership ambitions.

In 1925 Zinoviev published *Leninism: An Introduction to the Study of Leninism*. He no longer supported the NEP and now attacked 'Socialism in One Country', supporting Trotsky's view of the importance of international revolution.

Stalin packed the 14th Congress, in December 1925, with his own supporters. He defeated Kamenev and Zinoviev's group.

The struggle against the united opposition

At the 14th Congress, Zinoviev had called for all oppositionists, who had left active Party life, to combine to oppose Stalin.

An alliance of Trotsky with Zinoviev and Kamenev was tried. It was unsuccessful. Trotsky and Kamenev were removed from their Politburo membership in October 1926 after denunciation from the Party and the press.

In early 1927, they organised public demonstrations against the government. Stalin had Kamenev and Trotsky expelled from the Party in December 1927.

Trotsky was sent into internal exile at Alma Ata and, a year later, into foreign exile. Kamenev and Zinoviev were sent to Kaluga, but were readmitted to the Party the next year.

The struggle against the Right opposition

In January and February 1928 Stalin resorted to forcible grain collection. He was criticised in private by Bukharin, Rykov and Tomsky, who also condemned his policy of rapid industrialisation.

The conflict continued in private in 1928 and 1929. The Right was steadily undermined.

By late 1929 Stalin and his supporters launched an open campaign of denunciation in the press. The opposition signed a reversal of their views. The Central Committee removed Bukharin from the Politburo and censured Rykov and Tomsky.

> **KEY POINT**
>
> Stalin was left supreme as all the leaders with potential support in the lower ranks of the Party had been routed.

Collectivisation

AQA B	✓
EDEXCEL A	✓
OCR B	✓
WJEC A	✗
WJEC B	✗
CCEA	✓

Stalin's intentions

By 1928 the peasantry was refusing to supply grain in the quantities necessary to feed the towns, because they could not buy goods in exchange.

Stalin sent out requisitioning squads in a return to the practices of War Communism, worsening the problem, and effectively ending the NEP. He did this because…
- he saw the peasantry as an opposition group; they had never joined the Communist Party in large numbers

- he blamed profiteering by peasants for their refusal to supply grain, specifically the **Kulaks** (prosperous peasants)
- he needed to confiscate capital to pay for industrial change and the beginning of the Five-Year Plan.

Stalin wanted to…
- destroy private agriculture, forcibly establish collective farms and reduce peasants to tied agricultural workers
- destroy the Kulaks as a class.

By taking over all agriculture he would be able to run it more efficiently, supply grain to the towns more steadily and export grain in exchange for agricultural machinery. The government would dominate the countryside as never before.

The policy was unplanned, ill-informed and carried out in a confused way. In January 1930 the Central Committee said collectivisation had to be completed in major grain-producing areas by autumn 1930 or spring 1931. In other areas the deadline was autumn 1931 or spring 1932 at the latest.

Results of collectivisation

Collectivisation had the following results:
- There was a myth of popular enthusiasm. In fact it was met with sullen resentment and even armed opposition.
- Collectivisation was carried out forcibly: village buildings were destroyed and Kulaks arrested.
- The chaos was so great that, in March 1930, Stalin had to call a temporary halt. This meant that the proportion of the peasantry in the new collective farms fell by 60% in three months. The process was restarted after the harvest.
- Peasants destroyed livestock, produce and tools rather than surrender them to the state.
- Extensive grain procurements and a reduction in production led to famine in the Ukraine and North Caucasus in 1933. As many as 10 million people may have died.
- Party control over the countryside was established, and private ownership destroyed. Internal passports were reintroduced in 1932.
- Land was nationalised and production targets and delivery quotas set by the state. Never again would the peasantry hold the state to ransom.
- From 1935, private plots of land were allowed. By 1937 these produced 50% to 70% of marketable vegetables, fruit, meat and milk.

These figures compare production as a percentage of the 1913 level.

	Index	Grain harvest	Cattle	Pigs	Sheep	Goats
1913	100					
1928	124	74.5m tonnes	60.1m	22.0m	97.3m	9.7m
1933	101	69.5	33.5	9.9	34.0	3.3
1936	109	57.0	46.0	25.9	43.8	6.1
1940	141	97.1	47.8	22.5	66.6	10.1

The Five-Year Plans

AQA B	✓
EDEXCEL A	✓
OCR B	✓
WJEC A	✗
WJEC B	✗
CCEA	✓

The Five-Year Plans intended to...

- provide the **machinery**, such as tractors, to mechanise farming
- **catch up with the Western world**, to make Russia less dependent on the West for industrial goods
- ensure a **strong armaments industry** so that Russia could defend herself.

Stalin believed in state planning. The state would decide what was to be produced and how, when and where. It would decide prices and wages. Stalin decided on three Five-Year Plans.

First Five-Year Plan 1928–1932:

- Emphasised heavy industry (coal, oil, iron and steel and electricity) to lay the foundations for future industrial advance.
- A total of 1,500 new industrial plants were built and 100 new towns.
- Was completed within four years.

Figure 9.3 A Soviet poster of 1929: enemies of the Five-Year Plan

Second Five-Year Plan 1933–1937:

- Heavy industry remained top priority, but communications, especially railways, were important.
- Chemicals and metallurgy industries grew enormously.

Third Five-Year Plan 1938–1941 (cut short by the War):

- More and more resources were switched into armaments: tanks, planes and weapons.

Effects of the Five-Year Plans

	Total Index	Producer Goods Index	Consumer Goods Index
1913	100	100	100
1928	132	155	120
1932	267	424	187
1933	281	450	196
1937	588	1013	373
1938	657	1138	415
1940	852	1554	497

These figures compare production as a percentage of the 1913 level.

The Five-Year Plans had the following effects:

- There was a huge increase in the production of industry along with the building of railways, canals (Belomore Canal), dams (Dneipr Dam), gigantic factories (Stalingrad tractor works) and new cities (Magnetogorsk).
- There were a variety of social changes:
  - the urban population more than doubled
  - more than 9 million peasants left the land during the First Five-Year Plan alone: squalid urban conditions, poor transport and services and a serious housing shortage resulted.
- A lack of jobs reduced labour discipline, but the sabotage scare introduced fear into the workplace. The Stakhanovite Movement 1935–1936 tried to stimulate workers by producing positive role models.

> **KEY POINT**
>
> Within the economy, industry became the dominant sector and the government became the dominant power.

Stalin's purges

AQA B	✓
EDEXCEL A	✓
OCR B	✓
WJEC A	✗
WJEC B	✗
CCEA	✓

Stalin consolidated his power as dictator of the Soviet Union in much the same way as Hitler did in Germany. He exerted totalitarian control through...

- terror imposed through secret police and labour camps
- state control of education, arts and sciences, propaganda and censorship
- a single-party state.

During the 1930s the huge disruption to the population and economic life caused by industrialisation and collectivisation created great political controversy, but Stalin secured his position by making it too dangerous to criticise the government publicly. He extended his terror into the factories (in his campaigns against sabotage) and against Party rivals (in the Great Purges).

Sergei Kirov

Kirov had been popular in Leningrad since the 1920s (Petrograd was renamed Leningrad in 1924).

In 1934, when the collectivisation crisis was over, many thought it was time to slow down economic change and improve relations with the peasantry. Kirov championed these views at the 17th Party Congress and emerged as the popular alternative to Stalin. Shortly afterwards he was shot inside the Party offices in Leningrad.

Stalin gave him a state funeral, but there is little doubt who was responsible. The murder was the excuse for a spate of arrests.

The 1936 purges

In 1936 Stalin began a greater purge of all those he suspected within the Party.

Zinoviev and Kamenev were accused with 14 others of the murder of Kirov and of supporting Trotsky.

In the show trials, watched by the world, they confessed to laughable charges, such as that they had tried to murder Lenin. Despite their 'confessions', Zinoviev, Kamenev and the others were all executed.

Later purges

Thousands of other Communist Party members were denounced from 1936 to 1938.

In 1937 there were show trials of senior officials accused of sabotage and spying. In 1938 Bukharin, Rykov and Yagoda were shot.

Results of the purges

The results of the purges were:
- Over one fifth of the membership of the Communist Party was expelled or shot.
- Of 1,961 delegates to the 17th Party Congress in 1934, 1,108 were arrested.
- Of 139 Central Committee members, over 90 were shot.
- Five out of 11 Politburo members in 1934 died.
- Marshall Tukhachevsky and seven other generals, heroes of the Civil War, were shot.
- 90% of all Soviet generals and thousands of army and airforce officers were shot or imprisoned, with the result that Soviet armed forces were left in a desperate situation at the beginning of the Second World War.
- The purges slowed in 1938, but by 1939 it is estimated that over 20 million Russians had been transported to labour camps.
- Stalin's position was unchallengeable.

PROGRESS CHECK

1. By what name was the opposition to Trotsky in 1923 known?
2. Which peasant group did Stalin destroy as a class?
3. Name three great constructions of the Five Year Plans.

3. **Any three from:** Belomore Canal; Dniepr Dam; Stalingrad Tractor Works; Magnetogorsk.
2. The Kulaks.
1. The Troika.

Sample GCSE questions

(a) In 1917, which political party had a majority of the support in Russia as a whole and among which group was it particularly strong?

The Social Revolutionaries, who had particularly strong support from the peasantry. **(4)**

> It is important to answer both parts of the question.

(b) Why did the Bolshevik Party win the Civil War?

They had geographical advantages of being central with a large population and good communications. They dominated the railway system and had most of the heavy industries in Moscow and Petrograd. Bolshevik leadership was very effective. Trotsky set up the Red Army and took risks to deal with Kolchak while ignoring Denikin in 1919. Lenin took the risk of losing peasant support by running War Communism, which gave the Reds the supplies they needed. Red propaganda was better than the Whites'. The Reds convinced everyone that they were fighting for Russia against the foreigners. Lenin had given the peasants the land and they didn't want to lose it. The Reds used mass communication from Agitprop trains, plays, films and posters. The Whites tried to return land to landowners and attacked the Jewish populations. **(6)**

> There are three good reasons here with plenty of extra examples.

(c) 'The New Economic Policy was a serious setback for the Communist Party'. Do you agree with this statement? Explain your answer.

In one sense, the NEP was a serious setback for the Communist Party. They had won control in the Civil War and the NEP would reverse this to give comparative freedom in economic life. Whereas War Communism had given the Communist Party control of both the factories and the output of the peasant farmers, the New Economic Policy reversed this, so that the peasants were allowed to make profits like capitalist farmers, and pre-revolutionary managers regained control of most of Russian industry.

> This case represents a clear point-of-view, but also evaluates it in the last sentence.

Lenin called the NEP `one step backward to take two steps forward'. It was not the NEP itself that caused the setback, but the impossible position in 1921, when industry was at a standstill, the peasantry was in revolt, the Communist Party was shrinking and there was a serious chance that the Party would lose power unless it followed more popular policies. The NEP was a constructive response to this because it won a short period of truce during which the economy could recover and the Communist Party could rebuild its power. By 1926 the Soviet economy had achieved the output of 1913, and by 1928, when the next crisis came, the Communist Party was able to dominate the situation.

> Here the opposite point-of-view shows that the NEP was the only way forward.

Seen as a short-term policy, the NEP was remarkably successful for the Communist Party, though it was not a direct route to real communism. **(10)**

Exam practice questions

1 **(a)** Who opposed Stalin's rise to power during the 1920s?

....

....

....

.... **(4)**

(b) Why did Stalin decide to collectivise agriculture?

....

....

....

....

.... **(6)**

(c) How successful was Stalin's programme of collectivisation?

....

....

....

....

....

....

....

....

....

....

....

....

.... **(10)**

You may need to continue your answers on a separate sheet of paper.

10 Germany 1918–1945

The following topics are covered in this chapter:

- **The weakness of the Weimar Republic**
- **Hitlers rise to power**
- **Nazi control of Germany 1933–1945**
- **Life in Nazi Germany 1933–1945**

10.1 The weakness of the Weimar Republic

LEARNING SUMMARY

After studying this section you should be able to understand:

- how defeat gave the new German Republic little chance of success
- how the Weimar Republic was able to survive during its first disastrous years
- how the work of Gustav Stresemann helped to restore stability in the mid 1920s
- how weak the Republic remained when it was struck by the Wall Street Crash in 1929

How defeat caused a Socialist Weimar Republic

AQA B	✓
EDEXCEL A	✓
OCR B	✓
WJEC A	✓
WJEC B	✓
CCEA	✓

Defeat

Germany had refused President Wilson's Fourteen Points and in 1918 gambled on her first major offensive since 1914, the Ludendorff Offensive. The result was disastrous. By November she could fight no more and she surrendered unconditionally in the Armistice on 11th November.

> The end of the First World War and the Treaty of Versailles are explained in detail in Chapter 3.

Disaster

The Kaiser had fled to Holland. Ludendorff organised a parliamentary republic, but also thought that Germany had been let down by the Socialists and war profiteers, who would now form the new government. This is the origin of Hitler's myth of the 'stab in the back'.

Economic and political chaos

The war had caused economic and political chaos:

- Germany had **lost two 2 million men** and over **6 million had been wounded**.
- Her **currency had lost 75% of its value** between 1913 and 1918.
- Germany was **split between the extremes** of the Independent Socialist Party, on the Left, and the Fatherland Party, on the Right.

- After the 'turnip winter' of 1917–18, Germany suffered a major flu epidemic, with thousands dying each day at its height. **In 1918, 293,000 died from starvation and hypothermia**.

Revolution

In October 1918 the **sailors of Kiel and Wilhelmshaven mutinied**. Prince Max of Baden handed control to Friedrich Ebert, a moderate socialist, to try to maintain control while agreeing to the surrender.

In January 1919 a further wave of **Spartacist (communist) unrest** made it impossible to convene at the new National Assembly in Berlin. It met at Weimar, in February 1919, and had drawn up the Weimar Constitution by August.

> **KEY POINT**
>
> The Weimar Republic refers to government under the Weimar Constitution. It does not refer to a political party.

The impact of the Treaty of Versailles on the Republic

AQA B	✓
EDEXCEL A	✓
OCR B	✓
WJEC A	✓
WJEC B	✓
CCEA	✓

The new Weimar Republic had to shoulder the blame for the disastrous Treaty of Versailles.

The Treaty of Versailles

Germany rejected the Treaty of Versailles but was forced to sign it in June 1919. The alternative was war and total destruction. People were shocked by the Treaty:

- **Millions of Germans were given to neighbouring states**, while they were left with too few soldiers to defend themselves.
- Their government had been excluded from the negotiations, and the Treaty was imposed.

> **KEY POINT**
>
> Adolf Hitler called The Treaty of Versailles a '**Diktat**' (dictated peace) and thought it should be destroyed.

- **War guilt** was imposed upon Germany in order to justify making her pay **reparations** to the Allies. The final reparation bill was decided in 1921: a staggering £6,600 million in gold or manufactures.

Political instability

The Weimar Republic was blamed for Germany's humiliation at Versailles, which weakened the new democracy. Its first years were troubled by constant instability.

January and March 1919	**Spartacist rising** in Berlin: more than 1,200 killed by the army, under General Groener. A **Soviet Republic** was declared in Bavaria.
March 1920	**Wolfgang Kapp** led rightist nationalist Freikorps (disbanded soldiers) in their own bid for power in Berlin. They were defeated by a general strike. The communists formed the Ruhr Army (50,000 workers) to resist the Freikorps and the army. Ebert granted concessions, and then used the army. Over 1,000 workers and 250 police were killed by 1923.
June 1922	Assassination of the Foreign Minister, Walther Rathenau, by right-wing terrorists. They disliked his Jewish origins and he had attempted to improve the Treaty of Versailles.
January 1923	French and Belgian troops invaded the Ruhr to extract reparations by force.
Summer 1923	Economic collapse followed by communist strikes in Saxony, suppressed by government troops in October.
November 1923	The Munich Putsch (see page 169).

Constitutional problems

The Weimar Republic was also undermined by its own constitution, based on **proportional representation**, which was unable to provide support for strong measures. Socialist support plummeted from 38% in 1919 to 21% in 1920 and couldn't hold governments together for long.

> **KEY POINT**
>
> Proportional representation and coalition government: members of the Reichstag were elected in exactly the same proportion as the votes cast for them in the election. This often led to weak coalition governments made up of an unstable group of parties.

Hyperinflation

> **KEY POINT**
>
> Hyperinflation is rapidly accelerating inflation in which prices rise ten or one hundred-fold within a month.

In 1923 the German mark lost its value. War debts, the impossibility of selling goods to a poverty-stricken population and the invasion of the Ruhr by the French and the Belgians had destroyed the economy.

Date	1914	1919	1920	1922	1923 Jan	1923 Jul	1923 Sep	1923 Nov
Marks to the $	4.2	8.9	14.0	191.8	17,792	353,412	98,860,000	200,000,000,000

The recovery of the Weimar Republic 1923–1929

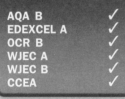

AQA B	✓
EDEXCEL A	✓
OCR B	✓
WJEC A	✓
WJEC B	✓
CCEA	✓

During the period 1923–1929 the Republic seemed to overcome its difficulties.

Gustav Stresemann

In August 1923, Gustav Stresemann, the leader of the German People's Party, became Chancellor.

> **KEY POINT**
>
> In Germany the **Chancellor** is the Prime Minister.

Stresemann...
- put down communist governments in Saxony and Thuringia
- ended the hyperinflationary crisis by issuing the **Rentenmark** (in November 1923)
- defeated Hitler's Munich Putsch.

Although his government fell, Stresemann was able to remain influential as Foreign Minister:
- April 1924 – he reorganised reparations in Germany's favour in the **Dawes Plan** (see below).
- 1925 – he made peace with France in the **Locarno Treaty**, guaranteeing that each country was safe from invasion by the other and finally sending home French troops from the Ruhr.
- 1926 – he took Germany into the **League of Nations**.
- June 1929 – he renegotiated the foreign loans in the **Young Plan** (see below). Prosperity began to look secure. Then in October 1929 Stresemann died. On 29th October came the Wall Street Crash, which plunged Germany and the world into depression.

> The Dawes Plan was negotiated by the Allies and bankers organised by the American Charles Dawes.

The Dawes Plan 1924–1929

The Dawes Plan...
- did not reduce the huge reparations bill, set in 1921
- reduced the initial payments to allow German industry to re-equip itself
- allowed reparations schedules to be met by loans
- helped stabilise the new Rentenmark
- said that after five years, a second negotiation would decide on repayment of loans and reparations.

The Dawes Plan bump-started the German economy, at the expense of the country, raising even larger loans. During this period more was lent to Germany than was repaid. Certainly, Germany seemed better off in the short term.

The Young Plan 1929–1932

The Young Plan...
- reduced the reparations from 132,000 to 37,000 million marks
- reduced annual payments further, spreading them out over 58 years
- ended Allied control of the railways, Reichsbank and customs duties
- withdrew Allied troops from Germany.

The weaknesses of the Weimar period

The Weimar period lasted until Hitler became Chancellor in January 1933, but the last years, from 1929 to 1933, were a period of increasing economic and political crisis.
- **The early years of democracy had shown that the Weimar Republic was weak** and could be coerced. Hindenburg, who became President in 1926 on the death of Ebert, was one of many who did not believe in democracy.
- **The Dawes Plan stabilised the regime to some degree, but at the cost of mortgaging the future** and persuading many that the Allies should not be bought off by agreeing to the Versailles Settlement.
- **Prosperity was uneven.** There was an unemployment crisis in 1926; the rate of industrial growth was low and Weimar had proclaimed an ambitious Welfare State, for which it was unable to pay in the longer term.

10.2 Hitler's rise to power

LEARNING SUMMARY

After studying this section you should be able to understand:

- how Hitler's early life prepared him to become leader of Germany
- why the Nazi Party gained little success in the 1920s, but much during the Depression
- what led to Hitler becoming Chancellor of Germany
- how Hitler was able to move from Chancellor to Führer between 1933 and 1934

Hitler's early life

AQA B	✓
EDEXCEL A	✓
OCR B	✓
WJEC A	✓
WJEC B	✓
CCEA	✓

Adolf Hitler...

- was an Austrian Catholic born in 1889
- worked hard at first, but later became unmanageable and left school early, in 1905
- drifted to Vienna, where he failed to gain entry to the Vienna Academy of Fine Arts, and then to Munich in 1913
- was quick to join a Bavarian regiment when war was declared in 1914.

> Munich is in Bavaria, a state in southern Germany.

His army career

In the German army, Hitler found his purpose in life:

- He was an exemplary soldier, a battalion messenger.
- He won the Iron Cross twice.
- He rose only to corporal because he was thought to lack leadership qualities.
- He was wounded in 1916, gassed in 1918 and in hospital when he heard of Germany's defeat.

How he joined the Nazi Party

Hitler...

- was an 'education officer' in the Bavarian army's political section
- joined **Anton Drexler's** German Workers' Party (DAP)
- drew up the Twenty-five Point Programme with Drexler in February 1920 and changed the Party's name to the Nazi Party.

What the Nazi Party stood for in the 1920s

AQA B	✓
EDEXCEL A	✓
OCR B	✓
WJEC A	✓
WJEC B	✓
CCEA	✓

The Nazi Party Twenty-five Point Programme

The Twenty-five Point Programme showed that the Nazi Party believed in…
- anti-semitism
- survival of the fittest (Social Darwinism)
- German nationalism
- authoritarian leadership.

> **KEY POINT**
>
> Anti-semitism means hatred of Jews.

The Beer Hall Putsch

> **KEY POINT**
>
> Putsch means the taking of power by a small, armed group – a coup d'état.

By 1923 the Nazi Party had 55,000 members in Bavaria with its own paramilitary force, the SA. Hitler was disgusted that Stresemann negotiated payment of reparations, apparently agreeing to the Versailles Treaty. He tried to take power in Bavaria.

To find out why Ludendorff was famous, see Chapter 2 on the First World War.

8th November	• Hitler and his SA burst into a meeting held by **General von Lossow** (Army commander in Bavaria) and **Gustav von Kahr** (Head of State of Bavaria) in a beer hall in Munich. • He demanded their support for his seizure of power and his replacement of von Lossow with General Ludendorff as army commander. • Thousands of SA arrested other members of the Bavarian Government, but failed to gain control of the army barracks.
9th November	• President Ebert declared a national state of emergency. • Ludendorff persuaded Hitler to march into Munich as the first step to Berlin. • About 2,000 SA marched towards the military base in Munich where armed police and soldiers met them; 14 Nazis were killed. • Hitler fled: Ludendorff was arrested.
11th November	Hitler was arrested; Nazis were banned.

In early 1924 Hitler was tried for treason. He turned the trial into a platform from which to attack the Weimar Government. The trial, just before the elections, allowed the Nazis to become the third largest group in Bavaria.

Ludendorff was acquitted and Hitler was sentenced to the minimum five years in prison for treason. He was released after only nine months in December 1924. He used the time to write *Mein Kampf*, 'My Struggle', which was published in 1925. Between 1933 and 1945 it remained the best-selling German book, a mixture of autobiography and statement of beliefs. Hitler grew wealthy on the profits.

Nazi failure before 1930

AQA B	✓
EDEXCEL A	✓
OCR B	✓
WJEC A	✓
WJEC B	✓
CCEA	✓

Strength of the moderate parties in the Weimar Republic

The Nazi Party made little headway during the 1920s, when the Weimar Republic was strong.

- **After 1923 the Weimar Republic was more stable**, with no attempted coups or assassinations between 1924 and 1929.
- After 1924, **voters switched** back to voting for the moderate parties, which supported the Weimar Constitution.
- The government was strengthened when the **Nationalist Party** (DNVP), representing the most influential and propertied part of the population and the army, threw its weight behind the Constitution.
- **Hindenburg**, the new President, did not really believe in the Republic, but was now under oath to protect it.

Weakness of the Nazis

The Nazi Party was weak during the 1920s:

- While Hitler was in prison, the Nazi Party fell apart.
- On his release, Hitler was banned from public speaking until 1927.
- The Nazis were only well-known in Bavaria and had no organisation in the rest of Germany.
- British historian Ian Kershaw called the Nazi Party a 'fringe irritant'. The Reich Ministry of the Interior in 1927 said they were: 'a numerically insignificant… radical-revolutionary splinter group incapable of exerting any noticeable influence on the great mass of the population and the course of political events.' (Ian Kershaw, *Hitler, 1889–1936*)

Reorganisation of the Nazi Party

> There was not enough time for these changes to take effect during the 1920s, but they allowed the Nazi Party to take advantage of the Depression later.

On his release from prison in December 1924, Hitler changed Nazi Party tactics away from revolution and towards gaining democratic control:

- He took supreme power over the party, asserted the **Leadership Principle**, and reorganised the Party's structure, strategy and symbols (e.g. he designed the **Swastika flag**).
- He used Weimar democracy to gain control, rather than attempting another putsch.
- He used propaganda to target specific grievances, using local speakers.
- He used the Nazi Party's own newspaper, the *Völkischer Beobachter* to spread its ideas.
- He extended party organisation throughout Germany, and so changed the emphasis of the Party from being a southern German and specifically Bavarian party, to being a national party.

> **KEY POINT**
>
> The Nazi Party had concentrated its efforts in Bavaria, a largely Catholic area in southern Germany. The Catholic Church had its own party, called the Centre. When the Nazis extended their efforts into Protestant, agricultural and small town areas in the north of Germany (Schleswig-Holstein) they began to have success.

Hitler developed a powerful message. He...

- stressed the national community of all Germans
- promised to solve economic problems and provide bread
- paid special attention to the needs of the small trader and the peasant, who would be saved from 'the clutch of the Jewish moneylenders'
- promised to smash the Weimar Constitution and provide strong leadership
- preached nationalism and promised to destroy the Versailles Treaty.

These strategies eventually brought success, but not until the Weimar Republic was destroyed by the Depression.

Success in elections 1928–1933

AQA B ✓
EDEXCEL A ✓
OCR B ✓
WJEC A ✓
WJEC B ✓
CCEA ✓

Changes in Nazi tactics and the growth of unemployment transformed Nazi fortunes.

The effects of the Wall Street Crash on Germany

By 1929 Hitler and the Nazi Party were well placed to benefit from any disaster suffered by the ruling coalition. Between 1929 and 1932 the Depression hit Germany particularly hard. This was because it was so dependent on foreign loans and the government was so indecisive.

	1929	1932
Unemployment (millions)	1.4	5.6
Wages (1913 = 100)	169	113
Government income 1928–9 (bn RM)	9.0	6.6
Government expenditure on Welfare Services (per person in marks)	102	106

> Between the elections of May 1928 and July 1932, the percentage of votes cast for the Nazi Party in Reichstag elections leapt from 2.6% to 37.4%.

No one could afford to buy goods. Unemployment rose but unemployment pay was cut. This caused major disagreements and the fall of the government. Although government expenditure on welfare services increased a little, its income fell by one third. By 1933 Germany appeared bankrupt.

> **KEY POINT**
>
> Deflation is the opposite of inflation. Goods become worth less because there are too many of them.

The weakness of the government

Between March 1930 and January 1933, **none of the three governments of Brüning, Papen and Schleicher was able to rule with a majority** in the Reichstag. President Hindenburg had to use his powers under the Weimar Constitution to rule by decree. This was because parties would not agree over whether to tax workers or employers in order to pay the unemployed. Others argued that unemployment benefits should be cut.

In 1930, Chancellor **Brüning called an election**, allowing remarkable gains for the extremist Nazi and Communist Parties, and **making the Reichstag even more unmanageable**.

Although **President Hindenburg** acted constitutionally, it is quite clear that **he preferred to rule by decree** rather than allow Communist or Nazi Parties into power. He refused Hitler's demand to be made Chancellor.

Hitler's tactics

Hitler **gained support from industrialists** such as Alfred Hugenburg and Fritz Thyssen because of their reaction against the Young Plan. This provided money and media coverage. However, most financial support still came from ordinary people's contributions at meetings.

The **Sturm-Abteilung (SA) founded in 1920, gave invaluable support**. They provided over 100 'martyrs' to the cause and focused attention against the communists. Their disciplined militarism attracted the German people.

> **KEY POINT**
>
> By 1930 the SA was a huge army of young men and ex-soldiers. Led by Ernst Roehm, they were provided with free brown shirts, meals and sometimes accommodation in hostels. They distributed propaganda leaflets, protected Nazi meetings from disruption and tried to destroy the communists.

Hitler, himself, was important to Nazi success. He used his own oratorical power to sway vast crowds. He refused to co-operate with any other party unless he was given the Chancellorship and power to rule without the Reichstag. The Nazis were not involved in the failure of other parties during the Depression. Support for the Nazis rose at each election.

He used the latest **technology**: loudspeakers, slide shows, films and the first aerial political campaign, 'Führer over Germany' in the 1932 presidential election.

The bargain that brought Hitler to power

April 1932	• President **Hindenburg** had been re-elected President. He **dismissed Brüning's government**. The new government, under **Papen, had support from less than 10% of the electorate**. In an election in July, the extremist Communist and Nazis Parties won over half the Reichstag seats between them. • **Hitler demanded to be made Chancellor**. He also demanded an Enabling Act to allow him to rule by decree (reducing the President's power). Hindenburg refused. • Papen could not control the new Reichstag, which was suspended after only one day. • Papen wanted to rule without the Reichstag, but Schleicher, leader of the Nationalists, tried to create a 'diagonal front' uniting some of the trade unions and the Nazis. Schleicher persuaded Hindenburg to dismiss Papen and appoint himself Chancellor, but his attempts to unite left and right failed. Hindenburg rejected Schleicher's request to be allowed to rule by decree.
November 1932	• There was another election. The **Nazi vote fell to 33%**. • The new Reichstag was as impossible to control as the old. • Papen constructed a government around Hitler. **Hitler would be Chancellor**, Papen Vice Chancellor, and General von Blomberg Defence Minister (for army support). • Hindenburg had no other alternative but to appoint Hitler Chancellor, but neither he nor Papen appreciated that they would become puppets.

Democracy was not working, even before Hitler destroyed it.

Hitler's consolidation of power 1933–4

AQA B	✓
EDEXCEL A	✓
OCR B	✓
WJEC A	✓
WJEC B	✓
CCEA	✓

30th January 1933	Hitler appointed Chancellor	Only three Nazis in the government.
27th February	Reichstag fire	Probably started by Dutch communist van der Lubbe acting alone, but Hitler blamed it on the Communist Party.
28th February	Decree of the Reich President for the protection of the nation and the state	• Hindenburg suspended all civil rights. • People could be held indefinitely in protective custody. • Used to repress the Communist Party.
5th March	Elections	• Nazi opponents intimidated. • Nazis won 44% of the vote. Their allies, the Nationalists, gained 8%.
24th March	Enabling Act	• The Reichstag met in the Opera House. Members were intimidated by SA (see page 172) and SS (see page 176). • Gave emergency powers to the Government to issue decrees and rule without the Reichstag for four years.
7th April	Law for the restoration of the professional civil service	The first anti-Jewish measure: Jews and other 'aliens' were purged from administration, courts, schools and universities.
1st May	May-Day holiday	International Labour Day made a public holiday. The day after, trade union offices were abolished.
14th July	Law against the formation of new parties	Germany became a one-party state.
12th November	New elections	Nazi Party won 92% of the vote.
January 1934	Law for the reconstruction of the state	State governments overthrown and replaced by Nazi governors.
30th June	Night of the Long Knives	SS shot von Roehm and many other leaders (e.g. Schleicher) who were seen as a threat.
2nd August	Death of President Hindenburg.	Hitler became Führer (Chancellor and President: Leader).

10.3 Nazi control of Germany 1933–1945

LEARNING SUMMARY

After studying this section you should be able to understand:
- how the Nazis controlled Germany
- how the Nazi state tried to purge itself of racial minorities and the disabled
- the effects of the Second World War on Nazi power

The Nazi revolution in government

AQA B	✓
EDEXCEL A	✓
OCR B	✓
WJEC A	✓
WJEC B	✓
CCEA	✓

Hitler made himself a **dictator**. He demanded complete obedience to his own will.

The forcible co-ordination of the state

After the Enabling Act in March 1933, Hitler was able to issue decrees. He alone was thought to understand what Germans really wanted. By the time Hindenburg died, in 1934, Hitler had transformed an ailing democracy into a dictatorship:

> The Reichstag tamely renewed the Enabling Act every four years.

- The Reich Chancellery became the central institution of the state.
- The Cabinet faded into insignificance.
- Local government was destroyed.
- The civil service and judiciary accepted Nazi authoritarian rule.
- Only the army remained a potential source of independent thought.
- Hitler took supreme command of a new High Command of the Armed Forces.

In 1938 both General Blomberg, Defence Minister, and Werner von Fritsch, Commander in Chief, were removed from their posts along with over 100 other generals.

A one-party state

By 1940 there were two million full-time party officials. They formed an efficient network of control:
- A **Gauleiter** was in charge of a region.
- A **Blockleiter** was in charge of 40–60 households.

The structure of power

Hitler believed in the survival of the fittest. He expected state departments to compete for his favour. This resulted in chaos, not efficiency. He encouraged overlapping of administrative responsibilities and rivalry between his key leaders:

- **Rudolph Hess** (Hitler's deputy up to 1941)
- **Martin Bormann** (Chief of staff to Hess from 1933–1941 and head of the party Chancellery from 1941)
- **Hans Heinrich Lammers** (Chief of the Reich Chancellery, 1933–1945)

Opposition and control

AQA B	✓
EDEXCEL A	✓
OCR B	✓
WJEC A	✓
WJEC B	✓
CCEA	✓

Passive opposition

Most opposition was **passive**: grumbling and non-co-operation; refusing to join the Party; refusing to make the 'Heil Hitler' salute or telling anti-Hitler jokes. People who resisted were...

- coerced by the Gestapo and the SS (see below)
- kept ignorant of events through the control of the media.

Unpopular policies were often moderated. Most people's quibbles seemed minor and after all, the Nazis had gained power through democracy.

Open opposition

You need to be able to give examples of each type of opposition.

Communists	Rote Kapelle smashed 1942
Workers	400 strikes 1933–1935
The Army	General Beck in 1938 Von Stauffenburg in 1944
Youth Groups	Swing Youth Edelweiss Pirates White Rose Group
The Church	Martin Neimoller, Dietrich Bonhoeffer, Cardinal Galen

It is estimated that 1.3 million Germans were put into concentration camps. About 300,000 left Germany between 1933 and 1939.

The destruction of opposition

Totalitarianism demanded the active co-operation of many in the population. Hitler used two particular agencies to impose fear and control:

The Gestapo:

- In 1933, **Heinrich Himmler**, was put in charge of the Gestapo. Basic individual freedoms were removed and thousands of Germans were rounded up and sent to concentration camps. Courts were coerced so that no authority could protect the population from the secret police.
- From 1936 it was the most important security agency, able to decide for itself what the law was.
- Its power was dependent on the consent and co-operation of ordinary German citizens.
- 80% of investigations stemmed from voluntary denunciations.

The SS:

- The **Schutzstaffel** began as Hitler's bodyguard, led by Himmler. From 280 members in 1929 it grew into a huge organisation. By the end of the 1930s it was involved in most aspects of the state.
- With the Gestapo it was the most hated and repressive organ of Nazi Germany.
- The Emergency Power Decree of February 1933 allowed the SS to take suspects into 'protective custody'.
- After the Night of the Long Knives in 1934, the SS became the chief enforcers of the Nazi Party.
- By 1939 162,000 were in 'protective custody' without trial, and 225,000 had been imprisoned for political crimes.
- By 1939 the 240,000 SS members were organised into the **Waffen-SS**, (primarily a military organisation) and the **Deaths Head Formations** (which administered the concentration camps and mass extermination).

Was the Nazi state successful in destroying opposition?

The regime was certainly not able to repress all opposition, but most opposition was effectively deterred, and overt opposition was dealt with.

Propaganda and control

AQA B	✓
EDEXCEL A	✓
OCR B	✓
WJEC A	✓
WJEC B	✓
CCEA	✓

Propaganda

Much **culture** (art, architecture, music and literature) was conveyed to Germans through the mass media (newspapers, radio and film). The Nazi government used culture and the mass media to spread **propaganda** (the point of view of the government) and to exclude differing opinions.

Josef Goebbels became party propaganda chief in 1928. Probably the greatest propagandist of all time, he became the Reich Minister for Propaganda and Enlightenment in 1933.

Figure 10.1 Josef Goebbels

Cultural control

You need to be able to give examples of the different types of propaganda and the ways in which it was used for control.

Art	Jewish, abstract or intellectual art was replaced by 'healthy' Aryan art. Nazi art created a myth of perfection. Licences to teach could be withdrawn.
Drama	Weimar experimentation abruptly ended. Bertholt Brecht, Ernst Toller and many others emigrated. Entertainment was escapist. Subsidised theatre brought to workers by **Strength through Joy**.
Music	Experimental music banned: many musicians emigrated. The Reich Chamber of Music controlled production. Wagner, Strauss and Bruckner replaced Mendelssohn. Hitler encouraged the Bayreuth Festival, dedicated to Wagner's operas; it celebrated German folklore. Carl Orff completed Carmina Burana based on medieval German songs in time for the 1936 Olympics.
Literature	20,000 books destroyed in Berlin to purify the new Germany. Famous novelists such as Thomas Mann, Stefan Zweig and Erich Maria Remarque, went into exile. Novelists were expected to promote Nazi ideals or to be neutral.
Architecture	In Hitler's view architecture was the most important artistic form of propaganda. Neo-classical style strengthened respect for authority. Plans for Nuremberg and 30 German cities, including Berlin. Domestic buildings and youth hostels in folksy style in contrast.

Control of the mass media

The press	Rigorously controlled: editors were made personally responsible for their papers. Nazi publishing house took over most papers.
Radio	Radio was the 'spiritual weapon of the totalitarian state'. Mass production of the cheap 'people's receiver'. By 1939 70% of households owned a radio. Mostly used for light entertainment but transmitted Hitler's main speeches to estimated audiences of 6 million.
Meetings and rallies	The atmosphere at meetings and rallies was similar to pop concerts using light, uniforms, mass movements, stirring music, striking flags and symbols. These made people wish to belong. 12 annual festivals, mass gym displays, Berlin Olympics, etc.
Film	Mass entertainment: audiences quadrupled by 1942. **In 1942 all film companies were nationalised**. The Reich Film Chamber regulated the content of films: Goebbels was personally responsible. The most famous producer was Leni Riefenstahl.

The persecution of minorities

AQA B	✓
EDEXCEL A	✓
OCR B	✓
WJEC A	✓
WJEC B	✓
CCEA	✓

Nationalism held the state together. The Nazis believed in the superiority of the German race and thought they could only achieve victory and domination by purging the nation of weak groups. They thought this justified persecuting such groups:

- **Gypsies** were considered non-Aryan and workshy. In 1935 intermarriage between Gypsies and Aryans was banned. Many had already been sterilised as a result of a law of 1933. **From 1936 Gypsies were sent to concentration camps** with other 'workshy' tramps and beggars. From 1938 they had to be registered by the state, and many were sent to **Buchenwald** concentration camp. **Only 5,000 survived the war (out of 30,000 in Germany)**. In all, about 500,000 European Gypsies were exterminated from 1942–1945.

- **The mentally ill**: The Nazi policy of compulsory sterilisation was applied to the mentally ill from 1933. In 1939 the Nazis began a **'euthanasia'** or mass murder campaign. Starvation, lethal injections or carbon monoxide gas were used to murder 6,000 patients in the first year. Gas chambers were built in six mental hospitals, and the campaign was only stopped by public opinion in 1941. **By then about 72,000 people had been murdered**.
- **Jews**: They were persecuted from the very beginning of Nazi rule.

1933	Official boycott of Jewish shops, doctors and lawyers.
1935	The **Nuremberg Laws** banned marriages, forbade sexual relations between Jews and Aryans and removed Jewish citizenship.
1937	Jewish businesses were confiscated.
1938	All Jewish property was registered (to aid confiscation), Jewish doctors and dentists were forbidden to treat Aryans and Jewish passports were stamped with the red letter, 'J'. In November came **Kristallnacht**: the SA, under Goebbels' orders, destroyed synagogues, Jewish homes and shops.
1939	All Jews were forced to use the first names Sarah or Israel and **emigration was promoted 'by every possible means'**. From 12th March 1939, the first mass arrests of Jews took place: 30,000 were sent to concentration camps.

The war turned mass persecution into genocide. Over 3 million Polish Jews had to be dealt with, and it was impossible to do so by emigration:

- The first answer was to herd them together: **500,000 died in the Warsaw ghetto**, mostly from starvation and typhus. The invasion of Russia meant that millions more Jews had to be dealt with.
- Special SS murder squads, **Einsatzgruppen**, murdered a further 500,000 during 1941.

> **KEY POINT**
>
> It is important to realise that extermination of the Jews was not even mentioned until 1939 and not agreed upon until 1942.

In early 1942, leading Nazis met at **Wannsee** in Berlin to work out a 'final solution'. **Death camps were built in Poland**. There, Jews and others were worked to death or gassed. Jews were moved from all over German-occupied Europe towards the Polish death camps. Some were used in hideous experiments. **Nearly 6 million Jews were killed, along with political opponents, homosexuals, Jehovah's Witnesses, anti-social elements, Russian prisoners of war and Gypsies.**

Was Nazi Germany a totalitarian state?

AQA B	✓
EDEXCEL A	✓
OCR B	✓
WJEC A	✓
WJEC B	✓
CCEA	✓

> **KEY POINT**
>
> A totalitarian state is a country where the government seeks to control nearly all aspects of life to ensure that the people become committed members of the state.

How much control was there?	How much freedom was there?
The power of the state in Nazi Germany was frightening: • The SS or the Gestapo were not legally restrained in their use of power. Hitler's right to make law by decree was unlimited. • Only the Nazi Party was tolerated. • Through the complete control of information, culture and the mass media, the state even tried to dictate the thoughts of its citizens. It is clear that the Nazi state aimed to be totalitarian.	The power of the state was limited: • There was confusion of overlapping ministries. • There were a limited number of Gestapo personnel. • Above all there was a need to rule with the consent and participation of the people.

The term 'totalitarian' does not mean complete control of all aspects of life and thought, but rather the wish to control. The Nazi state was totalitarian in that it tried to force uniformity. There were practical limits to their control, however, as there would be in any totalitarian state.

PROGRESS CHECK

1 What Act gave Hitler the power to rule by decree?
2 Name two army officers who opposed Hitler.

1. The Enabling Act.
2. General Beck; Von Stauffenburg.

10.4 Life in Nazi Germany 1933–1945

LEARNING SUMMARY

After studying this section you should be able to understand:

• how the Nazi government tried to influence and control young people
• how the Nazis tried to gain the confidence of women but restrict their opportunities
• how the state promoted the family and divorce
• how the economy was strengthened and weakened

Young people

AQA B	✓
EDEXCEL A	✓
OCR B	✓
WJEC A	✓
WJEC B	✓
CCEA	✓

The Nazis wanted to completely indoctrinate German youth, from the time children were three years old. They used school and youth groups to do this.

Nazi youth groups

Boys	Girls
• 6–10 **Pimpfen** – Cubs • 10–14 **Deutsches Jungvolk** – Young German Boys • 14–18 **Hitlerjugend** – Hitler Youth	• 10–24 **Jung Mädel** – Young Girls • 14–18 **Bund Deutscher Mädel** – League of German Girls • 18–21 **Glaube und Schönheit** – Faith and Beauty

Hitler Youth became less successful as more uncommitted people joined it.

Hitler Youth was founded 1926 and expanded rapidly after 1933. **Baldur von Schirach** was appointed Nazi Youth Leader in 1931, aged 24. After 1936 all other youth organisations were banned. Membership of Hitler Youth became compulsory, though many managed to avoid it.

Figure 10.2 Hitler Youth in Nuremberg Stadium, 1933

Education

Nazi education taught that the state was more important than the individual. Under Nazi policies the state took over education:

- **National Socialist Teachers' League membership** was made almost compulsory for teachers.
- A Nazi curriculum was introduced:
  - **Nazi ideas were incorporated into biology and history**.
  - Physical exercise increased to at least two hours per day.
- **Higher education declined**. This reflected the Nazi downgrading of academic education.
- **Mixed schooling was discouraged** to ensure that the sexes received appropriate education: girls took needlework and music, language and home crafts.
- **Special schools were established to train leaders**. National Political Institutes of Education and Adolf Hitler Schools for boys aged 10–18 were set up. These were taken over by the SS in 1936, and provided a military-style boarding education. The best students progressed to the **Ordensburgen** (Castles of Order). These housed 1,000 students aged 25–30 and 500 staff.

Women and the family

AQA B	✓
EDEXCEL A	✓
OCR B	✓
WJEC A	✓
WJEC B	✓
CCEA	✓

In 1933 Nazism was less popular among women than men. Nazism did become more popular among women, in time, for complex reasons.

Why Nazi policies attracted many women

Nazi policies attracted women for the following reasons:
- Nazis wanted to **reduce female employment** in industry and commerce.

Historians disagree as to whether women supported the Nazi régime more strongly than men.

- Marriage loans were given to women who gave up their jobs from 1933: men were preferred in the civil service.
- Nazis wanted to **increase the birth rate** of Aryan families: divorce became easier in order to end unproductive marriages.
- Nazi organisations supported the family by...
  - distributing food aid
  - giving medals to prolific mothers
  - providing maternity homes for the weeks after childbirth
  - running kindergartens to look after children while their mothers worked.

KEY POINT

Women tended to be more conservative and hated violence. Many who did vote Nazi were attracted by promises to get Germany back onto its feet and to 'do social justice to the poor' by increasing employment.

Why their success was limited

The Nazi policies were not entirely successful:

- From 1933–9 the **birth rate rose slowly**, but then it declined. It never reached figures of before 1928.
- Nazi racial and **sterilisation policies reduced the potential growth** of the population.
- The Nazi **government dared not force women out of employment** 1933–39.
- During the war, **women were less mobilised than in Britain or the USA**:
  - Hitler refused female conscription.
  - The government had to reverse previous policies and encourage female employment.

The economy and living standards

AQA B	✓
EDEXCEL A	✓
OCR B	✓
WJEC A	✓
WJEC B	✓
CCEA	✓

Most people voted for the Nazi Party in 1933 because of poverty. How far did the Nazis solve Germany's economic problems?

Jobs created

The Nazi government took action to create jobs, by increasing government expenditure and investment:

- Hitler extended public works schemes (e.g. autobahns, housing).
- He provided orders for private companies.
- Tax concessions to newlyweds stimulated demand.
- Trades unions were destroyed (industry benefited from cheap labour).
- Subsidies were given for hiring more workers.
- The civil service grew.
- Some groups were pressurised out of employment (e.g. women and Jews in the public service).

KEY POINT

Agricultural workers could not register for employment, so figures for their unemployment ceased to be kept. The Youth Service and conscription removed an age group from the jobless total.

Confidence increased

Brüning had ended reparations. **Hjalmar Schacht** was appointed as Economics Minister in 1934 (which inspired the confidence of financial institutions).

Economy controlled

By 1934, imports were rising alarmingly. Hitler agreed to Schacht's **New Plan**, which regulated and reduced imports. Schacht made profitable agreements with other countries to provide strategic raw materials on an exchange or barter system. Even so, it was very difficult to keep down demand for foreign products.

The Four Year Plan was to get Germany ready for war. Targets were set for private industry. Germany must be made self-sufficient (**autarkic**). **Goering** (Commander of Luftwaffe) was put in charge of the Four Year Plan in 1936.

Production increased even more

Albert Speer reorganised the economy for total war from 1942–1945. The invasion of Russia in 1941 had changed the nature of the conflict. Speer established a central planning board, composed of industrialists, and increased output until 1945.

Success of Nazi economic policies

Success	Failure
• Unemployment fell from 6 million to 1.6 million by 1936. • Germany recovered from the Depression extremely fast.	• Recovery had begun before 1933. • Other policies may have provided more sustained and faster growth. • The mass of German people failed to benefit greatly from economic growth. • Autarky was never achieved. • Rearmament was wasteful and disorganised until 1942. The Third Reich did not achieve a growth rate above the average in inter-war Europe.

Did most Germans benefit from Nazi rule?

AQA B	✓
EDEXCEL A	✓
OCR B	✓
WJEC A	✓
WJEC B	✓
CCEA	✓

This is a difficult question to answer, since the evidence is so biased:
• Should we measure benefit in the eyes of people at the time, or from our own point of view?
• How can the immoral persecution of minorities be balanced against the general prosperity of most Germans by 1939?
• Mass bombing, strains on the German economy and the holocaust would demand a very different answer after 1939 from before.

PROGRESS CHECK

1. Name the two Nazi youth groups for boys and girls aged 14–18.
2. Why did many women initially not support the Nazis?
3. Why didn't unemployed agricultural workers show up in Nazi unemployment statistics?

3. Because agricultural workers were not allowed to register for employment.
1. Hitler Youth and League of German Girls. 2. Conservatism and dislike of violence.

Sample GCSE questions

(a) Name the two main groups that sought to take power from the Weimar Republic before the end of 1920.

The Spartacists, who were Communists, in March 1919 and the Freikorps in the Kapp Putsch in March 1920. **(4)**

← Keep these short: one mark for each group named, plus one for developing it a little.

(b) Why did the Nazi Party dislike the Weimar Republic 1921–23?

The Nazi Party blamed the Weimar Republic for signing the Treaty of Versailles. In 1923, in the Munich Putsch, Hitler led a rebellion because the government was about to sign the Dawes Plan, to make the payment of reparations possible.

← Two good reasons should be enough here, but explain each in its own short paragraph. The candidate has developed each of these sufficiently.

Hitler thought that the Weimar Republic was weak because it was democratic and no party could gain a majority in the Reichstag without a coalition. **(6)**

(c) 'The most important reason why the Weimar Republic was weak was the unfairness of the Treaty of Versailles.' Do you agree with this statement? Explain your answer.

The Treaty of Versailles was not the only reason for the weakness of the Weimar Republic before 1929. In many ways Germany had brought weakness on herself, rather than having it imposed on her. The loss of the war, the abdication of the Kaiser, the creation of the weak Republican constitution and the extremism of German politics would have made Germany weak, even without the Treaty.

← The question spans the whole period from 1919 to 1933. There are two periods of weakness and two arguments: for and against the Treaty of Versailles. For high marks you need to include a little detail to show that you know the period adequately, but it is most important to include reasons. This candidate has come to a definite conclusion.

However, the Treaty did shock the German nation. The loss of so many Germans to other states, such as Poland, was an important reason for nationalists such as Kapp and Hitler to blame the government. The restrictions on German armed forces, especially the army, meant that the Republic could not police itself properly. Communism was bred by poverty, which in turn was prolonged at least by the need to pay the reparations demanded by the Treaty. After 1929, the determination of Hindenburg to rule by decree was important, but the Wall Street Crash and the effects of the Depression on Germany were important too. The fact that the Depression hit Germany so hard was because of the web of loans set up to allow the payment of reparations, e.g. the Young Plan. Hitler was also able to profit by promising to destroy the Treaty of Versailles: nationalism was the cement that bound the Nazi Party together.

So, though Germany would have been weak even without the Treaty of Versailles, the Treaty was probably the most important cause of its weakness. **(10)**

Exam practice questions

1 **(a)** How did Hitler change the Nazi Party during the late 1920s?

....

....

....

.... **(4)**

(b) Why did Germans vote for the Nazi Party in the elections in 1932?

....

....

....

....

....

....

.... **(6)**

(c) To what extent did Hitler come to power through the support of the German people?

....

....

....

....

....

....

....

....

....

....

....

.... **(10)**

You may need to continue your answers on a separate sheet of paper.

The USA 1919–1980

The following topics are covered in this chapter:

- Boom and slump in the USA 1919–1941
- The 'Great Society' 1945–1980

11.1 Boom and slump in the USA 1919–1941

LEARNING SUMMARY

After studying this section you should be able to understand:

- how the USA isolated itself from alliances and the world economy
- the boom of the 1920s
- the crisis on Wall Street and how it affected the whole of US society
- how President Hoover failed to pull the USA out of the crisis
- how Roosevelt turned the tide with the New Deal

The growth of isolation 1919–1922

AQA B	✓
EDEXCEL A	✓
OCR B	✓
WJEC A	✓
WJEC B	✗
CCEA	✓

Woodrow Wilson (Democrat) President 1913–21

- Between 1914 and 1918, **the USA had profited** hugely by supplying food, war and consumer goods to Europe.
- In 1919, at the Paris Peace Conference, Wilson had a formative influence on the Treaty of Versailles and the formation of the League of Nations. However, **Congress refused to agree to the Treaty or join the League.**

> Congress had gone Republican. Wilson became ill while trying to change its mind.

Warren Harding (Republican) President 1921–23

- In 1922, Harding organised the **Fordney–McCumber Tariff**. It taxed imports from foreign countries. At first it protected US farming and industry, but later foreign countries kept out US goods.

During the inter-war years, the USA tried to steer clear of entanglements abroad and to promote peace and disarmament.

The boom of the 1920s

AQA B	✓
EDEXCEL A	✓
OCR B	✓
WJEC A	✓
WJEC B	✗
CCEA	✓

KEY POINT

In a boom, products are in demand. Industry thrives and unemployment falls.

The economy grew quickly during the 1920s:

- Profits from the war and huge resources were used to create new industries.
- At first there was little competition from European industry and farming.
- A growing population was further increased by immigration.
- Republican policies cut taxes on profits and industry.
- Technological change, especially mass production, worked in America's favour.
- There was a huge expansion of credit: consumers could easily borrow in order to buy.
- Confidence in the USA was high: people spent their savings, invested in industries and lent money easily.

Growth industries

The following industries grew rapidly in the 1920s:

- **The motor industry**: Private car ownership grew from 9 million to 26 million from 1919–29. Ford's Detroit plant produced one car every three minutes, using the **production line** and paid its workers $5.00 a day. This stimulated huge growth in the glass, rubber and steel industries.
- **Mass media**: Radios became common, from 60,000 in 1919 to 10 million in 1929. The film industry grew. Cinema attendance more than doubled.
- **Transport**: The mileage of paved roads doubled. The number of trucks tripled. Railways declined, but civil aviation grew from nothing to over 150,000 flights by 1929.
- **Communications**: There were 20 million telephones in use by 1929.
- **Consumer goods**: Refrigerators began to appear and vacuum cleaners became popular. These changes were provoked by mass advertising, chain stores, easy delivery and hire purchase.

Changes in US society during the 1920s

AQA B	✓
EDEXCEL A	✓
OCR B	✓
WJEC A	✓
WJEC B	✗
CCEA	✓

Mass production, mass marketing, easier communications and increasing wealth changed some parts of society during the 1920s.

The roaring '20s

- The motor car widened people's horizons, making day trips, holidays, commuting and shopping much easier.
- The radio service began in 1920, and by 1930 40% of homes had one. New ideas spread much more quickly and popular music was really born.
- Clubs and dancing became popular in towns.
- Jazz became popular, moving from an African American audience to general acceptance among the young.
- Sexual conventions loosened. Sex outside marriage became more common.
- The cinema affected everyone: everyone wanted to live like the stars (Rudolf Valentino, Clara Bow, Theda Bara).

BUT

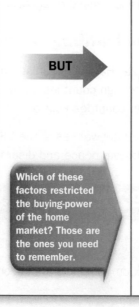

Which of these factors restricted the buying-power of the home market? Those are the ones you need to remember.

- The Ku Klux Klan worked to keep rural African Americans poor.
- Prohibition (the Volstead Act) produced lawlessness.
- There was general fear of communism, caused by strikes and bombs. This led to the Palmer Raids.
- Agriculture declined gradually through oversupply and low prices.
- African Americans as a whole were unable to enjoy the boom, isolated in rural or urban poverty.
- Some industries declined: cotton, coal, tin and copper.

Causes and consequences of the Wall Street Crash

AQA B	✓
EDEXCEL A	✓
OCR B	✓
WJEC A	✓
WJEC B	✗
CCEA	✓

Causes

The Wall Street Crash was caused by the following factors:

- By 1929 agriculture was in decline.
- Industry was suffering from foreign competition and tariffs, and the failure of the domestic market to grow fast enough.
- The long boom on the Wall Street Stock Exchange came to an end, when investors who had raised money 'on the margin' now realised that share and stock prices would not continue to rise as industry expected lower profits. Instead of buying, they sold at a loss.

> Buying 'on the margin' meant that investors borrowed 90% of the cost of shares from the banks.

The Wall Street Crash

Over about ten days in late October 1929 the Wall Street Stock Exchange crashed. The worst days were...

- 'Black Thursday', 24th October, when nearly 13 million shares were sold
- Tuesday 29th October, when over 16 million shares were sold. Stocks and shares had become worthless.

> While you will not be examined on details of the Crash itself, it is useful to remember that speculation had assisted in the rise of the market, and it also accelerated its fall.

The consequences

The Wall Street Crash had the following results:

- Banks that had lent money to investors 'on the margin' lost huge amounts. Over 5,000 closed from 1930–1933.
- Industry suffered when shares became worthless and consumers stopped buying goods (many factories were taken over or shut down).
- Farming suffered as less food was bought (there was already a surplus) so prices fell. Farmers couldn't invest in fertilisers and this worsened the 'Dust Bowl' problem (where the land was so dried out and impoverished that it blew away).
- Farmers and businesses went out of business, creating unemployment, which rose from 1.6 million to 14 million by 1933.
- Consumers lost their money in the banks and suffered as interest rates rose. Many became homeless and destitute and lived in 'Hoovervilles' (shanty towns).

> **KEY POINT**
>
> In a slump there is oversupply of products and not enough money to buy them. Unemployment rises. When it seems impossible to climb out of the slump, it is called a depression.

Government reaction and attempts at recovery, 1929–33

AQA B	✓
EDEXCEL A	✓
OCR B	✓
WJEC A	✓
WJEC B	✗
CCEA	✓

Herbert Hoover (Republican) President 1929–1933

In 1928 Hoover had promised 'two cars in every garage and a chicken in the pot'. He thought the economy should be left to right itself, but as the Depression mounted, he was forced into several actions:

- The Smoot–Hawley Tariff 1930: This increased import taxes as high as 50% to encourage people to buy US goods. But people couldn't afford to buy anyway.

- The **Hoover Dam** and other construction projects cost the government $423 million. They were a small step in the right direction.
- **The Farm Board bought up surplus farm produce**, but couldn't buy enough to make a difference.
- **The Reconstruction Finance Corporation 1932**, provided $1,500 million in loans to big business.

> **KEY POINT**
>
> Probably few governments would have reacted well to the Wall Street Crash and the beginning of the Depression. However, voters became bitter about Hoover's failure because he did not appear to care for the individuals caught in poverty.

Hoover relied on voluntary agreements with industrialists to keep prices up. He refused to provide relief for the hungry and homeless. State governments and charity were not enough help in this catastrophic situation. This had the following results:

- Increasing numbers of **strikes and lockouts**.
- A march on Washington by First World War veterans (the **Bonus Marchers**) in 1932. They demanded the pension due in 1945. **The government met them with tanks**.
- Spreading poverty and starvation.
- **Hoovervilles**.

The crisis came to a head during the Presidential election of 1932.

The 1932 Presidential election

AQA B	✓
EDEXCEL A	✓
OCR B	✓
WJEC A	✓
WJEC B	✗
CCEA	✓

Herbert Hoover: Republican	Franklin D. Roosevelt: Democrat
<ul><li>Believed businesses would bring prosperity without government interference.</li><li>Thought relief should be provided by the individual state governments and by charity.</li><li>Thought to be cold and detached: 'In Hoover we trusted and now we are busted'.</li></ul>	<ul><li>Promised government schemes to provide jobs and revive industry and agriculture.</li><li>Promised federal aid to the poor and unemployed.</li><li>Promised protection for workers from employers.</li><li>Promised to end Prohibition.</li><li>Understood that the poor needed help.</li></ul>

The election was a landslide victory for Roosevelt, with a **7 million majority**.

The New Deal

AQA B	✓
EDEXCEL A	✓
OCR B	✓
WJEC A	✓
WJEC B	✗
CCEA	✓

Roosevelt's contribution

In 1933 Roosevelt became President. His inaugural speech...

'...was one of the turning points of American history. In a few minutes Roosevelt did what had so wearyingly eluded Hoover for four years: he gave back to his countrymen their hope and their energy...'

(Hugh Brogan, *History of the United States of America*)

Roosevelt said...

'...the only thing we have to fear is fear itself – nameless, unreasoning, unjustified terror which paralyses needed efforts to convert retreat into advance...'

Roosevelt promised the following:
- **Relief** of poverty – to stop people losing jobs and farms, and to feed the starving.
- **Recovery** of industry – to get everyone working again.
- **Reform** – to provide unemployment insurance, old age pensions and to help the sick.

Roosevelt **spoke directly to the people in 'fireside chats'** (radio broadcasts), the first only eight days after taking office. He brought together a group of people (the Brain Trust) to decide on actual measures, while only being sure of the general direction himself. He put the **whole resources of government into the creation of the New Deal programme**, to make a decisive difference. Congress was so alarmed at the state of the country, that they were prepared to give him emergency powers. **He persuaded the country that he would take measures irrespective of party or class loyalties.**

> **KEY POINT**
>
> In contrast to Hoover, Roosevelt did appear to care. He inspired confidence, both in the financial markets and among the poor. Confidence was important in restoring normality on the Stock Exchange and in financial life generally.

The First Hundred Days

In 1933 Roosevelt took the following actions:
- He shut all the banks for a 'four day holiday'. Their books were checked and the government decided which were safe and could reopen. This restored confidence so that money flowed into banks again.
- He ended Prohibition. This deprived organised crime of its profits and allowed the alcohol industry to be taxed again.
- He created the '**Alphabet Agencies**'. These provided employment and support.

Figure 11.1 President Roosevelt stands in the middle of a group of children playing ring-around-the-rosie, symbolising the New Deal programme he created.

The Alphabet Agencies

Farm Credit Administration (FCA)	Made loans to farmers so that they were safe in their farms.
Agricultural Adjustment Agency (AAA)	Paid farmers to produce less food, so that prices went up.
Civilian Conservation Corps (CCC)	Gave conservation work to young men. This took them out of the job market and gave them worthwhile jobs to do: planting trees to anchor soil and providing flood control.
Civilian Works Administration (CWA)	This was an emergency measure to get through the first winter. The agency tried to employ as many as possible, clearing leaves, building roads, etc.
Public Works Administration (PWA)	Spent $7 billion on lasting public works: buildings, bridges, sewerage, dams, etc.
Federal Emergency Relief Administration (FERA)	Spent $500 million on soup kitchens, clothing, schools and employment schemes.
Home Owners' Loan Corporation (HOLC)	Lent money to stop people from losing their homes.
National Recovery Administration (NRA)	Aimed to increase wages, increase prices and give workers a fairer deal. Employers had to sign a code for their own industry and were then allowed to display the NRA Blue Eagle.
The Tennessee Valley Authority (TVA)	Aimed to improve the vast Tennessee Valley by building 33 dams, improving the soil, planting forests and improving river communications. As a by-product it provided hydro-electricity.

These measures put new heart into the American people. The measures started to regenerate trust and confidence and began the long journey back to prosperity.

How the New Deal changed after 1933

AQA B	✓
EDEXCEL A	✓
OCR B	✓
WJEC A	✓
WJEC B	X
CCEA	✓

Roosevelt had never been sure of the details of what would be needed, so after the First Hundred Days there were still more measures.

The Works Progress Administration 1935 (WPA)	Provided work on roads, public buildings, schools, bridges, tunnels, sewers and erosion control.
The Social Security Act 1935	Gave a state pension to everyone over 65, supported handicapped people and mothers with young children. It helped to provide unemployment insurance.
The Wagner Act 1935	Gave freedom to form unions and prevented employers from sacking trade union members.
The Resettlement Administration 1935	Helped to resettle sharecroppers, tenants and farm workers when they had become unemployed through the reduction in agriculture. This was replaced by the Farm Security Agency in 1937, which gave loans to sharecroppers and tenant farmers to buy their own land.

Opposition to the New Deal

AQA B	✓
EDEXCEL A	✓
OCR B	✓
WJEC A	✓
WJEC B	✗
CCEA	✓

Republicans opposed Roosevelt because...
- many thought that paying money to the unemployed would make them lazy
- it was said that money was being wasted
- they resented the higher taxation that was needed
- they accused Roosevelt of communism as he had taken so much power to solve the crisis.
- they doubted that he had the right to dictate to business.

Figure 11.2 'Priming the Pump': an American view in 1933

Business thought like Republicans, but also...
- they were angry at Roosevelt's support for trade unions
- they thought the TVA competed unfairly with privately-owned businesses.

The **rich** resented having to pay high taxes.

Huey Long, Governor of Louisiana, wanted to increase taxes on the rich. He proposed...
- to redistribute wealth over $5,000 in his 'Share our Wealth' scheme
- a minimum wage.

Huey Long was assassinated.

In 1935 the **Supreme Court** decided that the NRA was unconstitutional because the government could not control businesses. In 1936 it declared the measures taken by the AAA were unconstitutional because agriculture could only be regulated by state governments.

However, in the 1936 Presidential Election, Roosevelt won with an astounding 27 million votes. Only 16 million voted Republican. Roosevelt **then attacked the Supreme Court** by trying to appoint six new judges and gain a majority. **Even his own supporters thought that he had gone too far**, and he was forced to back down, but as a result the Supreme Court moderated its opposition. Further depression hit the economy in 1937, and by 1939 Roosevelt admitted that the New Deal was over.

Inequality under the New Deal

AQA B	✓
EDEXCEL A	✓
OCR B	✓
WJEC A	✓
WJEC B	✗
CCEA	✓

Many parts of American society were hardly touched by the New Deal:

- **African Americans continued to suffer severe discrimination**. They were prohibited from living in areas around the TVA dams. They found it very hard to find jobs. By 1935 about 30% lived on relief. Roosevelt depended on southern, white, Democratic Congressmen for his political support. They would not support civil rights or anti-lynching laws. However, African Americans did benefit from the CCC programme and new housing that was built after slum-clearance projects. Some gained jobs in the administration.
- **Women were not employed to any great degree** in the manual labour programmes, but their employment did rise during the 1930s, because they provided labour. They benefited to some extent from the Social Security Act. Some, like Mary Macleod Bethume (head of NYA) and Frances Perkins (Secretary of Labour) rose to prominent positions in the administration.

While both groups benefited, they did not benefit as much as white men.

Success of the New Deal up to 1941

AQA B	✓
EDEXCEL A	✓
OCR B	✓
WJEC A	✓
WJEC B	✗
CCEA	✓

Everyone agrees that the New Deal was very important but historians disagree about how important it was in promoting recovery.

Successes	Failures
• The New Deal was certainly successful in reviving businesses and reducing unemployment. • It **stopped the situation from getting worse** and prevented communism from spreading. • It **provided relief** for those who could no longer help themselves.	• It cost **billions of dollars** of government money but it failed to permanently fix the problem. • When the government reduced its support in 1937, **unemployment rose** steeply again. • Continual **support remained necessary** until, in 1941, the Second World War provided work for all. • Some parts of society benefited more than others.

PROGRESS CHECK

1. Give three examples of consumer products popular in the 1920s.
2. Name three industries, which did not enjoy a boom in the mid-1920s.
3. Which two Alphabet Agencies helped farmers?

3. FCA and AAA.
2. **Any three from:** cotton, coal, tin, copper, farming.
1. **Any suitable answers, for example:** Radios, refrigerators, vacuum cleaners.

11.2 The 'Great Society' 1945–1980

LEARNING SUMMARY

After studying this section you should be able to understand:

- how important the lessons of the New Deal were for post-war America
- how the Cold War affected politics at home
- the impact of civil rights and race relations on politics
- the political disruption of the Vietnam War
- the importance of corruption in the Watergate Scandal

The impact of the Second World War on US economy and society

AQA B	✓
EDEXCEL A	✓
OCR B	✓
WJEC A	✓
WJEC B	✗
CCEA	✗

The USA's economic resources had dominated the last part of the Second World War, but there was a real fear that afterwards she would sink back into depression. The expected slump did not occur though:

- There was a **huge pent-up desire for consumer products**, which US industry was quick to supply.
- Returning US soldiers were quickly reintegrated into society by the '**GI Bill of Rights**' (Servicemen's Readjustment Act, 1944). This gave returning ex-servicemen financial help for further education or to set themselves up in business.

Truman's problems at home

Truman was Roosevelt's Democratic successor in 1945.

President Truman faced a number of problems when he became President in 1945:

- **Prices**: There were severe problems when Truman failed to impose price controls on Congress. Prices shot up by 30%.
- **Congress**: Truman was unpopular at home and, from 1946, was opposed by a Republican Congress. Most New Deal measures remained in force, but Truman failed to widen it into the 'Fair Deal' he had promised in 1945.
- **Trade Unions**: In 1947 there were severe labour disturbances. This forced Truman to pass the **Taft–Hartley Act in 1947**, which restricted the freedoms given in the Wagner Act of 1935. It restricted union rights and allowed unions to be sued for damages by employers.

In 1948 there was another Presidential election. **Truman was expected to lose**, but he just squeaked home, probably because by then most people were feeling more prosperous again. Even after the election, the Republican Congress refused to pass Truman's Fair Deal measures.

McCarthyism and the 'Red Scare'

AQA B	✓
EDEXCEL A	✓
OCR B	✓
WJEC A	✓
WJEC B	✗
CCEA	✗

The beginning of the Cold War and the risk of **spying alarmed the Senate**. Several incidents particularly provoked them:

- In 1945 the publishers of the communist-sponsored magazine *Amerasia* were found in possession of secret American State Department documents.

- Canadian citizens passed American nuclear secrets to the Soviet Union in 1946.
- In 1950 the Senate found that Dr. Klaus Fuchs (British) and his accomplices, Julius and Ethel Rosenberg (American) had systematically turned atom bomb secrets over to the Russians between 1943 and 1947.
- The government reacted by imposing new loyalty and security checks on officials in 1947.

The House Unamerican Activities Committee

The House Unamerican Activities Committee began to ferret out communists from the trade unions, Hollywood and the government:
- It was biased and publicity-seeking.
- It accepted the testimony of informers and professional ex-communists to start a witch-hunt among the intellectuals of the USA.
- Not all those accused were innocent: in 1948 Congressmen Richard Nixon exposed the spy Alger Hiss, who had been a senior State Department official.

In September 1950 Congress passed the **Internal Security (McCurran) Act**. This…
- required the **registration of communist** or communist-front organisations
- **forbade the employment** of communists in defence plants
- **barred** anyone belonging to totalitarian organisations **from entering the USA**
- authorised the provision of **concentration camps for communists** in time of war.

McCarthy

In February 1950 **Senator Joseph R. McCarthy** claimed that scores of communists were still at work in the State Department. His sensationalism won him re-election to the Senate in 1950, when two of his critics failed. Over four years, his campaign spread to state and local administrations.

Figure 11.3 Senator Joseph McCarthy started the 'Red Scare'

Several thousand people lost their jobs and hundreds were imprisoned. Passports were denied to communists, resident aliens were persecuted and public life was poisoned. The reputation of the USA abroad was severely damaged.

McCarthy's downfall

In 1954 **McCarthy accused members of the army** of being communist. The proceedings were televised. Public opinion was outraged at the brutal bullying. Congress gave McCarthy a vote of censure and his career was over. Though he died unremarked in 1957, the scars of his era took a long time to heal. The McCurran Act was not ruled unconstitutional by the Supreme Court until 1965.

The Civil Rights Movements and their impact on US society

AQA B	✓
EDEXCEL A	✓
OCR B	✓
WJEC A	✓
WJEC B	✗
CCEA	✗

The position of African Americans in the South

KEY POINT

After the abolition of slavery in the USA, African Americans were kept down by...
- intimidation or terror
- segregation or racial separation
- discrimination or denying them equal opportunities as white people.

In the southern states of the USA, African Americans had to suffer the **Jim Crow Laws**, which were designed to keep them in their place by denying them civil rights:
- Registered voters **must be property owners** (which African Americans were usually not).
- Registered voters **must pass a literacy test** (which most African Americans could not).

All-white southern state governments then **passed laws to separate African Americans from white people** in all spheres of life: schooling, residence, public transport, and restaurants. This was underpinned by the fear of the **Ku Klux Klan**, especially in the inter-war years.

In the northern states, **there was no need for segregation** because the numbers of African Americans were small enough for ordinary discrimination at work and through housing to be effective.

The beginning of change

The war years began to break down discrimination because...
- many African Americans were able to gain jobs in the northern states
- the status of newly-skilled and returning ex-servicemen was higher
- Truman proposed reforms (although Congress refused to pass them).

Under Eisenhower, in 1954, the Supreme Court made an important judgement in **Brown v. Topeka Board of Education**:
- They declared separate but equal education to be unconstitutional.
- By implication, the rest of the Jim Crow separations became illegal too. However, change had to be enforced.

1955	**Montgomery, Alabama**: A bus company nearly went broke when Martin Luther King organised a bus boycott over about a year to stop segregated seating.
1957	**Little Rock Arkansas**: Federal troops had to force entrance for African American children into a white high school.
1963	**Washington DC**: Martin Luther King organised a 'march of poor people' after which President Kennedy promised laws to guarantee black voting rights and an end to social discrimination.

Figure 11.4 Rev. Martin Luther King: 'I have a dream...'

Victory

Final legal victory was won by the following Acts:

- **Civil Rights Acts in 1964 and 1968** made racial discrimination in employment and housing illegal.
- **Voting Rights Act in 1965** allowed federal investigation of areas without their correct proportion of African American voters.

Since 1965 African American voters have gradually been coaxed to the polls so that black voting power has become a reality.

'New Frontier', 'Great Society': the roles of Kennedy and Johnson

AQA B	✓
EDEXCEL A	✓
OCR B	✓
WJEC A	✓
WJEC B	✗
CCEA	✗

See details of Kennedy's foreign policy in the section on the Cold War Chapter 6.

John F. Kennedy (Democrat) President 1960–1963

Kennedy was only just elected with a margin of 0.1% in 1960. It was one of the closest elections in US history. He was only 43 years old and appointed a young administration. His brother Robert (Attorney General) and Robert S. McNamara (Secretary of Defence) were even younger.

Abroad: Kennedy involved the USA in **Cuba** at the **Bay of Pigs** and later the **Missile Crisis**; in **Berlin**, which he promised to defend, and in the escalation of the war in **Vietnam**.

At home: Kennedy **accomplished very little**. He acted very cautiously and lacked effective support in Congress. Many of the important parts of his New Frontier programme were either blocked or killed outright, for example:

- **health insurance** for the aged (medicare)
- **federal aid to education**
- reform of the **immigration laws**
- creation of a **Department of Urban Affairs**.

Margins of defeat were narrow and many think that Kennedy was too distracted by foreign policy to be successful at home. Kennedy was forced to give priority to curing inflation. **Growth failed and unemployment remained high**. Kennedy was then frustrated when Congress refused to allow tax cuts. He was slow to take a stand on **civil rights** and did not at first propose legislation. However, he did do the following:

- He **appointed African Americans to high office**: Carl Rowan became ambassador to Finland, Thurgood Marshall became a US Circuit Court judge and Robert C. Warren became Head of The Housing and Home Finance Agency.
- He **sent troops into Mississippi** in 1962 to enforce a court order, which directed the state university to admit African Americans. In 1963 he **sent more troops into Alabama** to protect a civil rights worker.
- Robert Kennedy vigorously used the courts to speed up **desegregation** in bus terminals and schools, and to expand black voting rights.

African American leaders remained unimpressed: Martin Luther King accused him of only token support. So, in June 1963, Kennedy **supported a sweeping Civil Rights Bill**. His congressional support melted away, but his commitment was irrevocable. By late 1963 Kennedy's domestic programme was hopelessly deadlocked. He hoped for a change after elections in 1964, but was **assassinated** in Dallas on 22nd November 1963. While he was idealised after death, really his achievement has been exaggerated.

Lyndon B. Johnson (Democrat) President 1963–1968

Johnson was helped by the national guilt caused by Kennedy's assassination. Within a few months he had achieved the following:

- He forced Congress into supporting nearly all of Kennedy's **New Frontier** proposals.
- He secured approval for a **Tax Reduction Act**, mass transit legislation and a **Higher Education Facilities Act**.
- He defeated a six-month delay by southern Congressmen to secure the Civil Rights Act of 1964, which was the most far reaching ever passed. The Act...
  - **stopped discrimination** in hotels, restaurants and theatres
  - allowed the government to refuse financial support to agencies practising discrimination
  - allowed the prosecution of anyone discriminating at the polls or in school
  - set up an **Equal Opportunities Commission** to put an end to discrimination on the basis of sex, religion or race.
- He passed an **Economic Opportunities Act** to provide work experience and training for the unemployed.

He regarded these measures as the first step in creating a **'Great Society'**. After his victory over Barry Goldwater in the 1964 Presidential election, Johnson went on to pass the following Acts:

- The **Medicare Act 1965** provided medical care for the elderly.
- The **Elementary and Secondary Education Act 1965** made education a federal responsibility and authorised $1 billion expenditure on schools. Church schools now received state aid.

- The **Voting Rights Act 1965** was to stop continuing southern efforts to keep African Americans from the polls. Along with this, the **Twenty-fourth Amendment to the Constitution in 1965** outlawed the use of poll taxes. This caused the registration of African American voters to rise.
- Other Acts on immigration, highway beautification, air and water pollution, and federal slum clearance were passed. He also created a Department of Housing and Urban Development. These '**Great Society' policies** were aided by the Supreme Court which, under **Earl Warren** (Chief Justice 1953–1969), took an extremely liberal view. The Supreme Court...
  - ruled for **desegregation** of public parks, voting and housing
  - protected communists and those believing in theoretical revolution from being prosecuted for conspiracy
  - decided that prayers and Bible readings in public schools violated the principle of the separation of Church and State
  - wrote a new code of criminal procedure, establishing the suspect's right to silence and legal aid
  - insisted on the equalisation of electoral districts
  - took a very liberal line over censorship and obscenity.

Protest movements in the '60s and early '70s

AQA B	✓
EDEXCEL A	✓
OCR B	✓
WJEC A	✓
WJEC B	✗
CCEA	✗

Black militancy

Even Johnson's anti-discrimination laws were insufficient to head off the meltdown of the city ghettos in the mid-1960s. They **did not make people's lives immediately better**. Many black militant groups conspired to make themselves heard:

- The **Black Muslims** were a puritanical group, which rejected Christianity and taught that all white people were devils.
- The **Student Non-violent Co-ordinating Committee**, under Stokely Carmichael, soon ceased to be non-violent.
- The **Black Panthers**, founded in California, confronted the police, and were associated with Eldridge Cleaver
- The **Organisation for Afro-American Unity** under Malcolm X (assassinated 1965) were very vocal.

Figure 11.5 Two members of the Black Panther Party on the steps of the State Capitol in Sacramento, 1967

These groups all believed in **Black Power**, arguing that **white people would never give equality unless forced to do so**. They did not agree with 'turning the other cheek' as preached by Martin Luther King.

Their tactics were to build up Black Power in the ghettos, challenge and replace the white profiteers who preyed on them there, make African American children proud of their own history and even arm and train youths to take on the police. The **Vietnam War** intensified their militancy because they thought that African Americans were doing a disproportionate share of the fighting. The result was a series of riots that were more serious than anything seen since the American Civil War.

1965	**Watts, Los Angeles**, 34 dead, more than 1,000 injured, $35 million worth of damage.
1966	More riots in **Chicago**.
1967	Disturbances in more than 100 cities, especially **Newark, New Jersey, and Detroit**. At Detroit over five days the death toll was 43, and damage more than $500 million.
April 1968	The assassination of **Martin Luther King** set off a new wave of violence.

In 1967, Johnson had set up a Commission of Enquiry, to find the causes of the trouble. It reported in 1968, blaming segregation in employment, education and housing. It concluded that a massive government effort was needed. The government passed an Open Housing Law to outlaw discrimination in housing, but did almost nothing else as it was distracted by Vietnam.

Against Vietnam

Almost from the beginning, American involvement in the Vietnam War had provoked opposition at home. Both the far Right, believing in isolationism, and the Left, believing in human rights, opposed US involvement. Was the USA overextending itself? Did it have a real reason to be concerned in South East Asia? Was the war distracting attention from real problems at home? TV brought the full horror of the war to everyone's sitting room.

The **hawks** were the group of people that supported the war; the **doves** opposed the war:
- From 1965 there were anti-war demonstrations among college students, many of whom resented their liability to be drafted, and were 'doves'.
- In Congress a group of 'doves' emerged: J. William Fullbright, Robert F. Kennedy and Eugene McCarthy.

Replacement of Johnson: Vietnam became the dominant issue in the 1968 Presidential election. The Democratic Party was divided between those who supported **Hubert Humphrey** and the war, and the Peace Democrats. Humphrey was chosen as the Democratic candidate, but the anti-war group was never reconciled. **Richard Nixon** was, therefore, returned for the Republicans and won the election. He promised to bring the war to an early and honourable end.

Under Nixon there were sporadic demonstrations, but the disruption was never as bad again until eventual withdrawal in 1973.

The Watergate Scandal and its impact

AQA B	✓
EDEXCEL A	✓
OCR B	✓
WJEC A	✓
WJEC B	✗
CCEA	✗

Richard M. Nixon (Republican) President 1968–74

At home Nixon **made war against inflation** and, in 1971, imposed short-term wage and price controls and devalued the dollar. He tried to gain support from southern conservatives by **soft-pedalling civil rights and slowing down desegregation**. These tactics worked and he won a second election in 1972.

Things started to go wrong when the Democratic Party's headquarters in the Watergate Building were burgled by two members of Nixon's **Campaign to Re-elect the President** (CREEP). Two *Washington Post* reporters, (supported by a Congressional Committee of Enquiry) later exposed this 'dirty trick'.

Nixon had helped to cover up the crime, and as evidence of his complicity mounted, he tried to conceal incriminating tape recordings, until forced by the Supreme Court to reveal them. Eventually, under threat of impeachment (removal by Congress), Nixon resigned in 1974, the only US President to do so.

Nixon was immediately 'pardoned' by President Ford, but several of his agents, who had already been sent to prison, were not pleased and published 'the truth' about the scandal in the following years. The results of the crisis were very far-reaching. More than 40 members of Nixon's administration were **prosecuted** for various crimes and measures were put in place to stop the **abuse of Presidential power**:

- In 1974 Congress reasserted its control over public funds.
- Congress controlled the amount of election expenses (but these controls were overturned in 1976).
- In the War Powers Act 1973 Congress insisted that, though the President could declare war, Congress had to be consulted each time a war was escalated.
- There was a drive towards freedom of information laws at state level, reinforcing the Freedom of Information Act 1966.
- There was Congressional investigation of the CIA and FBI.

KEY POINT

It is generally agreed that Nixon's was the most corrupt administration ever in the USA, which led Gerald Ford to distance himself and the Republican Party from his predecessor.

PROGRESS CHECK

1. What were two main reasons for the beginning of the McCarthyist purge of communists?
2. In which years were the two most important Civil Rights Acts passed to destroy segregation and discrimination?
3. What were the four main areas of President Kennedy's failed New Frontier programme?
4. Who, as Chief Justice, aided Lyndon Johnson's efforts to end segregation?
5. Why did President Nixon finally resign as President?

1. The Cold War and spy scandals, McCarthy's wish to be re-elected. 2. 1964 and 1968.
3. Health insurance (medicare), education, immigration and to create a Department of Urban
Affairs. 4. Earl Warren. 5. He was threatened with impeachment.

Exam practice questions

1 **(a)** Which were the two major political parties that dominated US politics in the 1920s?

....

.... **(4)**

(b) Why did prosperity turn into poverty in the late 1920s?

....

....

....

....

....

....

.... **(6)**

(c) 'The New Deal failed to solve any of the deep-rooted problems of the American economy.'
How far is this statement true?

....

....

....

....

....

....

....

....

....

....

....

....

....

.... **(10)**

You may need to continue your answers on a separate sheet of paper.

Exam practice questions

2 **(a)** Why was the USA so scared of communist spies by 1950?

....

....

....

.... **(4)**

(b) How was racial discrimination enforced in southern states of the USA until the mid-1960s?

....

....

....

....

....

....

.... **(6)**

(c) 'Though Kennedy had the reputation of being a great reformer, Lyndon Johnson actually achieved more for civil rights than Kennedy ever would have done.' How far do you agree with this statement? Give reasons for your answer.

....

....

....

....

....

....

....

....

....

....

....

.... **(10)**

You may need to continue your answers on a separate sheet of paper.

Exam practice answers

Chapter 2

1. a) Give two differences, each with some detail: The biggest difference is that this German soldier is not living and sleeping in a trench, as British soldiers did. He has a dugout, (Source A) 'Our dug out became more and more complete' which I know British soldiers did not. They had to be satisfied with 'foxholes' in the side of the trench most of the time; only officers got dug-outs. The German soldier obviously expected to be there for some time: 'with wooden shelves for the dixies and nails in the roof to hang the bread and sausages on, so that the rats could not get at them.' British soldiers were always told that they were moving forward, so trenches were temporary. Rats were common to both sides.

b) Gauge reliability first, followed by usefulness: This is a graphic description of the wreckage of the first day of the Somme assault. The commanding situation of the German front line is well-known and is clearly described here, as are the problems in assaulting it. The writer, who was clearly there, dwells on the problem caused by the barbed wire, which is very useful in view of the disaster, but others would add the problems of artillery and machine guns, so that this extract is not quite complete. The extract would be useful for the general problems suffered by the British attack and for the specific fate of the 37th Brigade, though it suffers from the narrowness of view of a first-hand account.

c) You need to use your knowledge to explain the references in the source: We know that this was from 1918, and by then air warfare had developed a great deal: 'I spray the area with both guns and let go two Coopers [bombs]'. Here the pilot is firing machine guns, probably synchronised through the propeller, to strafe troops (a late development) and dropping bombs (also a late development). Equally anti-aircraft guns were only invented to counter the threats from the air during the war.

d) Try to be balanced in your judgement: This account is a caricature of the First World War general. Like most sketches, it is both tellingly accurate, exaggerating the conservatism and ineffectuality of the generals, and quite unfair because those generals did allow and even encourage innovation. After all, the First World War was a war like no other before: mechanised, hugely destructive and even scientific. As early as 1915 the Germans used gas on the Western Front and by then flame throwers had been invented. By 1916 Britain was trying out the tank and aeroplanes were changing from reconnaissance to attack. No one could accuse General Byng of Vimy Ridge fame of being old fashioned or impervious to change. However, change was not instant and generals were blamed for being 'out of touch'.

Chapter 3

1. a) Two marks for a principle explained with an example, to the maximum of four marks overall:
- Free access to the sea for all
- Disarmament of all countries
- Self-determination for people in Eastern Europe and the Turkish Empire
- A League of Nations to settle disputes between countries

b) Two marks for each good reason given, the second mark being for extra information. The maximum is six marks overall:
- Because Germany was regarded as the leader of the Central Powers, whose policies had started the war and whose military power had been the most important element in their opposition.
- Because Germany had expanded far beyond her historic borders, taking Alsace and Lorraine in 1871, Belgium, Poland and much Russian territory between 1914 and 1918.
- Because Germany needed to be restrained to stop her becoming dominant in Central Europe, i.e. the states that surrounded her must be strong enough to resist her, her military power must be restricted (Rhineland and disarmament) and her economy must be weakened (reparations).

c) To score up to eight marks, the answer should be balanced and factual. To score ten marks you need to assess how convincing each case is: It is true that the Treaty of Versailles

punished Germany more than any other losing nation, i.e. neither Austria nor Hungary had to pay nearly as much in reparations or had their military power so greatly reduced, though they did have to pay reparations and they did lose territory and have other restrictions imposed. Germany felt singled out because she lost territory of historic significance to her, e.g. the Polish Corridor and thought that the principle of National self-determination should be applied to keep Germans in Germany rather than losing Germans to Poland, Denmark, Belgium, etc. In addition, the £6,600M reparations bill was so huge that they should have been condemned to poverty for 50 years, while they were unable to defend themselves because of the military restrictions. So, Germans thought that the Peace was unfair, particularly since they had expected something more from President Wilson. The case for unfairness was made forcefully by Adolf Hitler and became a main justification for his expansionist policies in the 1930s, i.e. it was only in 1939 that Germany annexed populations that were not primarily German.

However, the failure of the Treaty of Versailles was far more complex than this. A losing nation would always have expected to be treated unfairly, as France had been in 1871 and Russia in 1918. What mattered was whether the Treaty could be enforced. This again depended on whether the victors had lasting reasons to take armies to war to keep Germany in check. By the 1930s this just was not so: The League of Nations was weakened by the Depression, Britain and France wanted Germany to form a strong defence against communist Russia, the principles of disarmament and avoidance of war seemed more important than going to war to restrain Germany. Above all, the only reason to control Germany was idealism, while every nation was set on self-interest. It would be reasonable to suggest that, if the Treaty of Versailles had been harsher on Germany, with more gains for the victors, then Britain and France may have enforced it more effectively. So, if Germany would always have resented the Treaty, it follows that the victors' lack of determination to enforce it was the key factor in its failure.

Since no nation gained enough from Versailles to want to enforce it, Germany was helped to dismantle it, through the policy of appeasement followed by Britain and France. At the time this seemed better than going to war.

Chapter 5

1. a) Any four of:
- Soviet defeat confirmed the division of Germany for the next 41 years.
- US determination showed that there would be no easy resolution of the differences between them and the USSR.
- NATO had been constructed during the crisis and eventually the Warsaw Pact developed to oppose it in 1955.
- American B29 bombers were deployed in British airfields for the defence of Europe.

b) Any three of:
- Communist North Korea had invaded the South in 1950.
- President Truman's policy was to contain communism, which had lately taken over China in 1949.
- North Korean expansion seemed to threaten US influence in Japan and later elsewhere like a set of dominoes as each state fell.
- This was the first real challenge for the United Nations in which countries united to resist aggression.

c) This needs a balanced answer with each case evaluated: US policy was now for the containment of communism. The construction of different alliances all over the world (SEATO, CENTO) helped to project US influence as more and more countries became dependant on the USA for defence. At the same time US influence in South Korea was made permanent as the peace was never confirmed by a final treaty so that South Korea thought itself threatened. Increasingly the Pacific seemed to be an area of US influence suggesting that a direct confrontation with China or the USSR was likely. Finally, US victory had partly been

Exam practice answers

through success in the United Nations, where Soviet influence was marginalised and US policy was for the first time pursued under the cloak of the UN. While this victory was not immediately possible to repeat, it was the precedent for US policy for the future. In all these ways US policy appeared to triumph.

However, these apparent victories were at the cost of the reputation of the United Nations, which lost its reputation for impartiality. It would become a forum for confrontation rather than the resolution of conflict, with real diplomacy taking place between world leaders outside the UN. The decision to use nuclear weapons in Korea had not been taken, despite MacArthur's determination to do so, which showed a weakness of resolution in US policy, allowing the Cold War confrontation to persist. The possibility for the escalation of the Cold War into direct confrontation between the USA and the USSR had been avoided, which could similarly be seen as weakness of will or sensible moderation. There were clearly limits to US success. It was the gradual breakdown of Soviet–Chinese relations that allowed stability in the Pacific, which was not a result of the war. Lastly, the formation of the Warsaw Pact in 1955 seemed to strengthen the Soviet Union, limiting the effects of the Korean War. Rather than a US victory, the Korean War seemed just another action in which the world was divided between the superpowers without either being able to defeat the other.

Overall, the USA had succeeded in maintaining the position at the beginning of the war without making the world any safer.

Chapter 7

1. a) Three good reasons with corroborative detail:
- Khrushchev was criticising Stalin, which opened the floodgates for other leaders to do so too.
- The point about 'imposing his concepts' seemed to relate directly to Eastern Europe and promise a change of attitude.
- 'Stalin's despotism' had been spread to Eastern Europe in the previous ten years, where peoples had been subjugated. The expansion of Soviet influence had helped to cause the Cold War. Now Eastern European states, such as Poland and Hungary demanded change from the USSR in the expectation of US support.

b) Start clearly by giving the message, then explain the evidence:
The message was that, in 1968 Stalinism was entwining even Dubcek of Czechoslovakia although Stalin was long dead (in his grave). Dubcek carries cutters capable of cutting the brambles, but has not yet done so. This relates to the popular support that Dubcek had within Czechoslovakia and in the West. Would he be able to disentangle Czechoslovakia from the bonds of communist domination, or would he be enmeshed? At that point, Dubcek had been called upon by other Warsaw Pact states to maintain stability, but Czechoslovakia had not yet been invaded.

c) This is a matter of opinion: give a balanced answer: Certainly other Eastern European countries thought that Dubcek was going too far and that demands for free speech and the liberties he had given to workers and managers in industry would spread and destabilise the rest of the Warsaw Pact. Brezhnev particularly feared Dubcek's effect on Yugoslavia, which already seemed too loosely tied to Eastern Europe under Marshal Tito. Brezhnev feared that Czechoslovakia would become a democracy and would leave the Warsaw Pact, providing a direct invasion route to Russia. These hopes were shared by Western countries, in which there was huge support for the freedoms Dubcek appeared to offer. However, Dubcek probably didn't intend this.

Dubcek was a convinced communist and, like Gorbachev at a later time, he thought that communism could be reformed and made popular. It didn't need dictatorship to function, but could have 'a human face'. Equally Dubcek was committed to the Warsaw Pact and had no intention of leaving it. He was more committed to communism than to Stalinist dictatorship, and that is where he made his mistake: his colleagues in Eastern Europe were Stalinists first and communists after that. No, he would not have considered cutting Czechoslovakia's ties, but his colleagues doubted him.

Chapter 8

1. a) Irish, Jewish, Polish, Eastern European.

b) Three good reasons, each developed with an example:
- Many Jamaicans on the Empire Windrush had served in the British forces during the Second World War and knew that there were more opportunities in Britain.
- The British Government had appealed to Caribbean workers to fill vacancies, particularly in hospital and transport services.
- Textile firms in London and the north of England encouraged skilled workers from India and Pakistan.

c) You need a balanced and thoughtful answer:
At first immigrants were very well received, as they often had been before the Second World War. Press comment was universally supportive in the early 1950s, and public opinion reflected this, recognizing the labour shortages that had caused the initial immigration and curious to find out about such different people.

Unfortunately, after about ten years, a small number of people began to react against the immigration, posting 'no coloured' notices on factories and boarding houses. Complaints were heard that immigrants were attracted by welfare benefits, rather than to work, while immigrants were blamed for the housing shortage. The Commonwealth Immigration Act of 1962 restricted immigration imposing a voucher scheme, but its effect was to make matters worse because there was a surge in immigration before it came into force. Discussion over this and the later Race Relations Acts (1965 and 1968) actually heightened alarm at immigration, which was given added importance by Enoch Powell's 'Rivers of Blood' speech in 1968. The economic downturn of the 1970s was most obvious in poorer immigrant areas. The police were blamed for harassing the black community and serious riots broke out in 1981 in Bristol, Birmingham, Brixton and Liverpool. By then it was clear that considerable tension had built up between communities and that policies would have to change.

It is clear, therefore, that immigrants were well-received at first, but as numbers rose and the economic situation worsened the welcome turned sour.

Chapter 9

1. a) Give four opponents, or two opponents with explanations:
- Kamenev and Zinoviev (both thought they should be leader after Lenin died, opposing first Trotsky, then Stalin).
- Trotsky took his own importance too much for granted and tried to lead the party against 'bureaucratisation' and 'Socialism in One Country'.
- Bukharin, Rykov and Tomsky condemned rapid industrialisation.
- The peasantry refused to sell food and brought on a crisis in 1928, which caused collectivisation.

b) Give three reasons with explanations, for example:
- Stalin saw the peasantry as an opposing group, deeply conservative and running their farms like little capitalist businesses. He needed to destroy them to bring on socialism.
- Stalin needed to use food for export to pay for his Five Year Plan, so he needed to get control of the harvests and force the peasants to produce more.
- Stalin needed to expand communist control into the countryside by reorganising farming under the control of communist managers. This would enable the kind of political and economic control necessary in a centrally planned dictatorship.

c) Give a thoughtful, balanced answer:
Politically, collectivisation was very successful, even though Stalin took great risks that his cruelty would result in his own downfall. By the mid 1930s opposition in the countryside had been stamped out, the independent and capitalist farmers (kulaks) had been

destroyed, most farms had been collectivised under communist managers and were dependent on communists in tractor stations. The dictatorship now had control of the countryside, so the revolution had been completed but, more usefully, it could export the harvest to pay for change in industry. And yet, political control had come at the expense of output.

By 1936 the grain harvest had fallen from 74.5 million tonnes in 1928 (a poor year in itself) to 57 million tonnes. There had been a huge decline in livestock at the same time, so the Russian standard of living fell abruptly. The export of food made this change even more serious and forced a man-made famine onto the Ukraine and Caucasus where, in 1932–1933 as many as 10 million people starved to death. Change had been at the expense of the most productive class in the countryside, the successful peasant, whose expertise was lost to the collectives as they were starved or transported to the Gulag. This destructive policy took time to be successful and left terrible scars on the Russian population that are still visible today.

Stalin justified collectivisation as being necessary to push Russia into the 20th Century, but it was at huge cost. Collectives never proved as profitable as expected, so the real gain was in political control rather than in economic progress.

Chapter 10

1. a) **Four clear ways:**
    - He took control and applied leadership over the party: the Leadership Principle.
    - He decided to use Weimar democracy to take power, rather than violent revolution.
    - He used propaganda through the party's own newspaper to target specific grievances.
    - He extended party organisation throughout Germany so that it could challenge the government in elections.

    b) **Give three reasons, each with corroborative detail:**
    - The Weimar Republic had proved unable to solve the problems of the depression because the socialist parties would not reduce unemployment pay while the nationalist parties could not get majorities to rule. The result was continuing economic crisis and lack of direction.
    - The Communist Party was growing much stronger, which meant that many Germans voted Nazi to keep them from power.
    - Hitler promised firm leadership, the destruction of the Versailles Treaty and nationalism, all of which were popular in comparison with the unstable government.

    c) **'To what extent' always asks for a balanced answer:** There is no point in denying that Hitler and the Nazi Party were a popular alternative to communism in 1932 and 1933, but Hitler became Chancellor in January 1933 because von Papen had persuaded von Hindenburg that the Nazis were the only party around with whom a nationalist coalition could be formed to keep the communists out, i.e. Hitler initially came to power by a 'backstairs bargain' rather than through an electoral majority. In the second election in 1932, Nazi support had actually decreased for the first time and perhaps that was significant in persuading Hitler to accept power. If he had not accepted the Chancellorship then, the likelihood was that the Nazis would lose popularity as Bruning's economic measures began to work. In 1933 the Reichstag Fire was significant in persuading Germans to vote Nazi, but even then they did not have a majority, needing the Nationalists to join a coalition to give them control. Only after all pretence of democracy was over, after the Enabling Law, was Hitler able to gain a 99% majority, which no one believed was real.

    On the other hand, many Germans did support Hitler, and without this support, Hitler could not have been picked as the candidate of the Right. Germans voted against unemployment: Hitler promised full employment. They voted for leadership, which Hitler had imposed on his own party and promised the country, clearly speaking against the lack of decisive government produced by democracy. Germans, therefore, expected dictatorship. They also voted for nationalism: they knew this meant tearing up Versailles, but they didn't necessarily expect war. They just wanted Germany to stand up for herself internationally. Hitler was the only leader that represented this, as the communists would have made Germany take Russian leadership and the socialists had allowed the other powers to impose reparations and loans during the 1920s, which had ended in Germany's disastrous bankruptcy in 1929. It isn't surprising that Hitler's promises were taken seriously even though they did not, in themselves, get enough support to take him to power.

    While Hitler did have a large measure of popularity, he was not really voted into power. The inadequacy of the Weimar constitution allowed a series of bargains and coalitions to take place, which gave Hitler control. The Nazi majority had to wait until he could fix the elections to get it in 1933.

Chapter 11

1. a) The Democrats and the Republicans.

    b) **Give clear reasons:** The boom of the 1920s had been in consumer industry, while mining, farming and cotton had declined. The government had imposed import tariffs to protect US industry, but these backfired when other countries shut out US goods. The booming industries had saturated a smaller and smaller market. When speculators noticed this, they began to sell shares on the Wall Street stock exchange, which then crashed. Banks had lent money to speculators and many went bust. Industries were unable to raise money or sell goods, so many closed. More and more people were put out of work and poverty spread.

    c) **Make a balanced argument:** From the Republican point-of-view, the huge amount of government aid that Roosevelt gave through the Alphabet Agencies was money wasted. They did not believe that paying people relief through FERA or removing their responsibility for their homes or farms through FCA or HOLC should be allowed to reduce people's self-sufficiency. As if the removal of incentive was not enough, the administration had increased costs to industry through high taxation and the high wage legislation of the NRA. It was only because of the billions of dollars pumped into the economy that things appeared to improve before 1936. When Roosevelt later reduced his subsidies, the whole improvement was seen to be false, as unemployment rose again.

    The Democratic argument was quite different. Though they agreed that subsidies and high taxation were normally to be avoided, they also realised that by 1933 many people could not help themselves. People had become so poor that stimulating them into productive and self-sufficient work would not provide enough money in circulation to pay for the food or goods that they may produce. Only the 'priming of the pump' by the government spending and giving away money in relief would begin to get the economy moving. The spread of communism was feared, and in any case poverty had become so pronounced that private charity and state governments could no longer cope. Roosevelt's efforts would have been more effective if they had not been restricted by the actions of the Supreme Court, and in any case, they saved the USA from still worse depression than was actually seen.

    Each group saw different problems, but both were partly right.

2. a) **Two reasons with some detail or four reasons should be sufficient:**
    - The publishers of *Amerasia* magazine had been found in possession of secret documents in 1945.
    - Canadian citizens had passed American nuclear secrets to the Soviet Union in 1946.
    - Klaus Fuchs and the Rosenbergs had given atom bomb secrets to the Russians in 1950.
    - The Korean War was being fought, which threatened conflict between communist states and the 'free world'.

b) **Three ways with some explanation are necessary. One mark for each way and one for each explanation:**

- The 'Jim Crow Laws' restricted African American rights by allowing the vote only to property owners who were literate. Most African Americans were neither of these.
- States passed laws to segregate African Americans from white people in schooling, public transport and restaurants. There were clearly separate black and white areas.
- The Ku Klux Klan enforced segregation through terror of the fiery cross on the front lawn or mob lynchings.

c) **You need to assess the effectiveness of both points of view, coming to your own judgement:**

Most of Kennedy's policies failed to gain support in Congress, e.g. he failed to get health insurance for the aged, federal aid for education or to reform the immigration laws. None of these proposals were relevant to civil rights. At first Kennedy attempted very little change, appointing a few African Americans to high office, but doing little else. On occasion he sent in troops to enforce desegregation, e.g. of the university in Mississippi in 1962, but this was not enough. Martin Luther King accused him of only token support for black civil rights, which stung him into proposing his Civil Rights Bill. At that point he found his congressional support ebbing away and the Bill became hopelessly deadlocked.

Nothing more had been achieved before his assassination in Dallas on 22nd November 1963. So Kennedy's reputation as being a great reformer was not well earned.

Lyndon Johnson achieved rather more: he forced Congress into passing nearly all Kennedy's proposals, then passed Acts to enforce desegregation, e.g. the Higher Education Facilities Act. He also passed legislation to help the poor, many of whom were African American, e.g. the Tax Reduction Act and the Economic Opportunities Act. Above all, he passed the Civil Rights Act of 1964, which outlawed discrimination and created an Equal Opportunities Commission to put an end to discrimination. This was followed by the Voting Rights Act of 1965, after which he amended the constitution to outlaw poll taxes, which had been used to force African Americanss not to register to vote. Johnson was helped to achieve all this both by the effect of Kennedy's assassination and by the work of the Supreme Court, but in any case he had achieved much more than Kennedy.

Kennedy's reputation was altered by his assassination, after which no one would believe anything bad about him, whereas Johnson's reputation was harmed by the Vietnam War, after which no one would say much good about him. Johnson, however, was a real reformer in his quest for the 'Great Society'.

Acknowledgements

Images

p7 ©Mary Evans Picture Library/Alamy; p8 ©by permission of the Imperial War Museum Q 81819; p9 ©Hulton Archive/Getty Images; p11 ©Bernard Partridge/Punch; p13 ©Hulton-Deutsch Collection/Corbis p16 ©by permission of the Imperial War Museum Q 27854; p18 ©by permission of the Imperial War Museum IWM PST 0414; p20 (left) ©by permission of the Imperial War Museum IWM PST 12052, p20 (right) From the collection of Anthony Langley/www.greatwardifferent.com, used with kind permission; p28 ©istockphoto.com; p44 ©Leonard Raven-Hill/Punch; p46 ©Bettmann/Corbis; p53 ©Ernest Howard Shepard/Punch; p54 ©David Low Cartoon/©Solo Syndication; p63 ©Oasis/Photos 12/Alamy; p65 ©Keystone/Getty Images; p66 ©by permission of the Imperial War Museum D 2593; p68 ©Corbis; p73 ©Oasis/Photos 12/Alamy; p81 ©Bettmann/Corbis; p92 Huynh Cong/AP/PA Photos; p95 Arpad Hazafi/AP/PA Photos; p96 ©Sipa Press/Rex Features; p97 ©epa/Corbis; p98 ©Alain Keler/Sygma/Corbis; p106 ©Martyn Turner; p108 ©Bettmann/Corbis; p119 ©Bettmann/Corbis; p120 ©Sean Adair/Reuters/CORBIS; p121 ©The Times, Kenneth Mahood, N I Syndication; p126 ©Central Press/Hulton Archive/Getty Images; p128 ©Mike Chitty, Wavertree Society; p132 ©Bettman/Corbis; p135 ©Hulton-Deutsch Collection/Corbis; p136 ©David Hoffman Photo Library/Alamy; p138 ©Collection/Rex Features; p146 ©INTERFOTO/Alamy; p156 ©Mary Evans Picture Library/Alamy; p159 Courtesy of the Gareth Jones Archives –©Gareth JONES, www.garethjones.org; p176 ©Mary Evans Picture Library/Alamy; p180 ©Stapleton Collection/Corbis; p189 ©Corbis; p191 Peter Newark Pictures/The Bridgeman Art Library; p194 I Have Here In My Hand – A 1954 Herblock Cartoon, copyright by the Herb Block Foundation and used with permission.; p196 ©Bob Adelman/Corbis; p198 ©Bettmann/Corbis

All other images ©2009 Jupiterimages Corporation and Letts Educational.

Text

p20 C used with the kind permission of Sheila Angelini; p20 D David Lloyd George Memoirs vol 1 p.64, used with kind permission of the Parliamentary Archives on behalf of the Beaverbrook Foundation; p35 A from War by Ludwig Renn, translated by Willa and Edwin Muir, published by Secker & Warburg. Reprinted by permission of The Random House Group Ltd, p35 B used with the kind permission of Sheila Angelini, p35 D ©AJP Taylor, extract from Sarajevo to Potsdam, Thames and Hudson, used with permission of David Higham Associates; p68 E ©AJP Taylor, extract from The Second World War – An Illustrated History, Penguin, used with permission of David Higham Associates; p69 F Most Secret War: British Scientific Intelligence `939-19456 by R. V. Jones (Hamish Hamilton 1978) Copyright ©R. V. Jones, 1978.; p121 C ©Alan Woods, reproduced by kind permission of www.marxist.com; p170 Hitler 1889–1936 by Ian Kershaw (Allen Lane The Penguin Press, 1998) copyright ©Ian Kershaw, 1998; p188-189 ©Hugh Brogan, History of the United States, published by Pearson Education Ltd, used with kind permission

Index

Index